Understand Russia

Stories about Everyday Life in Russia

Tanya Golubeva

© 2019 Tanya Golubeva. All rights reserved.
Visit the author's website at https://understandrussia.com
Cover design by Nick Popov
ISBN: 978-1-0723844-1-0
Independently published

Table of Contents

Preface ix

1. **FAQ ABOUT RUSSIA** 1
   - 1.1. *Is It Always Very Cold in Russia?* 1
   - 1.2. *How Do We Cope with Long Winter?* 2
   - 1.3 *How Much Vodka Do Russians Drink?* 4
   - 1.4. *Visiting Russia – FAQ* 6

2. **PSYCHOLOGY/HABITS** 15
   - 2.1. *Perceptions of Hard Work vs. Luck in Russia* 15
   - 2.2. *Why Russians Don't Smile?* 18
   - 2.3. *Small Talk – Does It Exist in Russia?* 21
   - 2.4. *Do Russians Believe in Superstitions?* 24
   - 2.5. *Why Russians Do Not Believe in Insurance?* 29
   - 2.6. *The Mysteries of the Famous "Russian Soul"* 31
   - 2.7. *The Impatient Side of Russians Uncovered* 34
   - 2.8. *Money in Russia* 36

3. **RELATIONSHIPS** 39
   - 3.1. *Friends Are Forever!* 39
   - 3.2. *Gender Stereotypes in Russia* 42
   - 3.3. *Dating in Russia* 47
   - 3.4. *Flower Etiquette in Russia* 51
   - 3.5. *Age Stereotypes in Russia* 53

4. LIVING IN THE CITY — 55
- 4.1. Russian Clouds Have a Silver Lining — 55
- 4.2. What Does It Mean to Be a Muscovite? — 56
- 4.3. Small Towns of Russia — 60

5. HOME — 63
- 5.1. Russians Take off Their Shoes at Home — 63
- 5.2. Balkon, Dacha, Pomoika (Balcony, Country House, Garbage Can) or the Lifecycle of Things — 64
- 5.3. Apartments or Houses? How Urban Russians Live? — 66
- 5.4. "Euroremont – Interior Design of Post-Soviet Russia — 69
- 5.5. What's Behind the Russian Steel Door Culture? — 73
- 5.6. Dacha – More Than a Country House, Rather a Passion — 76
- 5.7. Spring Cleaning in Russia — 80
- 5.8. If You Are Invited to a Russian Home – Russian Hospitality — 84

6. FOOD — 89
- 6.1. What Russians Eat for Breakfast — 89
- 6.2. What Russians Eat for Lunch and Dinner — 91
- 6.3. From Russia with Love – Pie Recipe! — 94
- 6.4. Russian Soups – Comfort Food for Cold Weather — 95
- 6.5. Okroshka – the Most Bizarre Summer Soup — 99
- 6.6. Festive USSR Style Dinner — 101
- 6.7. How Spicy Is Russian Food? — 104
- 6.8. Why Russians Love Sour Cream and Mayo? — 105
- 6.9. Do Russians Eat Fish? — 106
- 6.10. Do Russians Really Eat Russian Salad? — 109
- 6.11. Do Russians Have a Sweet Tooth? — 110
- 6.12. All You Need to Know About Russian Blinis — 112
- 6.13. What Are Some Favorite Junk Foods in Russia? — 114
- 6.14. How the Self-Imposed Food Embargo Impacts Russia — 117
- 6.15. Serving Food – the Russian Way — 120

Table of Contents

7. HEALTH/WELLBEING — 123
- 7.1. How Do People Keep in Shape in Moscow? Part I – Fitness — 123
- 7.2. How Do People Keep in Shape in Moscow? Part II – Diets — 124
- 7.3. Preventing Colds – the Russian Way — 127
- 7.4. Home Remedies in Russia — 128
- 7.5. Healthy Lifestyle – a New Trend in Russia — 131

8. TRANSPORT — 135
- 8.1. Ways to Entertain Yourself in Moscow Traffic Jams? — 135
- 8.2. Why Russians Are Crazy Drivers — 138
- 8.3. Why Dash Cams Are Popular in Russia — 141
- 8.4. The Advent of the Unofficial Taxi in Moscow — 143
- 8.5. How to Travel in Russia – by Car, Plane or Train? — 145
- 8.6. Metro – the Underground Wonder — 150

9. EDUCATION/ENTERTAINMENT/CULTURE — 153
- 9.1. Cultural Life I – Literature — 153
- 9.2. Stay Tuned to Music — 155
- 9.3. Movies from Soviet Time and Now — 157
- 9.4. Robots Among Us — 159
- 9.5. Russian Language Is Difficult Even for Native Speakers — 161
- 9.6. Learning Foreign Languages… and Not Speaking Them — 165
- 9.7. Facts and Legends About Moscow State University — 168
- 9.8. 25th of January – Student's Day and Tatiana's Name Day — 170
- 9.9. How Tatiana Becomes Tanya – Russian Names Explained — 173
- 9.10. Mushroom Picking – Russian Tradition and Passion — 178
- 9.11. Russian Pets — 180
- 9.12. Iron Madness or What Russian Tourists Want — 181

10. HOLIDAYS — 183
- *10.1. How Holidays Disrupt Business in Russia* — *183*
- *10.2. 8th of March – International Women's Day* — *186*
- *10.3. Maslenitsa – Time to Eat Russian Blinis!* — *190*
- *10.4. Back to School – Russia* — *191*

11. DOING BUSINESS IN RUSSIA — 197
- *11.1. What Are the Do's and Don'Ts in Russian Business Meetings* — *197*
- *11.2. Are Russians Good Public Speakers?* — *201*
- *11.3. Storytelling in Russia from Tolstoy to Modern Days* — *202*
- *11.4. Time Is Fluid in Russia* — *207*
- *11.5. Role of Branding in Russia over the Last Century* — *213*

12. USSR — 217
- *12.1. How Lenin Brainwashed Children* — *217*
- *12.2. Kolbasa – the Food Symbol of the USSR* — *220*
- *12.3. Packaging in the USSR or Why We Keep Plastic Bags* — *223*
- *12.4. Space – Russians' Greatest Pride Revisited* — *224*
- *12.5. A Typical Apartment of the Soviet Time* — *228*
- *12.6. Communal Flats in Russia – Shared Life* — *231*
- *12.7. Carpets as Carpets and Carpets as Symbols* — *237*
- *12.8. Life Hacks from Soviet Time or the Story of a Deficit* — *238*
- *12.9. What Do Russians Think About the USSR Now?* — *242*
- *12.10. Propaganda in Russia and Abroad* — *244*
- *12.11. Guest Post: American Perspective on the Soviet Union* — *248*

Preface

Acknowledgments

This book would not have been possible without two groups of people – my friends, who encouraged me to start the Understand Russia blog and my readers, who kept surprising me by sending smart, fun, witty and sometimes totally unexpected questions about Russia. Thank you!

My Dear Readers,

Thank you very much for your interest in my book. It is exciting to welcome you here! I want to share with you the story of this book.

I am Russian, was born in Moscow at the time when the country was still named the USSR. I have traveled extensively around the world and lived for more than a decade in several foreign countries. I have been fortunate to meet and befriend people from all over the world with very different ideas about Russian life, and those same friends have taught me much about their own cultures.

One thing has always surprised me – questions that people ask me about Russia. These have been mostly questions about day-to-day life in Russia and the culture, habits, and mentality of Russian people. Although Russia is not a closed country anymore, it seems that most foreigners either get a "touristy" view of Russia and its people (Kremlin, Red Square, Saint Basil's, matryoshkas, and babushkas) or receive "official" information on politics and economics on their local news.

Preface

So, I thought about writing a book which answers questions about real people. I decided that the best way to motivate myself to write a book would be by starting a blog. For several years I wrote a blog, entitled UnderstandRussia.com. Having a blog proved to be more than a great motivation, via the blog I connected to my readers, received new questions and feedback on my posts. My favorite thing to do was to look in Google Analytics tool to see, what are the countries and cities, where my readers live. It was amazing to find out that people from more than 100 countries were reading Understand Russia. I often tried to imagine, sitting in my Moscow kitchen and looking at the snow outside, who are these readers from far places and what is their daily life like in South America, New Zealand, South Africa, Madagascar, and even Tasmania.

Finally, I believe that I have enough material to publish the book. How the book is structured – there are 12 thematical chapters and many sub-chapters in them. You can read the entire book or skip to the topics that interest you most. If you have any questions, you can always send them to me via the blog (I am not adding new posts at the moment, but still read and reply to comments and emails).

Before I let you go and read, I want to say that I am not a cultural expert or academic, these are my subjective observations and opinions about life in Russia, specifically about my life in Moscow. It's important to remember that Russia is a big country, with diverse geographies and peoples. So, when I refer to "Russian culture" it is relative to my own experiences.

I sincerely hope you enjoy my stories!

Yours,
Tanya

1. FAQ ABOUT RUSSIA

Two most typical questions about Russia are: "How much vodka do Russians drink?" and "Is it always very cold in Russia?" Then come a series of questions about visiting Russia.

1.1. Is It Always Very Cold in Russia?

"Oh, you are from Russia? You must be really used to the cold!"

Yes, it is cold, and that is why we always wear those funny fur hats, called shapka-ushanka, which can literally be translated as a hat with ears, when walking our pet bears.

In fact, winter here is long indeed. And in some parts of the country, temperatures do get brutal. As I was writing this blog post, it was -47°C (-53°F) in Yakutsk. Weather.com said that it actually felt like -47°C. I was happy for locals that it did not feel colder. But can you imagine how -47°C feels? I cannot as it never gets that cold in the capital.

Weather in Moscow is quite warm and sunny from May to August, but it starts to get colder every day in September, and from November to March it is winter. However, it typically gets freezing (-25°C or -13°F) only for about a week or two during the winter. All other time, the temperature fluctuates from +5°C to -10°C (41°F-14°F), hanging around zero Celsius (32°F) a lot.

However, cold is not the biggest problem of our climate at all. Living in the city, you do not suffer much from cold. Apartments and offices are very well heated, your car has an excellent heating system and heating of seats as well. If you live in Russia, you know how to dress well – you wear winter boots, insulated with fur, fur coats or down jackets and hats, scarfs and gloves. We have a saying that there is no bad weather, only the wrong clothes. One cannot get used to the cold but can learn how to dress well. Also, Moscow is NOT a windy city at all so, unlike in Chicago – snowflakes slowly fall down instead of getting in your face parallel to Earth and with high speed.

There is usually a lot of snow in winter. The first snow (in October or November) is always beautiful, but after a couple of months, it starts to get on your nerves. Most apartment buildings do not have indoor garages, so your day begins with 15-20 minutes of the intense workout of carving your car out of the snow. Driving in the snow is also no fun. Most people know how to drive in deep snow really well, and all vehicles change into winter tires, but traffic is very slow, and there are many accidents on the road.

Still, snow is also not the biggest problem here. The biggest problem is the lack of sunshine. Sun disappears in October, and next time you see it in late March. It's not like we have a polar night here in Moscow, we are not that far north. But the sky is covered with clouds most of the time, and it gets dark very early. The only days when you might see the sunshine during winter are actually those really cold days when there is high atmospheric pressure. And we like those days a lot, because it is crispy cold and sunny, and the center of the city looks gorgeous.

We do not treat weather as something special, though. All Russians consider absolutely normal to eat ice cream outdoors in winter. And many Russians do swim in frozen lakes either once a year on a religious holiday or regularly.

1.2. How Do We Cope with Long Winter?

1. Make Sure Your Car Is Well Equipped for the Winter

The most important part of your car in winter is your car battery. Just buy a new one every 2 years and your car will start every morning.

It is that simple. Also – buy a windshield washer fluid rated to minus 20°C. Use it the entire winter. Then – winter tires. Mine are with studs. Finally – 4WD SUV and better choose manual transmission. Every Summer I am thinking about getting a sexier car, sedan, coupe or even a convertible. Every Winter I am happy that I am driving a car, that is good for any terrain. I should wash it, though – I barely remember that it used to be dark blue…

2. Dress Well

That means both – dress warm and love your winter outfits. Several winter coats plus lots of scarfs and mittens and gloves and boots. Even if it is minus X and/or snowfall and a grey sky – nice looking clothes put you in a better mood.

3. Taxi Is Your Friend

A cab in Moscow is at your doorstep in 2 min. Day or night, thanks to the apps. If you do not feel like digging your own car out of snow or looking for parking – that is a great option!

4. But How Do You Wake Up, When It Is Dark?

Coffee? Good Music? Chatting with friends? If all that fails – I suggest a HappyLight lamp – that thing really works. 15 min of light of the right specter and, you forget your Winter Blues.

5. Participate in the Cultural Life of the City

Theaters, exhibitions, movie premiers – you name it. Best cultural events happen during Winter. Enjoy that!

6. 1 Hour + Commute to the Office?

Find an FM station broadcast, that makes you laugh in your car. Chat with friends, drink coffee, have breakfast. With the right state of mind this hour is not wasted, on the contrary, it could be the most enjoyable hour of your day.

7. Shop Until You Drop!

Best sales take place in winter. Take advantage of that!

8. Ski!

Easy to say, difficult to follow. Both Moscow and St. Pete are located on flat terrain. No earthquakes whatsoever, but no mountains as well, only some small hills. Fly to Sochi or to the Alps, both are close. You can wake up in Moscow in the morning and hit the slopes in the afternoon. How cool is that? Or you can skate in the city, which is cool too!

9. What If Nothing Works?

Plan a getaway to a sunny destination. Seriously. There are plenty of places on our planet, which have warm beaches, palms, seafood, etc. People there are waiting for your arrival! Don't make them wait!

10. Think About Spring Coming up Soon

3-5 months from now it will be all over, and Moscow (and other cities in Russia) will become a great place! Just wait for that!

Cheers from the Winter Wonderland! Stay warm!

1.3. How Much Vodka Do Russians Drink?

The fact that Russians start their day with vodka and have vodka at all business meetings has become such a cliché! How accurate is that stereotype?

Per capita consumption of vodka and other strong alcohol has always been scary. It does go down though – from 18 liters of pure alcohol per year in 2011 to 13,6 liters in 2018 (according to WHO). I may have an answer – why?!

First of all, not many young people drink vodka. Vodka is considered to be a drink for old people or for people of lower social and educational level. Girls and women almost never drink vodka. One of the most surprising things for me, when I moved to the US, was vodka (or vodka cocktails) ads in a Cosmo magazine. You can never find that in Russia.

What do people drink? Beer is popular among young people (legal drinking age in Russia is 18), wine is a drink of choice for people in their 30s. Men often like whiskey. I can understand why somebody may want a shot of ice-cold vodka, but I am never tempted to do one.

Another question I often get – do Russians drink vodka during most business meetings? I know that is a boring answer, but no. To make this text less boring, I will share with you the only story I have that relates to business meetings and drinking.

A long time ago I was working for a Canadian Ministry of Justice, Crimes Against the Humanity Department. We were working in Minsk, Belarus, investigating WW II cases. I still remember a meeting with one of the top government officials, which took place at our hotel at 8 am in the morning. That guy came into the room, carrying a briefcase. And immediately took a bottle of cognac, a chocolate bar, and lemon out of his briefcase and started to talk about Russia/Belarus hospitality and traditions. I was lucky to have a good excuse for not drinking – I was working as an interpreter in that meeting, but poor Canadian fellows had no excuse and had to enjoy the hospitality. That day had indeed looked like what you see in Hollywood movies about Russia.

Do we say "Na Zdorovie"?

No, never. We may raise a toast to the health and prosperity or to the hosts or to the success of mutual projects or to the great year or season. It is always a meaningful toast and sometimes a long one. We are raised in the culture of War & Peace, we put our hearts and thoughts in toast speeches. Best bet for you as a foreigner if you make a toast is to say – "Za vstrechu" (to our meeting) or to say "Za udachu" (to the luck)

Oh, and there are no bears on Moscow streets! I wanted to state that fact for a long time but could not find a place to mention it. When you visit Moscow, you will see that Moscow is much more similar to NYC or London than you think. The quality of a mojito and the quality of an ambiance will all be top-notch! And pricey. But drinks in fancy bars have become more pricey in both NYC and London too in the last 5-10 years! Just don't follow the per capita intake of alcohol and both you and your wallet will be fine! Enjoy!

1.4. Visiting Russia – FAQ

When to visit Russia?
May to August, when it is warm and sunny. If you are a tourist – you are outdoors most of the time, so you want comfortable weather and good pictures with the blue sky in the background for your Instagram.

Do I need a visa?
That depends on where you come from. Russian citizens need visas to most countries, and that is always reciprocal. If you hold a US or EU passport – you need a visa, if you are from South America – you do not need a visa. Google that question first as the time to get a visa, cost of visa and the list of required documents vary by country.

My visa application says I need a letter of invitation. Where do I get one if I do not know anybody in Russia? I also read that I will need to register somewhere upon arrival. Where?
The hotel that you have booked will give you the letter of invitation for the visa. It is ok to change your mind later if you want to stay in a different hotel. In any case, the hotel in which you will actually stay will give you all registration docs you need. Do not lose those they are important.

How safe is it in Russia for tourists? Do I need a bodyguard?
It is safe, and you do not need a bodyguard. You need to take the minimum precautions against the pickpockets. Also – in any big cities it is not wise to walk around deserted neighborhoods at 3 am in the morning. But I would say that in general Moscow is safer than Chicago, New York, London, Paris or Buenos Aires. It is especially safer than US

cities due to two reasons – it is illegal to carry guns here, and we do not have "bad streets or neighborhoods." Some really remote areas at the outskirts of the city may be less safe, but there is nothing there that may attract a tourist. Downtowns of all major Russian cities during the day are completely safe.

What is the locals' attitude towards tourists? Are locals nice or hostile?
Russians, in general, treat foreign tourists well and are curious about people, who come from different countries. Locals may seem hostile to you though because they typically don't smile at strangers. That does not mean they do not like you; it is just the custom here.

A lot of people asked me: "I am American, the relationship between the US and Russia is sour now. Will local people hate me because I am American?". The answer is no. Although a lot of Russians are brainwashed with the State propaganda the person who they hate is your president, not you. Russians get that you are not in charge of politics in your country and they like that you decided to spend your vacation to see their country.

Do I need to speak Russian to get around?
Russian is a difficult language to learn. So, nobody expects a foreign tourist to learn the language just for one trip. However, if you can learn 10-15 words and phrases (such as Hi, Thank You, Please, etc.) your life as a tourist will be so much better here. You will notice that making such a small effort will melt peoples' hearts. We love when a foreigner speaks even a bit of Russian and will go out of our way to help you and make your stay here more comfortable.

In general, most Russians do not speak English. If you are stuck and need help – your best bet will be to ask younger people. But even people, who do not speak English will try to help a foreigner with a map to find her way.

Navigation in the cities, even in Moscow, is not easy. Most signs are in Russian, and it may be really confusing. Downloading an offline city map would be very useful. Metro maps now have a transliteration of the stations on them, and audio announcements also are in both Russian and English. Some stations have very long names though, so I am not sure how helpful is the audio. For example, we have a metro station, Street of the year 1905. Guess, how it sounds in Russian? "Ulitsa tysyachedevyatsotpyatogo goda." Better follow the map, ah? The Metro map is actually quite simple, and trains never go to different places from the same platform as in the US or UK tube.

How expensive is travel to Russia?
It used to be super expensive, especially travel to Moscow. Moscow was #1 most expensive city in the world for expats for several years in the row. But the ruble collapse in 2014 made travel abroad more expensive for locals and made tourism to Russia quite cheap for tourists. If you compare Moscow to London, New York or Paris now – everything will seem to be very affordable in Moscow.

Can I pay with the credit card while I am in Russia? Or do I need to bring cash? In which currency? Where do I change money in Russia?
You can pay with a credit card almost everywhere in big cities. But even in Moscow, you will need to have cash on you for tips and some street markets. Best bet is to bring US dollars or Euros – you can exchange these anywhere where you see the tableau with the exchange rate or in any bank. It should be pretty safe. Never ever try to change money on streets even if a person seems reliable, as it is most certainly a trap.

Russia Is So Big! How Much Time Should I Plan for a Trip?
That really depends on how much vacation time you have and what would you like to see. Russia is a huge country, indeed. I am living here, and I still haven't been to so many places yet. Unless you take a 6-month sabbatical from work – you will not be able to visit everything. But you do not need to see the entire country in one go. For most

tourists – Moscow and St. Petersburg are the main attractions. And – believe it or not – you need just one week to see both capitals.

For the first visit to Russia, I would suggest starting with Moscow and St. Petersburg – do all the sightseeing, visit museums (Hermitage in St. Petersburg, Tretyakov Gallery in Moscow), go to the famous Bolshoi or Mariinsky theaters and explore the nightlife of the two capitals. You can actually do all that in one week since there is a fast train between the cities.

You can arrive in Moscow, spend 3 days here and then take a fast 4-hour train to St. Pete and spend 4 days there. Here is the suggested itinerary (which may differ, depending on your interests and preferences):

Day 1 – First Day in Moscow
- Red Square – "The heart of the country," the most important and the most famous square. Just being here will make your heart beat with excitement. It is old, full of history and is indeed beautiful (the name took origin not from the red color of the Kremlin walls, but from the old Russian word "krasny," which means both red and beautiful.

While you are at the Red Square – make sure you do not miss the following sites:

- Gorgeous Saint Basil's cathedral – legend says that the architect, who build it, was blinded so that he never creates anything as beautiful ever in his life. Make sure you go inside – St. Basil's has 8 tiny churches inside, which look like a fairy tale houses
- Look at the Lenin's mausoleum. Lenin is still there so you can go inside too
- GUM – #1 department store. Mostly western luxury brands inside now, but interesting architecture. And a great grocery store on the first floor, which looks like a typical Soviet grocery store (well, like a very posh ideal grocery store of that time). GUM also has a Bosco café, where you can have a super expensive coffee, but with the best view of the Red Square

- Before or after seeing the Red Square, you can go to Kremlin. Make sure it is before 4 pm, as Kremlin museums close early. There you can see:
- 3 gorgeous cathedrals – visitors are allowed inside, and it is the must-see
- Tsar (King) Canon and Tsar Bell
- A glimpse of office buildings, where Mr. Putin works. You will not be allowed to trespass, but if you are lucky – you will see a president's car or a helicopter

Kremlin and Red Square will take at least half day. After lunch, you can explore the surrounding area if you are not very tired – see one of the main streets – Tverskaya or walk to Bolshoi Theater, gorgeous Metropol Hotel, and former KGB building

Day 2 – Museums & Culture – Tretyakov gallery (great collection of Russian paintings) + maybe exploring that area (an old and interesting part of the city), and go to see opera or ballet in the evening in Bolshoi theater

Day 3 – Novodevichii monastery (very picturesque) and the campus of Moscow State University + viewing point nearby and taking a boat along Moskva river, stopping by the Gorky Park – the #1 park in Moscow and a very fun one. If you are visiting in winter – look for Radisson cruise boats, it is the only boat company, which uses icebreakers.

Explore nightlife in Moscow if you still have energy on all or some of these days.

St. Petersburg
Day 1 – Sightseeing in the center (cathedrals, Nevsky prospect, etc.)
Day 2 – Paul and Peter fortress and half day for Hermitage museum (However, I'd say that a half day in the Hermitage would probably be too short if you are a real fan of art. One can easily spend the entire week in Hermitage.)

Day 3 – Peterhof palace near the city (gorgeous)

Day 4 – Tsarskoe Selo palace (where the famous amber room is)

In St. Pete – watch the bridges open at night (while making sure you are on the same side as your hotel)

If you have more time (let's say a week for Moscow alone):

- Do the same as in the previous itinerary, but make it less packed – spend more time enjoying breakfasts and lunches at the open terraces of cafes, go for a walk without having a particular destination in mind, take more photos of street life
- In continuation of the previous point – you could spend the entire day at the Gorky Park (assuming you visit in summer and the weather is nice) – you can play all kinds of sports there, have a long walk, eat at one of the cafes or just read a book in a park
- Having more days in the city will allow you to go to more museums, concerts, theaters.
- Another interesting thing would be to visit one of the former factories in the center of Moscow, which are now centers of art, crafts, and entertainment. Check out TimeOut Moscow for ideas and the schedule of events
- If you are interested in the Soviet period of history – you may go to VDNH – it is a cool place, designed initially to showcase achievements of Soviet republics, so its large area contains 15 pavilions, built in honor of these republics and some additional pavilions. In the Soviet time each building hosted a thematic expo of the products, produced by those republics. After the collapse of the Soviet Union, VDNH was neglected for a long time, and buildings deteriorated and hosted markets. But they were recently renovated and even though, only some of them still serve the initial purpose (such as the pavilion of Space), there is a lot of life there. And the place itself is grand – with interesting architecture and fountains with sculptures.
- You can take a day trip(s) to the Golden Ring cities and look at beautiful churches, countryside and buy some authentic souvenirs

- Finally – you can spend several hours visiting the "sleeping quarters" of Moscow that is how we call the area which is outside the center and where most Muscovites live. To go there – just take a metro and go beyond a circular line. Stations, such as Belyaevo will give you an idea of a residential area.

How will I get around in Moscow and other Russian cities? Should I plan to rent a car or is there reliable public transport?

If you are a foreigner, I strongly advise against renting a car, especially in Moscow. Some of the Russian drivers are a bit crazy, and the traffic is dense. There is an abundance of public transport. Metro is probably the easiest way of transportation and, it is a gorgeous must-see tourist attraction as well. Trains arrive every 50 seconds during the day. If you need to take a taxi – Uber works here, but it is better to avoid taking a taxi during rush hours (5 pm – 8pm in Moscow) if you do not want to spend hours in the traffic jam.

To get from and to Sheremetyevo and Domodedovo airports using the train is convenient and inexpensive, and all taxi services also have a flat rate to the airport, so just ask your hotel concierge to book you a taxi.

What is the food like? Is the food spicy? Which dishes should I try? Is the street food safe? Is it safe to drink tap water?

Let's start with the water. Tap water in Moscow is considered safe to drink, but I suggest you drink bottled water because it tastes better. Tap water is still filtered with chlorine, which impacts the taste. So, even locals do not drink tap water. So, it is better not to take chances.

Food in Moscow and St. Pete restaurants is absolutely safe to eat, and there will be a lot of variety – from traditional Russian food to any kind of ethnic food. In both capitals there are a lot of fantastic restaurants now, for example, any restaurants from this company will delight you – http://en.ginza.ru/msk. If you travel outside of the cities though – you may need to be more careful. If the place does not look like a restaurant (if it is a street food kiosk) – refrain from any minced meat or shawarma. Also, Russians use too much mayo and sour cream. Food that is high in fats may be difficult to digest if your daily diet is less fatty.

All food will not be spicy… even the ethnic food, which is supposed to be spicy. Russians do not like spicy food. You can ask for pepper at the table or ask to make dishes spicier if you are at the ethnic restaurant.

Trying local food is a part of the immersive experience in any country. Read the chapter about food in this book and try as many items as you can and wish. But if you get tired of unusual food or just prefer to eat the same food as at home – you will find whatever you are used to in the big cities.

I have special dietary needs – gluten-free, vegetarian, vegan, kosher, halal, etc. Will I be able to find the food I need in Russia?
My advice is to do a lot of research before your trip. If you plan to visit only Moscow and St. Pete – with the prior study, you will find enough restaurants and grocery stores to cater to your needs. In all other places that could be a challenge. Most Russians will understand if you are a vegetarian, but awareness about other dietary restrictions is quite low.

If I were to spend a month or two traveling in Russia – where would you recommend that I visit?
Russia has a fantastic nature and culture. You can find everything from mountains to lakes and seas, meet people of different religions and lifestyles, see both the world-famous and the folklore art.

If you have a month or more – possibilities are really endless. Definitely try to go to Lake Baikal, the largest freshwater lake on Earth, which is amazingly beautiful. Altai mountains are another cool tourist destination as well – you can do a horse tour there or just go hiking. Kamchatka area (Far East) is one of the most unusual places on Earth – with mountains and geysers – but a trip there will be quite expensive. If you want to go to the seaside – it will be easy to visit Sochi, which hosted the Olympic Games in 2014.

Regarding planning the trip – you can easily design your trip to Moscow and St. Petersburg (and the vicinity) on your own and travel solo, but for all other trips – it is better to use a tour agency and go with a group. You will have a better experience, and all the logistics will be taken care of by the agency.

What about the famous Trans-Siberian train? I want to do that!!!
I am writing about that in more details in the Transport chapter. In brief – that is a dream of all foreign tourists and no Russian citizens. Why? It is a very long journey and, while it may seem exciting, landscape from the train window will stay the same for a very very long time. Also, unless you are planning to take the luxury train, you may experience some discomfort.

But if it is something you always dreamed of doing – go ahead, just read the other travelers' reviews beforehand.

Hope that you travel to Russia, whether it would be for a week or a month, will make you love and understand our country better!

2. PSYCHOLOGY/HABITS

2.1. Perceptions of Hard Work vs. Luck in Russia

There is always a duality in the Russian soul. Attitude to work is no exception. From one point of view – Russia was an agrarian country for many centuries, and people worked hard to get food, from the other point of view – there are some inner laziness and a firm belief in luck. Let's try to solve this tangle.

Russian Proverbs About Work

Most proverbs and sayings do talk about the virtue of hard work, such as:

> *The man, who does not work, does not eat.*
> *Without hard work, you won't even catch a fish.*
> *Patience and hard work will grind (overcome) everything.*
> *It is the feet that feed the wolf.*
> *No water flows under the lying stone.*

There are however some bizarre sayings, such as:

> *Work is not a wolf; it will not run from you to the forest.*
> *Horses die from work.*

There are many interpretations of the latter sayings, some of which tell that the original meaning did not imply laziness and skipping work. But the modern meaning certainly does imply precisely that.

In general, I would say that Russian people treat work as a necessary evil. Everyday hard work does not bring us personal pleasure. Unless there is a big idea behind the work in question, in that case, we can do wonders. Important, meaningful work is a huge motivator, sometimes bigger than monetary reward.

Attitude to Work Through Russian Fairy-Tales

Fairy-tales always reflect nation's mentality. A typical plot of the Russian fairy-tale is the following:

A guy is literally doing nothing (resting) until he is 33 years old. Then he catches a magic gold-fish or a magic bird, which can fulfill any wishes. Or, there are three sons in a family, and the youngest is considered to be not the smartest guy in the village. And then there is some hardship or war or battle for the princess and the youngest son becomes a hero. Not because he secretly trained to be the best soldier in the last 20 years and not because of other skills. Because of luck and a kind heart. Needless to say – princess has all the more reason to sit tight and wait for her prince. The country is very patriarchal, so traditional fairy-tales do not have strong female characters.

Take home message from these fairy tales is that Luck is a big part of the success if not the crucial one. Russians are very fatalistic and believe in luck and fate. If it is your fate – you will achieve the goal. If you will not reach the goal – that just wasn't your fate.

Country's History Influence

Russia was historically an agrarian country, and everyday work in the field is hard work indeed. That explains proverb – how well you work is how well you eat. Nobody could accuse old Russians of being lazy. Some playtime was always acknowledged though. Many sayings are telling us that after you are done with work, you are entitled to have fun.

However later, things started to change with the change of the society. Industrialization has brought new challenges, but at the same time made life a bit easier. Work and food still were directly correlated, but you did not grow your own food and life in the city was a bit easier.

Then we move to the Soviet era, during which everybody had guaranteed employment, and there wasn't much income gap. There were no opportunities for private business and superb performance at work did not result in a significant salary increase. That situation did not stimulate hard work. A popular joke of that time said: "We pretend we work, they pretend they pay." Of course, there were many brilliant people at that time as well, but they worked hard because they loved what they did, not because of money. Soviet people had an outstanding work/life balance. Combine a lot of free time with the scarcity of available entertainment, and you get people engaged in sport, hobbies, tourism, and arts.

I may be wrong, but it seems that the attitude towards work as the necessary evil and a shift in focus towards holidays, comes from the Soviet time. I think I hear the trace of those times every Friday from my car radio. DJ congratulates everybody that the hard and tedious workweek has ended and now everybody can go play.

The Heroic Act of Work

One key advantage that Russian people have and in which we may outrun the rest of the world – is our ability to "move the mountains" (do an enormous amount of work) in a very short time.

We are sprinters, not marathoners. If justified well – we can do a massive amount of work overnight. Sochi Olympics is one example; the way students study the entire course in last 3 days before the exam is the other. Even our fairy-tales showcase that – in many of them the father of the princess demands a glass bridge to be built overnight by the potential son-in-law. And the guy always manages to fulfill the wish.

The Soviet regime was not dumb. Psychologists have captured that national trait and used it to the full extent. The most famous example of that was a movement to achieve 5-year development plan of the country in four years. We, Russians, love such challenges and are always game to participate in them if we agree with the goal. Such heroic acts of work do make us happy.

Work Series vs. One-Time Exceptional Job

Continuing the previous topic, nothing makes us happier than working on the one-time extra cool and challenging project. A famous Russian legend tells about a craftsman, who managed to put a horseshoe on a flea. Not that we needed an army of fleas in horseshoes; it was a one-time deed.

We love innovation and the idea to be first in something that has never been done before. Take a man in the space for example. We often lose interest in the project once it goes into the boring implementation/mass produced phase, but we are fully engaged in the initial stage.

Having in mind these intercultural characteristics may be quite useful for business. If you motivate people in the right way – you will see glass bridges built overnight!

2.2. Why Russians Don't Smile?

Why nobody seems to smile on the streets, while most of the Russians I know are lovely, charming people who smile and laugh?

Smiling is one of the most essential communication behaviors. On the one hand, smiling is universal across cultures, on the other hand – a smile is a function of the context of a social situation, and that is the main reason Russians are always accused of being gloomy. We just smile in different social cases than people in the West.

The Science of Smiles

A smile reflects a vast array of emotions in different cultures. Not all smiles are genuine expressions of happiness. There are cultural differences in both how people smile and when they smile.

In Western society, smiling is a highly valued social behavior and people who smile a lot are perceived more positively. However, Western smile first of all signals politeness and Russians smile only when "there is a reason to smile." We even have a saying – "only fools smile without any reason."

When Russians Smile

(Based on research by I.A. Sternin, B. Notkin, and others)

- **When we see a friend, relative or acquaintance.** Not smiling to strangers is a cultural norm, since there is no particular reason why we should greet a stranger that way. Unlike Western people, who treat strangers as good people until some of them act as bad people, we handle all strangers as aliens until they prove that they can be trusted.

  In fact, if you start smiling to strangers on the streets in Russia – it will make locals uncomfortable. They might think that you are laughing at them (maybe they look funny because of their appearance or hairstyle or there is something wrong with their wardrobe). They will get confused and will not smile in return.
- **When we hear or see something amusing.** If somebody told a good joke or you are watching a comedy, you are expected to smile or laugh
- **When there is a particular reason why you smile, and people around you are aware of it.** (You just won a lottery or got engaged or received a promotion). If your colleagues see you smile, they may ask, "Why are you smiling? Did anything good happen?" And you are supposed to explain (give a valid reason). Personal questions and sharing personal information are considered ok even in the workplace since Russians are both very direct to ask and very open to share how they feel. If you do not have any special reason, you can say – "just have a good mood today, it's such a sunny day."

When Russians Don't Smile?

- **When you are around people, who experience any significant troubles, smiling is considered inappropriate.** In some cultures, smile is a sign of empathy and support, but in Russia smiling when somebody shares his or her bad news is considered highly offensive
- **If you have any troubles**, such as a work or family crisis, you are not expected to smile to others. In fact, you are supposed not to smile; otherwise, people will think you either are careless or act weird
- **A typical passport photo** is always "no smile." We joke that if you start looking too much like your passport photo – it is time for vacation.

- **Smiling in work/study environment is not appropriate** (except for employees of the Western corporate environment, who are usually expected to follow Western communication style). All other "serious contexts" are considered to be "not a place to smile." That starts from school. If a teacher hears giggles in her classroom, most often response would be: "Why are you smiling/laughing? Did I say something funny?" A boss in a typical Russian-style company may say the same in a business meeting. No wonder that immigration officers never greet incoming passengers with a smile. They are protecting the country border, it is a serious business. There is no place for laughs here.
- **Smiling/laughing at others is not polite**; ability to smile/joke at yourself, on the contrary, is a socially positive trait. However, it is critical not to smile/laugh all the time, otherwise, you may get a reputation for being a clown, and people will not treat you seriously. A good laugh is good, but when it comes to business or other serious stuff – "leave jokes aside."

Duchenne Smile vs. Social Smile

When we do smile though, you can be sure that this is a sincere smile. And it is quite easy to distinguish genuine or Duchenne smile (named after 19th-century French neuroscientist G. Duchenne). Duchenne smile involves not only muscles around the mouth, but also muscles around eyes.

When Russians travel abroad, at first, they love that people around them smile all the time. But quite soon they sense that these smiles do not mean that locals are extra happy to see them, that is just a social norm. And most Russians come back home saying that foreigners have "insincere smiles."

I wonder why no cosmetic company has yet come with an ad campaign of eye cream, using the idea of "your smile is always sincere, but you need an eye cream to fix those crow feet in the corners of your eyes. Because smiles are beautiful, but there is no need to pay for them with wrinkles". It could've worked so well in Russia.

Types of Smile

Types of a smile also differ across cultures. Since Russian smile is a natural one, parents never train kids how to smile (at most, they will ask a kid to smile when taking a photo).

Therefore, we do not have a universal Russian smile, but in most cases Russian smile is more like a grin, not showing teeth. That does rapidly change, however, as toothpaste companies are changing the "standard of smile" with their TV commercials.

2.3. Small Talk – Does It Exist in Russia?

Foreigners often say that Russians are too direct. One of the manifestations of that is going straight to the point at business meetings or in social situations. That makes people from some countries, especially Americans, very uncomfortable. Why don't we do small talk?

Small Talk Did Exist at the Aristocratic Salons of the Past

If you read classical Russian literature from the 19th century, you would notice a lot of descriptions of social evenings of aristocrats. They dressed up and rode in a carriage to the so-called "salons," where they engaged in conversations, danced and enjoyed their free time.

People, who were welcome at such events, belonged to a very thin layer of the society. Those were people from noble families, who received excellent education either abroad or in Russia, with the help of foreign tutors. They spoke several languages, often traveled abroad and had a lot of exposure to other cultures, especially to the French culture.

So, no wonder that they had excellent communication skills and could take part in the conversation pretty well. I wonder though, what percentage was that social layer from the entire population, mostly represented by peasants? For them life was far from easy, people worked a lot in a field. Not all children had the luxury to study in school;

instead, they had to help their families at work. Communication in this social circle was more direct and up to a point.

Soviet Time Style of Communication

It would not be correct to generalize Soviet time as one homogenous epoch as each of the decades had its' own communication characteristics. However, for most of the Soviet years' communication was skewed to being "in-circle," among close friends, at homes of each other. Networking and meetings at social events, where most people were strangers, were less common.

Unfriendly and hostile environment, both politically and economically, made close friendships extremely valuable. Close friends formed one's support networks; relationships among friends were becoming more and more profound. In the Soviet economy, the income gap among people was relatively small, a deficit of goods in stores made it easier to save than to spend. Soviet people had a lot of free time, a balance of work/life was excellent, and so people read and thought a lot. Being "deep," well-educated, well-read were the qualities that mattered.

And when you talk to your close friends, you do not need small talk. You talk about things that really matter and expect the other side to listen and contribute to the meaningful conversation.

Modern Time – Dealing with Foreigners

During the Perestroika of the 90s, one of the most frequently used words was JV – Joint Venture. International firms have made their way to the Russian market and were looking for local partners and employees, who could help them set up businesses here.

Intercultural differences became one of the most significant obstacles in that process. Ability or inability to do small talk may have been not the biggest of them. But still relevant, since Westerners are accustomed to using small talk for testing the waters, to have a feel for communication skills of the potential partner.

Peach vs. Coconut Cultures

The Dutch organizational theorist Fons Trompenaars popularized the theory that people from some cultures (i.e., Americans) could be viewed as peaches (soft on the surface and easy to connect with, but having a hard shell inside, which makes it more difficult to become close friends with them).

And people from other cultures (i.e., Russians) may at first seem as unapproachable as coconuts, but once you get through the outside shell, there is a soft center inside. Russians are initially closed to strangers, but then open and may become your best friends.

What to Expect When Trying to Small Talk with Russians

- Most Russians are not used to the concept of small talk and do not see value in it. That could be supported by the fact that there is even no direct translation of small talk. Google translate says that it is meaningless chit-chat, chatter or babble
- Russians either do not talk at all or talk about things that are important to them; Russians may go straight to the point both in business meetings and in social situations. To some extent that is justified by not wasting your precious time
- But be prepared that if you ask Russians some questions, their answer might be long and detailed. Even the basic question "How are you?" is not a greeting in Russia. It is a question, that deserves a thorough answer
- Russian conversation style is more descriptive and based on stories. Stories often have detours, which do strengthen the point or expand the conversation
- Small talking with strangers, shop assistants, waiters, etc. would make them feel uncomfortable. For them, it may even feel as if you are hitting on them or invading their private zone
- To approach complete strangers, you would usually need a good reason, such as asking for directions

- Some small talk is OK here. But if a person would small talk too much, Russians will think s/he is shallow or even crazy. We have a saying: "Words are silver, silence is golden"…
- If small talk happens at the business meetings, it usually only occurs at the beginning of the session. Appropriate topics are weather, traffic to the office and discussing the venue where the meeting takes place (especially if you are meeting at your Russian counterpart office and can compliment on something nice or interesting s/he has there)
- Using jokes for small talk at the beginning of business meetings or business calls is advised only if you already tested that joke with your Russian friends and they understood it, laughed and found it proper for the business context. Be very careful though – Russians treat business seriously, so even if the joke was funny and clean, it might still be perceived as an inappropriate way to start the business talk
- Do not expect much small talk (if any) at the end of the business meeting. Meetings in Russia are usually much less structured than in the West. And meetings would often go over the time limit and end when your counterpart glances at his watch and understands, he is late and needs to run to make it on time to the other meeting

As often happens with the intercultural differences – the key is to see and acknowledge such differences. That alone greatly helps in avoiding miscommunications. The next step is to adjust your own cultural communication style to the style of others, to make them feel more at ease and facilitate building a relationship. And finally, often both sides can learn something from each other.

2.4. Do Russians Believe in Superstitions?

It is quite funny that people of the country, which sent the first man in space, are quite superstitious. Some superstitions are the same worldwide, some are unique to Russians.

As in all other countries, we believe in superstitions and signs that bring bad or good luck. Russians are firmly convinced that their destiny is only partially under their control, but there are other external factors which they cannot control, and which make a significant impact on their wellbeing.

Signs of Bad Luck

The most famous bad luck sign is when a black cat crosses your way. 100% of Russians will either change their direction or wait until somebody else crosses the cat's path first. Cats are mystical animals in general and black cats are associated with dark magic. When people move to a new home, it is very likely that they will let the cat in first. The cat will take the spell on her.

Mirrors are thought to have magical power, no wonder they are often used in fortune-telling. Mirrors also play a part in the everyday life – when you forget something at home and return to collect it, you will look in the mirror on the way out to make sure you have not attracted bad luck. But most importantly – nothing can upset a Russian more than breaking a mirror – it is believed to be a prediction of death in the family. Same is believed, when a bird accidentally flies inside the house. Birds are considered to be quite mystical – for example, if Russian hears a cuckoo in a forest, he will ask – "Cuckoo, Cuckoo, how many years will I live?" And then he will count how many times the bird cuckoo. Most people will also never kill a spider in the house since that may bring bad luck.

Spilling salt on a dinner table is not good. People believe that it leads to a quarrel in a family and to cancel the hex you have to throw a pinch of salt above your left shoulder. Not many people know the origins of that superstition – many years ago salt was very expensive, so spilling such a precious product could have easily led to a quarrel among relatives.

Another dinner table superstition is to take away empty bottles from the table immediately. Even now most people do that. The origin of this tradition is in heavy drinking that was taking place in Russia, which often led to quarrels and violent fights. Having empty bottles on the tables was dangerous, in a row they could become deadly weapons.

Finally – most girls would avoid sitting at the corner of the table. It is believed that it brings bad luck in personal life – a girl will not get married for 7 years. I do not have a reasonable explanation for the origin of that superstition.

Signs of Good Luck

There are also plenty of superstitions referring to good luck. Finding a lilac flower with 5 petals is one of the most popular. In former times, when horses were the primary means of transportation, finding a horseshoe was believed to lead to good luck.

A very funny superstition of Soviet times was to get a "lucky" bus ticket. At that time people paid for a bus ride after boarding the bus and got a bus ticket which had unique 6 digits number. If the sum of first 3 numbers equaled the sum of last 3 numbers – such card was considered lucky. And…you had to eat it! Preferably after you get off the bus, otherwise you could get fined if faced with a ticket controller.

If we return to the dinner table superstitions – when something breaks (glasses in particular) – any Russian will immediately say – "it's for good luck." I assume that this superstition originated as a way of coping with the loss of glass – it is much nicer to let it slide than to quarrel about broken glass. But maybe there is a much more in-depth explanation since deliberately breaking glass at weddings is a tradition in many religions.

Some superstitions and signs are more difficult to explain. If you accidentally drop a fork or knife – it means that a man will unexpectedly visit your house, if it is a spoon – wait for a female visitor. You cannot however deliberately force more visitors by dropping objects. Or – the other superstition –if you have accidentally worn an item of clothes inside out – you have to change as fast as you can; otherwise, somebody will beat you.

Attracting Good Luck

Even though Russians think that luck is beyond our will – we have kept some of the ancient pagan traditions and believe that we can attract good luck or forecast who will have success this year by performing certain rituals.

To forecast – we do what many other nations do – put a coin or a button inside a pie, or inside one of the dumplings (pelmeni) and a person who gets this dumpling with coin inside is bound to be lucky. The more violent version of that game is the famous Russian roulette when just one bullet was put in the gun. Needless to say – it works the other way – a person would've gotten the bullet had really bad luck that day.

In general – Russians love to play with fortune and love fortune-telling. There are myriads of fortune-telling practices and rituals. Some deal with actively attracting good luck. Students have a lucky coin in their shoe when taking exams. Students also "call luck" the night before the exam. When you are tired from studying, you open the window and put your report card outside and shout three times –"Luck, come here." Then you close the report card (it is a small book) tightly and put it underneath the leg of your bed. You have caught the luck, and it should help you tomorrow.

Another example is the New Year's Eve rituals. You have to make a wish when raising a glass of champagne when kuranty (the main Red Square clock) ring 12 times and your request will come true in the next year (if you do not share what you wished with anybody!). Some people even write down their wish, burn the paper and drink a glass of champagne with ashes and if you managed to do all that while kuranty ring – your wish will come true. There are many other New Year superstitions – some are actually very reasonable – if you have a debt, you must pay it back before the New Year's Eve; otherwise, you will be in debt the entire year. That makes total sense, New Year is a chance to live a better life, to change, to better yourself and your fortune.

Returning to making a wish – if you are standing between two people with same names – you can make a wish, and it will come true. If you see an eyelash on your cheek – you take it and put it on the back of your hand, make a wish and blow. If the eyelash disappears – your wish will come true.

There are some things that you are not supposed to do – like whistling inside the house. If you do that – you will whistle all the money away!

Fortune Telling/Horoscopes

Many people in Russia love fortune-telling and horoscopes. If you sleep at the new place and you are a girl, you say "sleeping in a new place, may I see my groom in dreams tonight." Also, we believe that dreams from Thursday to Friday night are forecasting future.

In Russian literature, one can find lots of references to fortune-telling. In Eugene Onegin girls were throwing shoes outside the house on a particular religious winter holiday and asking the guy, who had found the boot first, his name. That name is going to be a name of your future spouse, so you better be attentive to that when you deal with your admirers.

It is interesting that modern Russians are developing new rituals and ways to attract good luck. Once I was taking a cab ride, and when the cab was going under the bridge, and a train was going above the bridge, cab driver started to fidget and finally found a coin and put it on the top of his head. I was stunned by that performance and asked for details. He said – that's the way to attract money. And that is not the funniest part of this story. From that day I do the same in such situations and all of my friends, whom I told this story also do that. You never know, if it helps, why skip the chance.

It is also quite popular to create your own secret signs and rituals. For example, I have a "lucky 2-digit number," and when I am driving, I pay attention to car license plates. If I see that particular number – it is going to be a good day.

But maybe even all these odd superstitions and signs have explanations if proper research is done. Examples above are very random, however, most signs in Russia have always been the ones, related to weather and agriculture (such as – if the weather is such and such on a particular day – it means cold or warm season ahead, etc.). In these cases, superstitions were just the first scientific observations. And sometimes even signs that relate to birds could be explained by science. For example – when swallows fly low – that predicts rain. No magic in that – pure science. Before the rain, atmospheric pressure is getting lower, and flies fly low, so birds also fly low to catch them.

But you know what? Friday the 13th was actually never among traditional Russian superstitions, and the number 13 is not considered unlucky (unlike in the States, where most buildings even do not have the 13th floor).

2.5. Why Russians Do Not Believe in Insurance?

Insurance companies have a tough time in Russia. Russians do not believe in insurance and equal it to Ponzi scheme. Sometimes that comparison is a correct one – the industry is working far from perfect, so buying insurance does not always guarantee a payoff should the case happen. However, the roots of such attitude are deeper...

Russians Are Fatalists

"Do what you can, but rely on fate," "what happens, is meant to happen," "One cannot escape his fate," these are just some of the 184 proverbs and sayings on that subject. My 100-year-old grandma always believed in fate, I could argue to the point of turning blue, but she just smiled and offered me more food (Russian grandmas always try to feed you).

"Can-Do" attitude is not welcome here. "The Man plans, but the God decides." That kind of attitude is very foreign to me, I am Russian, but have absorbed a lot of Western culture, living abroad for most of my childhood. Also – my parents never told me – "Tanya, do what you can, the rest is in God's hands." They always told me that I should study hard, get excellent grades, use my brain and then I will see the payoff.

Once I talked to a very famous local astrologer, whom I referred to as Lika the Great after she welcomed me at her house, where the first thing to see was her portrait, painted in oil by the most expensive Kremlin house artist. Lika the Great exhibited nobility, stature and confidence. She was wearing a long grey dress, made of wool, and a high hairdo. The reason I got entitled with her audience – I was writing the New Year (how to celebrate/what to wear/how to charm the year's mascot etc.) article for one of the glossy magazines with a circulation of one million.

Lika the Great breezed through the topic at such pace that made me thankful for not relying on my stenography skills and bringing the audio recorder with me. When we were done with "Taurus should wear blue and eat fish on the New Year's Eve," she graciously offered me to look into my fate. I was hesitant at first but gave in. She had looked at stars and planets and told me that things seem good – I will have plenty of marriages, and all of them will be happy (Go figure!). I will also always be wealthy and will continue to write.

I asked her – "Lika, do you believe in fate? How come you are so confident in what you say? What if I do nothing for the next year? Will planets still help me to achieve all that?". She immediately fired back: "No, planets are like muscles, if you do not work out, they atrophy."

Why Planets Do Not Need to Work out in Russia

Although Russians are fatalists, they are "fake fatalists." They believe that universe/god/fate plans the life of others, but they personally are the exception. They are the lucky ones, who will not get caught when violating the traffic rules and will not crush in the incoming traffic when driving the wrong lane.

That kind of behavior is so strong; there are even some words that do not have an adequate translation into English. One of the words is "avos' – 'Avos,' I will get lucky." I looked up Avos in Multitran dictionary – here is the closest translation and the definition: "blind trust in divine providence; blind faith in sheer luck; counting on a miracle ("Counting on a miracle, I decided to slip into the oncoming lane to get around the traffic jam"); usually unjustified dependence on success by chance or luck; faith in serendipity".

There is another word – "nebos'," which in the context could mean, "Most probably as in – most probably they will not catch me!" This word originated from two words "ne boisya" (do not be afraid). This short word has a deep meaning: "don't chicken, most probably everything will be fine." Avos and nebos are huge drivers of our behavior.

Having these insights – do you wonder any more, why Russians do not believe in insurance? Our fate is in God's hands, but most probably nothing terrible is going to happen to me personally! And, just in case, I will look into the daily horoscope for Taurus…

2.6. The Mysteries of the Famous "Russian Soul"

Dealing with Russians is often confusing. We have a duality in almost all aspects of our behavior. We do not smile to strangers but have a great sense of humor. We are pessimistic when things go well, but have great stamina and joke, when they don't. We believe in fate but will never cross the path of a black cat. Does the famous "Russian Soul" really exist and what is it?

It is impossible to describe Russian national character in one article adequately. Here are just some snippets that may help you better understand Russians.

Russians Are Very Direct

That is not necessarily bad – we do say what we think, and you can be sure we say what we mean.

But we are not born-diplomats at all. If we do not like your idea, we will rather say it is stupid then (like the British people) – that it is "interesting." We are often thought of as being rude because of that. We are not, we just give you honest feedback. You may argue that we are wrong in return, that is very acceptable. We love heated discussions!

PSYCHOLOGY/HABITS

Russians Are Rude to Strangers, Polite to Acquaintances and Rude to the Close Circle

That one is interesting. We do not care about you at all if we do not know you. But will be really nice to you if you are a friend of a friend and will go out of our way to help you. But if you are our spouse or a close friend – we will skip "thank you, please, would you be so kind, etc." You will think – what is going on? Why are we suddenly hostile? We are not. We just do not believe we need to say extra words if we are already close friends or more. We just omit the unnecessary reverences, but if you need us – we will always be there for you.

Russians Tolerate Cheating at Exams but Will Never Betray Friends

If you cheat on the exam – we would rather help you than turn you in. If you commit a bad thing at work and we know about it – we would rather keep silence than turn you in (even if we disagree and think it is bad). Turning somebody in – that is what is considered a crime. Questionable in the case of exams, but that is how ethics works here.

In the same time that behavior has its positives. You can always rely on your friends and be very open with them. They will tell you what they think about you and your stupid behavior but will try to help you to get out of any problematic situation. As we say – Russian will give the only shirt he has to a friend.

Russians Do Judge and Think That It Is Ok

We will judge how strangers dress their kids to school ("you are a bad mom, your kid is not wearing a hat"). We will tell you that your kid should wear a hat even if you do not ask our opinion. We will judge how you dress at work, how you live etc. We honestly think it is to your benefit and should be considered as valuable feedback. The terrible part of the character, which may have come from the Soviet times, when various committees at work or in school were allowed to judge unwanted behaviors publicly.

Famous "Russian Soul." Does It Really Exist?

Not all Russians have a mentality, described in Dostoevsky novels, but we all have a bit of a dark side in us. Reading too much and living without proper sunshine for 9 months a year makes one think about life and gives a lot of time to do so. From what I read about the correlation between happiness and the number of sunny days around the world – there is a strong correlation between these two parameters. Russians tend to overanalyze things and expect pessimistic outcome even if things go rather well. Long winter nights in our cold country give us a lot of time for self-reflection.

In the same time, if things are horrible – we pull ourselves together, get help from friends, believe that the dark stripe will always be followed by a white one and invent hilarious jokes about the situation. We are solid in the times of hardship.

So, what is a typical Russian soul? It is indeed more on a pessimist side. But with a firm belief in luck and magical forces that can make a difference. It is quite rare for a Russian to be in a super elevated mood and see the life through rosy lenses. There are so many things, which can go wrong, even when everything looks fine. One of the most famous modern sayings, which captures the essence of our attitude towards life was a saying from a former prime minister Chernomyrdin. He said – "we wanted to do our best, but things turned out as usual". Hell is full of good meanings and intents. But Russians are fatalists in their core. Unlike Americans with their "can-do attitude," we always expect that external forces will be against our best wishes and intents. In the same time, we believe that luck and other good forces can truly help us. This is an ongoing battle, and we do think about cause and effect a lot. Maybe even too much.

We are prone to analyze and over-analyze all our conversations with people. Very often we seriously discuss not the exact words that a person said to us, but what we think he or she really thought or felt at the moment. Non-verbal communication is something that we pay a lot of attention to. In most cases, it has nothing to do with open/closed postures or other scientific stuff. It is about – "I said this, and I felt that she was uncomfortable with the news. She answered that, but I think she felt the opposite". One of the popular Russian pop songs has the following text – "I glanced back to see if she had glanced back to see whether I had glanced back." That behavior is very typical for us.

If we consume alcohol – we do not become silly. Well, maybe for a moment. But after it – we become very serious and engage in lengthy conversations about the meaning of life. And nothing is more bonding than having an in-depth and quality discussion with a Russian, whether it is under the influence of alcohol or not.

2.7. The Impatient Side of Russians Uncovered

I travel a lot both for business and for pleasure. And noticed that many Russians are impatient when they travel. I do not know why that is so but let me share tell you a couple of stories.

A Culture of Standing in Lines for Everything

I do not remember much of Soviet time due to my age and living abroad during my childhood. But I know that standing in line for food or goods was a big part of living in the USSR. I think that people were used to that.

Now we do not have long lines for anything in Moscow, but from time to time you can have a glimpse from the past. For example – when I was recently sending some souvenirs to friends – I did stand in line at the local post office for 3 hours. It was a strange experience since all people were standing really close to each other. Feeling the breath of some stranger on my neck for 3 hours (and it was an old woman, not a guy if you have questions) made me feel quite uncomfortable. The line was like a monolith, no chance for the intruders to break in. That experience made me think that Russians are very patient.

Disembarking the Planes and Driving

In the same time, I had the opposite experiences with my fellow citizens. Let me share that with you as well.

When the plane lands, everybody on board is anxious to get off. But in most countries, people typically sit still until the plane reaches the terminal and even then – manage to wait for people in front of them to get their suitcases and other belongings and move row by row. Not in Russia! In Russia – as soon as the plane lands – people first burst in a round of applause (which is strange on its own) and then jump and start opening the storage areas and getting themselves ready to disembark. They do hear the announcements, which ask them to stay put and wait, but they do not pay any attention to that.

A similar thing goes on while driving. A lot of roads near Moscow have relatively wide technical side lanes, not paved with asphalt and not intended to be used as driving or walking lanes. When traffic builds up though – you can see a row of SUVs that drive on that side lane. They make all other cars dusty, and they do not gain much advantage as they still need to queue at some point.

Buying a Fridge in Moscow at 2am

Soviet grocery stores had lunch breaks from 1 pm till 2 pm. Other (non-food stores) typically had lunch breaks from 2 to 3 pm. Even restaurants had lunch breaks midday. Combine that with the fact that it was illegal to be unemployed (if you are unemployed, you are a **"tuneyadets"** – lazy person, who does not deserve his bread) and you see that all people worked on the same schedule as the store opening hours. Shopping and working did not go together well. And in the evening most stores were closed by 6-7 pm.

I guess that is the main reason most shops in Moscow now either work 24/7 or at least until 11 pm. IKEA, for example, is working until 2 am. MVideo (BestBuy of Russia) is open 24/7. Booze is no longer sold after 11 pm, but if you want to buy a dining table, gardening equipment or a fridge – you are welcome in the store at night. Insomnia and too long to do list are good for store owners. They will comfortably accommodate your lifestyle, whether you are a night owl or an early bird. And many of my Russian friends do post on FB after midnight that they are out there hunting for a shower curtain or furniture.

Does it make sense? Totally no. Who are the people who need cottage cheese, ice skates, grass cutting equipment or a dresser at 2 am in the morning?

So, How Did the Culture of Patience Turn into the Culture of Impatience?

I do not know the answer to that question. One guess is that the impatient people are all young people, who never experienced waiting. The other hypothesis is that all people have become tired of waiting and got used to the fast service. I think that Russian people often behave rudely because of such impatience and hope that it is a temporary thing.

2.8. Money in Russia

The relationship between Russians and money has never been an easy one.

Value of Money in Soviet Time and After

During the USSR time money per se was not as important as your network. You could be rich, but you still needed connections to buy simple things, such as good shoes or even a decent piece of meat at the grocery store. Retail was not as it is now, on the surface there was nothing good in the stores. Quality products appeared in the stores occasionally, accumulating long lines of people. But if you were friends with the manager of the store or with a salesperson – you could get the "deficit goods". That usually was a favor trade: you did not pay a commission, but you gave something in return. That could've been anything – for example, concert tickets in return for the Italian shoes. That usually depended on where you worked, to which "deficit goods" you had access to yourself. In addition to that, friends could always lend you some money or help you in some other way (move your furniture, take you to the airport so that you do not need to call a taxi, etc.).

Some people even despised wealth as a criterion for success. During the USSR time, criteria for success among intellectual élite were your achievements in science or other professional fields and in your hobby (if you were an artist for example). Criteria for success among less intellectual crowds still were material things such as carpets, crystal, etc. at your apartment. But these things showed not just that you have money, but that you have connections and are able to get "deficit goods."

As soon as Russia turned into "capitalist country" after Perestroika, things have changed. Suddenly, goods and services have become abundant, but most people did not have enough money to buy them, since a lot of people lost their savings during the money reform. In 1991 there was a crazy financial meltdown. Old bank notes were replaced with new bank notes, 50 and 100 Ruble notes issued after 1961 became invalid. People could only exchange their old bank notes during a 3-day window, but no more than 1000 Rubles per person. It was a horrible time and tens of millions lost nearly all their money.

During Perestroika of the 90s, the income gap has become really visible. A 17-year-old interpreter or 20-year-old person, who sells T-shirts at the street market could make ten times more money than an engineer with 20 years of experience. In the next 10-20 years, things more or less came in order. It has become more challenging to make a lot of money until you get a diploma. And even the most romantic souls now value money quite highly.

How Russians Invest Money?

For most people who live in Russia, that question is still rhetorical. They earn just enough to sustain their monthly expenses, so they do not experience the trouble of wise investing. They instead experience the difficulty of resisting too much credit. For the population that has never been exposed to credit cards, credit cards and loans became a big problem. People loved the idea of buying what they wish now and paying the debt later. Most of the people had no clue about interest rates, and at first banks played on that, did not disclose exact interest rates, etc. It was nearly the same problem as many of the US teens have with their first credit cards. The difference is that we are talking about tens of millions of adults in Russia. For many of these people, it will be complicated to return their financial freedom. They have bought household appliances or cars at the interest rate that sometimes was more than 30-40% a year and now have more debt than their annual income. Level of financial literacy is very low in general. A lot of people spend all their money, because they do not know how to save or just do not believe in saving even for the retirement.

However, there is a small percentage of Russians who manage to save. Some of them got an excellent Russian or Western education and work in big Russian or Multinational companies or are successful entrepreneurs. First of all, they prefer to keep most of their money in hard currency (either USD or EUR). Sometime ago, government created an effective way to make people trust banks again – deposits of approximately 20K USD per bank are guaranteed to be returned by the state insurance agency, even if the bank gets bankrupt. So, people put their money in different banks, making sure they are not exceeding the limit. Annual interest rates on deposits used to be very high in the last decade – up to 8%, and it was a guaranteed return on investment, unlike the stock market. Now interest rates are down to 1-2%, so investing in the stock market should rise.

3. RELATIONSHIPS

3.1. Friends Are Forever!

We have a saying – "Do not have a 100 Rubles, have a 100 Friends". Now, when a 100 Rub is approximately $1.50 it totally makes sense. But even when 100 Rub was a lot of money – a true Russian would still choose friends over cash. Friends play a vital part in the life of any Russian.

Why Is Friendship So Important?

In addition to the universal benefits of friendship, such as social support and companionship, friendship in Russia always helped to fight external forces. Brutal political leaders and governments that did not care much about the well-being of the ordinary people, wars, political and economic turbulence, harsh weather – are just some of the hardships that Russians had to overcome. External environment was always quite hostile and having friends to rely on made life so much better and lowered stress levels.

How Do We Find Friends?

Closest friends are usually friends made in school, university or even kindergarten, people whom you know for many years. We have a saying – One old friend is better than two new friends. Having lifelong friendship is indeed priceless because the collection of shared memories goes back to the time when you both were kids.

One of the reasons why life-long friendships are quite typical for Russia – people are less mobile, and many people live all their life in the same city, so the bonds do not break. That kind of friendship can be seen in some US States, such as Minnesota, where people also tend to have lifelong friends. But unlike the famous "Minnesota nice, Minnesota ice," a saying that describes that people there are very friendly to strangers but are quite reluctant to make more close friends since they already have a circle of friends – Russians are always open to more friends in their life.

There is a distinction between friends and acquaintances though. People believe that one cannot have many real friends. So, most people have one or several close friends and consider the rest – acquaintances.

How Different Is Friendship in Russia Compared to the West?

The most notable difference between friendship in Russia and the US is the level of intimacy between friends. According to the course "Understanding Russians: Contexts of Intercultural Communication" by Professor Mira Bergelson, in the US friends are familiars, in Russia friends are intimates.

In the US friends are people, whom you enjoy spending time with. You may also occasionally share with them some of your problems and ask for their advice and help, but you tend not to overload friends with too many issues. Russians allow friends very deep in their life, actively share both good and bad news and expect a lot of involvement from friends in finding solutions to problems. Shrinks are not popular in Russia. Why go to shrinks if you have friends?

Russians say that friend is a person whom you can visit at 2 am without prior notice to share good or bad news or if you just need to talk. It used to be so, but people everywhere became busier in recent years. Our demanding schedules affect how often we see friends and require prior planning. And quite often we substitute face-to-face meetings with email, texting or talking on the phone. But real friendships still exist here. Your friends will always be there for you and will always be at your side, and you can rely on your friends.

I wonder whether the fact that Russians allow friends to be so close has anything to do with the limits of personal space in Russia in general? Acceptable limits of private personal space depend on which country you are from. In a typical line in the US, there will be gaps between people, and in Russia, people will most likely stand right next to each other. If we allow strangers in our personal physical space so easily, maybe it is no wonder we allow friends to get so close to us in the emotional area?

Russians highly value "female friendship" and "male friendship," and there are certain rules and rituals for both. In the same time majority believe that friendship between men and women does not exist. That there is always a sexual context in such "friendship." This idea also exists in the West as we can see in a dialogue from the wonderful movie When Harry Met Sally.

Still, there are probably more similarities than differences since friendship is a universal type of relationship. And making friends with Russians is not that difficult and is worth it.

How to Become Friends with Russians If You Are a Foreigner?

- Having a good meal together helps a lot in building relationships in Russia.
- Be sincere and open
- Do not be afraid to show your weaknesses – it is very much accepted and will show that you are a human being
- Show your emotions – otherwise, it is difficult for us to understand what you think or feel
- Be as direct as you can in what you think, feel or want to do
- Avoid bragging – modesty is a highly regarded value
- Do not be afraid to ask questions

- Do not be scared to be funny, telling a story in which you acted clumsily or foolish will get you some bonus points
- Be genuinely interested in what we think and feel, be compassionate
- Be a good listener, even if our stories seem too long or highly unstructured
- Be interested in our culture and appreciate the achievements we are proud of (Ballet, Literature, Space exploration, etc.)
- Spend more time with us and do not be afraid to let us in your personal space
- Drinking together is optional if you do not drink, but long conversations at the dinner table are a must to become friends

Just be yourself! We like sincere and open people!

3.2. Gender Stereotypes in Russia

Many Russians are intolerant to any diversity. A person's behavior should fit in "age and gender appropriate" image. Let's explore what that means and why that happens, starting with gender stereotypes.

Gender Stereotypes in Russia

Woman: should be young and pretty, should spend a lot of time on grooming and never leave the house without make-up. Preferably – she should always wear feminine dresses and high heels. She should always be nice; assertiveness in women is usually viewed as aggressiveness. Best-case scenario – a woman takes excellent care of herself and looks gorgeous, is a fantastic wife and mother by the age of 25. If she has spare time – she may work, but she should not think that her career is more important than family. Family or trying to find a man to build the family with should always be her priority. She should treat her man as superior, do all household chores and still be pretty for him. She should love and want kids and take full care of kids when they arrive. Stepford Wives movie – that is the ideal image. Women are not expected to know how a screwdriver works or how to change a car tire. If a woman does any of that, it is probably because she is an unlucky spinster, who could not score a man. A woman is allowed to cry and be upset about silly stuff (such as lack of new dresses).

Man: Should be a breadwinner. His role is to make money, to bring that mammoth home. He should know how to use a screwdriver, a drill, how to change tires and how to do any other "manly" work at home. Ideally, he also has "manly hobbies," such as carpenting, hunting or fishing or working in his garage. Typically, all "manly hobbies" are done with other males and include beer drinking. How a man looks does not matter at all – he is allowed to be out of shape, unshaved and with a poor haircut ("a man should be just marginally better looking than an ape" is a popular saying). In fact – if a Russian man takes too much care of himself, it raises questions. Russian man should not be emotional, he is never allowed to cry or complain. At the same time – "he should treat women right" – open doors, help women carry heavy things, etc. And, always pay for women in restaurants and elsewhere.

Does That Make Sense? Are Both Men and Women Happy as a Result?

No, not really. I would say that being a woman in Russia is probably more difficult than being a man, but such stereotypes make life more difficult for both genders. Men are stressed out and cannot complain, which leads to drinking and early heart conditions. Women are chasing the youth and the stereotypes they should fit in.

There is no real reason for both.

70 years of Soviet Union may have had a lot of negative impact on many aspects of life. But there were also positives, such as liberating women. Women had equal rights to study and work.

Russian cosmonaut Valentina Tereshkova was the first woman in space. Women worked in all industries, and many of them managed to reach high profile roles. There is actually less gender discrimination at work in Russia than in many developed countries. Still, the most typical question people ask female cosmonauts of today is "how do you take care of your hair in space?" Not – "what are the most interesting scientific experiments you have done during your space mission."

In USSR everybody had a job, but after Perestroika many people lost their jobs. That created a lot of stress, especially for men, since they could no longer provide for the family. Men did not have a support network to complain about hardships and to discuss them, and spent days lying on couches, depressed. In the same time a lot of women started small retail businesses, bringing clothes from abroad and selling them at a market.

Now the workplace opportunities in Russia are more or less equal for men and women. A lot of people of both genders receive a good education and then use it to advance in their profession. But the old gender stereotypes are still in place. Here is the cycle.

Gender Stereotypes Cycle in Russia

Before the baby is born: Pregnant woman in Russia is treated as a person with severe disabilities. She is expected to downshift all social activities. I have seen a lot of happy pregnant women at an open swimming pool in Europe. You would not see Russian pregnant women at a swimming pool. Typically, pregnant women spend most of the time at home or engage in low-key activities. They are allowed to ask husbands to go to the grocery store at night if they want pineapples or pickles or anything else. Any Russian husband will do that if his wife has cravings.

When the baby is born: Russian men very rarely go with their wives in the hospital. And most of the time, it is a woman, who does not want to have a husband in a delivery room. Women are seriously concerned that they may not look great during the delivery of a baby and "men should not see them without make-up since that could negatively impact their sexual life after." So, the husband would bring the wife to a hospital and then start a 2-3 day drinking with his pals. When the baby is born, he is expected to visit his wife in a hospital. If the hospital allows visits – he might see the baby. Most hospitals though do not allow visits, so he will call her and ask her to come to the window to have a brief talk. Good husbands may "help" the mother-in-law to buy necessary things for the baby after he or she is born (most people do not buy any baby items before since it is considered to be bad luck). Why "help" in brackets – his involvement is considered to be help, not something that he has to do, but something he is graciously doing. The husband meets the wife and a newborn in the hospital when they are ready to go home.

Caring for a newborn: it depends. Sometimes both young mother and father take care of a newborn. But more often than that – it is the responsibility of the mother and grandmothers. If a father is involved, he is "helping." And you are "lucky to have such a husband."

Raising a child: is almost solely a woman's responsibility. A husband may "help," but the chores are almost never split equally. "He works, she stays at home," so he is a breadwinner and needs to rest after work.

What Is Wrong with Gender Stereotypes?

Ok, but isn't that a time, when a young mother could stop the vicious circle? And raise a child as she sees best? No, stereotypes are strong. Girls will be given dolls to play with, boys will be given cars. Pink and Blue. A mother might hate that grown-up men do not give place to women in public transport but will secure a seat for her son and will stand near him with heavy grocery bags. She will also tell her son that "he is a man, thus should never cry" and will tell her daughter that "she is a girl, so she should not be assertive." Girls will play with dolls and will help mothers to cook; boys will play their "manly games."

You see where I am leading with that. As a result of such upbringing, the cycle continues. Girls, who are told that they should be sweet and pretty and their mission in life is to find a good husband and have children may miss out on building the career. Boys, who are told they are kings of the universe, may expect women to be pretty rather than to be a soul mate or a partner.

When Are Russian Women Praised?

Any time they look good. They may be successful cardio surgeons, businesswomen or cosmonauts. If they do not look good, those achievements do not matter. If they do look good – no need to be a cosmonaut to get praise.

Any Russian woman can expect a man to pay for her meal in the restaurant, to get the door opened, to get help with her coat or with any heavy or not so bulky items that need to be carried. Also – with any kind of technical things, since "women are naturally not good in that." So, if you are a woman and have a flat tire in Russia – just stop your car and 5 min after a stranger will do his best to change the tire for you.

On the 8th of March. International Women's day is the day when men will take a shower, shave, dress well, cook you breakfast, bring flowers, do household chores and will praise you.

Men at your workplace will also praise you on 8th of March … for bringing beauty to the workplace. And 99% of Russian women do love that day! Imagine that! If a woman has any issues with all the above – she is most likely "a feminist," and that word has an extremely negative connotation here. People do not really know, who feminists are, but suspect they have short haircuts, hairy legs, and hate men.

Gender-Related Jokes and Stories

The most typical are stories about blondes. Even though Russian men adore blondes – there is a stereotype that blonds are dumb. And Russian men consider normal to tell jokes about dumb blondes, who for example, cannot park a car properly. And they will do that in front of their blond spouses without any hesitation. To say more – female blondes will also often tell jokes about blondes or even say proudly: "I am such a blonde, I have no clue how to park a car." They think that is cute, they are girls, blonde girls; they are not expected to know how to park a car or use a screwdriver. Men should do that for them.

Finally, my favorite story. I was late for an important meeting and took a taxi. It was an old shabby Lada car; driver most certainly did not have a shower that week and wore sports pants and sandals with socks. I was dressed in a suit and was about to sign a big contract. On our way, the driver was continually complaining about female drivers, who make driving in Moscow unbearable. I was sick and tired of hearing that and asked if he seriously thinks that women should not drive? He said yes. And lectured me on the fact that women have a smaller brain than men; thus, they should not be allowed to drive. He said that this fact has been scientifically proven. I have to agree with that. Women indeed have 100-150 grams less of the brain than men (on average). But there is no correlation between the size of the brain and how well it works. Einstein's brain was smaller than the average. But he certainly knew how to use it.

Of course, not all Russian people fit into those stereotypes. There are men, who care for their kids and are not afraid to show the sensitive side or express their feelings. There are women, who do raise their kids differently and are not scared to change a flat tire. And it looks like the younger generation is more free from gender stereotypes and that will make their life better in general.

3.3. Dating in Russia

Dating here is similar to dating elsewhere in many ways; people are people and people all over the world are looking for love. But the "Rules" are different in some ways.

Chivalry is a big part of dating in Russia – Russian admirers are very romantic, and they lavish objects of their affection with flowers, small and significant gifts, and romantic events. Men will be very polite, will open doors in front of women, help them into coats and do all other similar things. A man will never allow a girl to carry anything heavier than a tiny purse and will always pick a bill at a restaurant. The latter is expected in 100% of cases, so do not be surprised that the girl will not even offer to share. And if you offer to share – you will never see her again, and not because the only thing she wanted from you was a free dinner, but because that is against the cultural norm.

Flowers are a must, not only for important events but also for everyday dates. Make sure that you give an odd number of flowers since even number is for funerals only. Also, try to avoid yellow flowers – they are a symbol of separation or break-up. Long-stemmed red roses are a safe bet and the most appreciated flowers since they symbolize love. They are expensive, but no need to present a dozen or more – one red rose is considered equally romantic and will be much appreciated. If you think that red roses are too cheesy – go for tulips (in Spring) or irises or even for wild field flowers. Avoid orchids (also separation connotation), carnations (too formal and remind of Soviet time) and lilies (smell is too acute).

Girls are never expected to plan the date – it is a man, who thinks, prepares and surprises his princess. Typically, men date younger girls. Girls are supposed to be pretty, that is a skill that all Russian girls have mastered to the greatest extent. Be aware that a girl will start preparing for the date with you minimum several hours in advance and maybe even several days in advance. And she will invest a lot of money in expensive manicure and other beautification procedures and a lot of time and effort in choosing what to wear and on doing makeup. She will want to look perfect, and she will look her best. Most of the time that has nothing to do with her trying to look chic to extract any benefits from you (contrary to the popular opinion). That is just the upbringing and the habit here. However, she will expect a lot of admiration in return, so do not be shy to compliment her on her looks. Russian girl will always accept praise with grace and smile and will love that.

Good idea for a date with a Russian – to dress up a bit more than you would typically do for going out regardless of whether you are a man or a woman. For a man – wearing a jacket, for a woman high heels (if you feel comfortable wearing them) are most appropriate. A typical outfit for a date in the US for a girl – skinny jeans, high heeled boots, and a cute top, may be not enough in Russia. You may feel a bit underdressed and will feel more in place if you wear a more feminine outfit. That does not mean – you have to wear a mini but wearing a dress or a skirt and a top will be more appreciated than wearing jeans.

I get a lot of questions about "The Rules" of dating Russian men or women. In the US – there are plenty of rules, especially regarding appropriate topics for conversations at a first date, duration of the date and the progress (what is allowed and considered appropriate at each stage of the relationship). In Russia – there are much fewer rules, barely any rules. People act as they wish and are rather emotional than rational. Of course, being too intimate after one date is a "no-no" everywhere; one-night stands are never wise if you want a long-term relationship. But in general – people kiss if they feel like it and do whatever feels right at each particular moment. I know some cases when couples decided to get married after 2 weeks of dating and still are happy together after 10+ years.

Champagne is the drink of choice for any romantic occasion in Russia, not just for weddings and anniversaries

As for date behavior and conversations – expect the guys to act manly and the girls to act girly. A guy will talk about his business or his job a lot and will find a way to demonstrate his wealth by mentioning his car, house and other evidence of status. Sadly, wealth is valued more than good looks, and there might be too much emphasis on the wealth from the guy's side. A guy will also talk a lot about his manly hobbies – hunting, shooting, fishing, doing manly sports, jumping with a parachute, DIY projects, etc. Also, a guy is expected to be a good storyteller and to make a girl laugh.

Expect a girl to talk about being an excellent cook and mentioning her "girly" hobbies. I was stunned that guys in the US often brag about their great cooking skills to their dates. To me, that was so bizarre that I asked one of my American friends, why these guys do that? You will never hear a Russian guy, bragging about how he can cook a herb-crusted salmon or bake macaroons! And my friend said that otherwise, you will not get a girlfriend, that cooking skills are now among the expected skills for men. How cool is that! I frequently amuse my Russian girlfriends with that story!

In the US people usually avoid talking about politics, religion, and problems on a first date. In Russia all that is considered quite normal. Girls may tell about some minor disasters, which show them as vulnerable – how she got lost somewhere or her heel broke, or she had a flat tire and did not know how to change it. Girls will often downplay their intellect, education and professional status. She may have a Ph.D. in nuclear physics, but she will chat you up about baking pies or embroidery, especially if she is unsure whether you are an equal intellectually. She may also speak about problems in her family or about her past disasters in love life (that openness always surprises foreigners).

Man can also tell about that – how unfair love life has been for him so far. Or can even tell about problems at work or tell a story from his childhood, how he was bullied in school. You see a contradiction there – how the same man can act manly and portray himself as a winner and whine about something? There is no contradiction here – that is building a connection on an emotional level. In former times, in ancient Russia to love and to pity were synonyms. That mentality is still active – if a woman feels that a man is vulnerable, she will be more likely to fall in love with him. So, if you are dating a Russian girl – do not feel sorry about showing your vulnerability in limited doses.

There are no strict rules on how fast the relationship should move forward. It can progress to marriage very fast or stay at a dating stage for a long time, and both versions are considered normal. The big difference is that engagement rings appeared only recently (new habit, promoted by diamond makers). Before, a guy was just asking "for a hand and a heart" from a girl and asked for permission to marry her from her parents. The wedding usually happened in 1-2 months after the proposal, and that is when the bride and groom got wedding rings. To a large extent, marriages happened so soon because people used to marry in the early 20s, when they still lived with their parents and parents did not approve of sleepovers. But another reason is that Russians are emotional and impatient. If we decide that we have found a right guy or a right girl – why wait to be together?

3.4. Flower Etiquette in Russia

Flowers are beautiful. But what is more critical – flowers are symbolic. Flowers follow us on all special occasions. Knowing "flower etiquette" is vital, especially if you live in Russia. I am your guide, follow me!

Flowers – General Guidance

Always give an uneven number of flowers. Unless it is a funeral, in that case, you should bring even number of flowers (that rule is for up to a dozen flowers, but most people will follow it also if they give a big bouquet – such as 51 roses for the 50th Birthday)

Give a lot of flowers. Russian people love flowers. You cannot go wrong with too many flowers

Know which flowers are proper for which occasion.

Flowers – Love, Dating & Other Occasions

Love in Russia is strongly associated with flowers. Ideal boyfriend always brings flowers to a date. What kind of flowers? That depends on the girl's taste. Most women love long stem red roses, and only very few may think it is cheesy. To be on the safe side, you can start with white or off-white roses at the beginning of a relationship, and progress in a density of color as your love gets stronger.

Or just ask which flowers she likes (and if she likes roses – which color is best). Some girls love green roses or tea-colored roses. Some women would think though that roses are faux pax. In that case, opt for either simple field flowers or exotic ones.

Avoid yellow flowers – many people think they are a bad omen and lead to a break-up.

The least sexy flowers? Carnations! Why? Because this flower is associated with the Soviet holidays.

Make bouquets look classy. (no plastic, just a cute ribbon around) If in doubt – give as many flowers as you can – your date will love that!

Choose fresh flowers. We do believe that if flowers stay fresh long – it means they were presented with love and care.

However, think about the circumstances of the date. If you are meeting a girl in a café, waiter will find a vase for flowers. But if you are going to a movie theater – avoid bringing flowers. Your date will get tired of holding them during the movie and will get upset if flowers die without water.

Never ever bring your love flowers in a pot, unless houseplants are her hobby. Houseplants are a good present for families or older women, if you know they have houseplants at home.

Do not give a Russian man flowers unless he has died or has a big birthday (for example, 50th). If you decide to gift flowers to a man, make the bouquet look manly (dark, large flowers).

Some flowers are especially relevant for some occasions. For example – mimosa used to be a flower of the 8th of March, International Women's Day. Now though it seems like tulips are more welcome for that date

Flowers – Visiting a Russian Home

Bringing flowers is a very good idea. Give a nice bouquet of flowers to the lady of the house. Make sure that you bring wine or sweets too.

If you know that the family likes houseplants, those may be appropriate. But present flowers in pots only if you are sure. Some people do not want to care for houseplants. Also, if you present a plant in the pot, make sure you know people's tastes. Some people love orchids, some care about low maintenance succulents or violets.

Flowers for School

On September 1st all kids bring flowers to teachers in school. The most typical flowers for that occasion are gladiolus (3 bulbs) or astra (5 flowers). Any color works. For some reason, red gladioluses are the most typical.

Avoid lilies or other flowers which could cause allergies or just have an acute smell. Flowers will be in the classroom and at the teacher's home afterward.

Flowers – If You Visit a Friend in the Hospital

Make sure a hospital allows visits and accepts flowers first of all. Buy such flowers that do not smell, just to avoid allergies. I guess that is universal advice for any country though.

Most patients will be happy to see flowers, but what they would love to see even more – oranges or other fruit, chocolates, biscuits, and other food (from the allowed list) or something to read or watch.

3.5. Age Stereotypes in Russia

Age stereotypes are as strong as gender stereotypes in Russia. Age-appropriate behavior, clothes, hairstyles. Age discrimination at work. Are the age stereotypes internal or external? How far is Russia from Western countries on that dimension?

Senior Citizens Are Excluded from Social Life

Some time ago my mom and I went to movies and, while we were watching a Hollywood action film, a guy sitting next to her leaned in and asked: "Do you Really enjoy the movie?" She replied: "Yes! Do you?" I was angry at his tactless question since it implied that a woman of her age could not possibly enjoy such entertainment. And then I glanced over the audience and noticed that there were hardly any people older than 60 in the theater. My mom is in her 70s and, she is very active, travels abroad often and enjoys life. She and I often go to movies together and Really enjoy that. But the data shows that less than 1% of people her age go to movies.

The same thing is with concerts and other live events. After retirement, most people in Russia are not participating in social life as actively as when they were younger. There are several explanations for that, such as declining health and decreased income (average monthly pension in Russia in 2018 is $200). But another strong reason is age-related stereotypes, what is and what isn't appropriate for people of a certain age.

It is considered necessary to spend time with grandchildren, have such hobbies as jam making or knitting and watch TV at home. Attending a rock concert or going to movies is considered to be a thing for young people. That stereotype is most likely internal, and it deprives many people of fun social experiences.

Age stereotypes are also evident in how people dress, what kind of haircuts they choose. Glossy magazines often write about whether it is proper to wear certain clothes, makeup, and hairstyles when you are in your 30s, 40s, 50s.

Middle Aged People Have Hard Time Finding Jobs

Both the Russian Constitution and Labor Code prohibit discrimination against applicants and employees irrespective of their age. However, in practice, half of job postings list age preferences, usually capping the age at 40 or even 35. And even if age requirements are not listed, candidates over 40 will have slim chances to get a job.

What are the reasons behind cutting off candidates at the peak of their career? Incompetence of HR managers and lack of research that would show that companies miss out when they discriminate candidates and employees by age. Employees over 40 are experienced, mature, and are likely to have fewer personal distractions.

Age-based job discrimination stems from Perestroika times. At that time many young people had adjusted to the new market reality and quickly gained the new skills and people in their 30s and 40s were not as fast to adapt. But it was 25 years ago… Now people, who are in their 40s and 50s have the skills and experience, but they still suffer from age discrimination.

I do believe though those things will change with time, and when millenniums reach that age, maybe they wouldn't be discriminated against based on age, but rather would be evaluated based on their skills and work experience. Hopefully, the Russian laws would catch up and protect experienced employees.

4. LIVING IN THE CITY

4.1. Russian Clouds Have a Silver Lining

There are some things that we, here in Moscow take for granted. One of such things is that it is always sunny on major holidays. Clouds are eliminated. For us, it makes total sense. How else would we see the fireworks?!

Is That Real?

When I tell about that to my friends abroad, they think I am kidding. The government does what?! Planes spray silver on the clouds, so that you, Tanya, could watch fireworks?! Yes, that is exactly what my government does for me. After all – I do pay taxes and need to make sure my taxpayer money is invested well, right?

I must put a disclaimer though. That service is provided in Moscow only. I am just lucky to live here. It would've been a bit costly to manage weather at the entire Russian territory, even for special holidays.

How Exactly Do They Manage the Weather?

There are several methods. What all of them have in common is that to make the sky clear of clouds above the Red Square, one must convert these clouds in the rain, before these clouds reach Moscow.

The most typical method for doing that – to make up to 10 airplanes spray silver on the clouds. It is not pure silver though – it is AgI (Argentum Iodide), particles of which cause condensation of water. One can use cement for the same purposes as well, but AgI is more powerful, so it is cheaper. Even though that sounds bizarre. How could spraying silver be less expensive than spraying cement? I do not have in-depth knowledge about the process, I guess that you need much more cement to get the same result. And since you are using planes and fuel, maybe that is the reason it is cheaper to spray a bit of silver and not tons of cement.

How "Cheap" Is That?

Great question. Good weather for holidays is quite pricey indeed. According to media sources, the Moscow Government spent 430 M Rub (about $8.3 M) in 2014.

How Often Do You Have Fireworks in Moscow?

Unfortunately, not as often as in Chicago in Summer (not every week). Only on the major holidays.

I have a funny story about that from my childhood. As a child, I always loved fireworks and wanted fireworks to last longer. Once I asked my dad – how do people who make fireworks decide how long each firework is. My dad said that it takes a lot of time to make fireworks, so they work day and night and produce as many firework rockets as they can in between holidays. And I thought – it is ok to have fireworks only several times a year. That way each session last longer and is more memorable.

4.2. What Does It Mean to Be a Muscovite?

Who Is a Muscovite?

Muscovite is a person, who was born in Moscow. Distinguishing a Muscovite from a person from any other Russian city is actually pretty easy. Muscovites have a special kind of pronunciation, reducing "o" to "a" in many words. For example, when saying "moloko" (milk), I will pronounce it as "malako". There are also some words that are mostly used in the capital. And, of course no Muscovites would spend a New Year's Eve at the Red Square, the same way as no New Yorkers would go to the Times Square on the New Year's Eve. And a true Muscovite has a dacha.

What Is It like to Be a Muscovite for Me?

I love and hate Moscow at the same time. If you ask me in the sunny month of June – I do love the city. What not to be loved – great weather, gorgeous parks, hottest nightlife, lots of dining options, dozens of cultural events every day! But ask me the same question again in November – the answer will be different.

Most foreigners think that it is always freezing in Moscow. It does get cold in winter, but all the buildings and cars and public transport are well heated, so freezing is not the issue for us. And not because "we are used to cold" as most foreigners think, we just know how to keep ourselves warm. So, it is not the cold weather, but the lack of sun in winter months, that makes us unhappy.

However, the biggest problem of Moscow is overpopulation. Since most well-paid jobs are located in the capital, many people from other cities move to Moscow. As was said in one famous Russian movie – "Moscow is not made of rubber." Too many people create chaos for the transport system, that leads to traffic jams, air, and water pollution.

What Is Moscow's Identity?

Moscow used to be the center of the intellectual life of the country. And it probably still is – the Moscow State University is still located here; a lot of Muscovites still like to read. We are proud to have so many theaters and museums in our city. But living in Moscow is stressful, and commuting takes so much time daily, that most people only wish they went to theaters and art exhibitions at least once in a quarter. In reality, most people spend their life working and even if they have some free time, they often do not have the energy to attend cultural events.

Moscow is also an expensive city to live in. For several years it was among the top most expensive cities in the world. Now, after the collapse of our currency in 2014, living in Moscow became cheaper comparing to living in London, Paris and other cities. But it only became less expensive if your salary is in hard currency, which is not the case for most of local people. Moscow did become cheaper to visit, but more expensive for locals.

85% of Muscovites are now living in the city suburbs, which are called "the sleeping districts," and most of the historic center is demolished either during WWII or in the last 20 years. So, although what is left is beautiful, the majority of Muscovites are surrounded by a really dull visual landscape.

Moscow did change a lot in the last 10 years. Some changes are for the better, improving life of people, who live in the city. Some changes are to the worse – such as demolishing historic buildings. There are ongoing debates on those topics.

Is Moscow Becoming a Livable City?

- The most significant positive change, which happened in the last several years – better public spaces were created in the city. Public space is a new topic for Moscow, this definition emerged just several years ago, and the famous Danish urban design consultant Jan Gehl and his team did contribute a lot to that. Better public spaces mean more friendly parks, more bike lanes, more opportunities for outdoor fitness, more time people spend outdoors and enjoy that
- Parks are especially worth mentioning. The city seemed to master the science of turning ill-kept, unsafe and boring parks into the centers of recreation. Just cleaning the parks and planting flowers is not enough to make the park popular. Adding free wifi and smooth roads for rollerblading attracts crowds of young people. Having many people in the park at all times attracts businesses, that want to sell food and entertain park visitors. Free sports equipment attracts even more people, making parks safer, so moms with kids now also like to spend

time there. That sequence is best described by Jane Jacobs in one of the chapters of her book "The Death and Life of Great American Cities". It is great to see that Moscow is using best practices
- City responds to the lifestyle of people – it has become a 24/7 place, where one can find food, do a manicure or buy a refrigerator late at night. IKEA in Moscow is open until 2 am in the morning. That is both a bit crazy and very convenient. And other things add to the convenience although we, Muscovites, take them for granted – such as clearing the sky on major holidays so that we could enjoy fireworks
- A relatively recent initiative is a paid parking in the center. People who live in other big cities will be surprised, but even several years ago parking in Moscow was free and not regulated. One could basically park anywhere, and people did park their cars on pedestrian sidewalks. Now all that is gone, and traffic in the center got better. Also – currently it is always possible to find a parking space. Unfortunately, in some cases expensive parking has negatively impacted local retail
- Muscovites seem to have more control over the city now. Active Citizen app allows to vote for the right initiatives and ban the bad ones. Various apps allow reaching city officials when there are housekeeping problems. In the same time, unfortunately, Moscow government does not listen to people, when demolishing buildings in the historical center.
- As a lot of Muscovites, I think that Immigration is one of the most pressing issues in Moscow. I have nothing against migrants, in fact I vote for more diversity and skilled workers. But that program was not managed well. Thousands of people were moved from nearby countries (former USSR Republics) to work in Moscow. Most of them did move with an intention to work and started with a great enthusiasm. And I have seen the benefits of that in my neighborhood – for several Winters there was no snow on pavements and roads around my apartment building – it was all cleaned before I even woke up! But moving all these people was not thought through. A lot of them did not speak Russian and had trouble to integrate, many

received below minimal wage, none had any cultural integration training. That made life really difficult for them and for us, inhabitants of Moscow
- Another huge issue for me as a Muscovite is a "New Moscow". Government included a vast area outside of Moscow in the city. That idea was initially sugarcoated with the intention to move Moscow government there to improve traffic (Moscow officials do not take public transport, and streets are usually blocked for their daily commute). Moving them outside the city was a good idea, but no Muscovites believed that will happen from a very beginning. And we were right – Moscow government decided not to move from the city center, but for some reason we, Muscovites are now paying our taxes to expand the city limits

4.3. Small Towns of Russia

All small towns in the world have similarities – people know each other, the pace of life is slower than in large cities. Usually, living in small towns is nice. Is that true for Russia?

Russia is very much centralized around the capital – Moscow. Most of business happens in Moscow. St. Pete is the second most important city and is often called "the cultural capital" of Russia. Then we have 10 more cities with the population over 1 million. But Russia is a huge country and it has hundreds small towns. How is life there?

I haven't traveled within the country much. I used to do some work-related travel, but now my job does not need me to travel to regions. Still, let me tell you a couple of stories.

Bryansk

At the end of the 90s, I was helping Canadian producer to prepare radio show about a Russian town Bryansk, which is only 6-hour train ride away from Moscow. Bryansk is not a small town – it has over

400K inhabitants. This town's best time was in the Soviet times when 3 military factories were providing employment for people and rockets for the security of the country. When the plants got closed down, the majority of citizens lost their jobs. We have spent 12 hours in this town, during which we met with local people from all social levels – from the former director of the plant to retired folks to students. It was an incredible experience for me to see how people adjust to new circumstances. Some people supplemented the small pension, provided by state with whatever they can grow in their backyard – potatoes, carrots, etc. Some people started their own business (we met with folks, who began to sell ACs and computers), some people relied on their skills (mostly language or programming) to find a job elsewhere. I had very mixed feelings – on the one hand, I saw poverty, however – I saw a lot of energy.

Kasimov

The other small town that I want to write about is Kasimov, a tiny town (30K+ inhabitants), on the banks of Volga river. I visited this town several times for work. 350 km from Moscow (terrible road, drive takes 5 hours) and you are in a very picturesque place in terms of nature, but in the city that had seen better times. Churches, houses, infrastructure – it all looks like nothing was renovated in the last several centuries. The only modern facility there is the chocolate factory, and local people do love this business as it provides a steady income for many of the citizens. There is also another factory, which produces fishing nets, but I am not sure how many people they employ and how this business is doing.

I was writing this post from a small and very picturesque town in Montenegro and, I was thinking about a big difference between life in the small cities in Russia and in Europe. Even if you compare towns in more or less similar locations (in terms of weather, proximity to touristic sites and big cities, etc.) – Russian towns are much more impoverished, and people are much less happy. It is sad but true!

How to Bring Life to Small Towns of Russia?

I thought – what could be done to fix that? From the perspective of a marketing person – a lot could be done!

Let's take Kasimov as an example. Nature alone could bring tourists to the city during the summer. Volga river with sandy beaches is gorgeous. There is enough local food to feed an army. There are also some sights, and the town has a fascinating history of being both Russian and Tatar (half of the population is Christian, half is Muslim, and they live well together). There is also a fantastic samovar museum, one of a kind. That museum alone could've been a focal point of attracting tourists. People who live there do handcrafts, they could've crafted souvenirs.

Why is all that not happening? a) 350 km is not far but try to drive there! The road is terrible! SUV, driven by an experienced driver, gets there in 4-5 hours in Summer. Once I went there with a bus of media people in February during a snowstorm, and it took us 8 hours to get to Kasimov. b) Government does not support small business. Local people may have wanted to open shops or cafes or B&Bs, but taxes on small business are massive, and the procedure is complicated. That discourages people from launching new businesses. c) there is no marketing support for this tourist destination. Tourists are just not aware of it!

Any Best Practices in Russia?

Very few. The best "model case" is Veliky Ustiug – a town that was unknown for ages, but then somebody rebranded it to become a hometown of Russian Father Frost. Now, there are hotels and restaurants there, and it is not easy to book rooms and tables during the holiday season.

I believe that at least 1/10 of the small towns in Russia could be branded, promoted, helped with infrastructure, etc. People, who live in these small towns would get jobs and become happier, State would get its share in taxes. I wish that happens one day!

5. HOME

5.1. Russians Take off Their Shoes at Home

I always wondered about the custom of taking off shoes when you go to someone's place. For me, it appeared to be quite funny to attend parties, sometimes formal ones, and still to see people barefoot. Can you explain that?

One thing that really amazed me when we moved to Switzerland with my family was that you could wear black suede boots in fall/winter, and they wouldn't get dusty or dirty each time you go out on the street. At that moment, Muscovites heard what was considered to be a rumor – that in Europe roads are being washed with shampoo. That piece of knowledge really entertained us, it was in line with stories about people in some countries eating insects or paying for breathing pure oxygen.

So, the most obvious and probably correct answer is that the roads in Russia are less clean; hence, people remove their shoes to keep their apartments clean. It is also practical during a long winter season when it is freezing outdoors, so you wear warm boots, insulated with fur and it is hot indoors, so keeping your shoes on at home is not going to be comfy.

But we can also speculate on some more reasons. Comfortable footwear is quite a recent thing for Russian consumers. I am not talking about trainers and other sports shoes, I am talking about comfy shoes in general. In Soviet times shoes and boots produced by Soviet footwear industry were not comfortable, so people wanted to get rid of them as soon as they got home to give their feet some rest. Although now that is not an issue anymore, it might be the power of habit. And for girls, it still is an issue since 9 cm heels worn daily are tiring.

Finally, here is what amused me most about this question. Any Russian person would immediately recognize that this question is coming from a foreigner. I bet that not all guests at those formal parties were barefoot, some of them had "smenka" (change shoes) with them and felt in place with the situation. Smenka is something that Russians are used to from early age – kids in school always brought change shoes in a separate bag with them to school, adults used to bring shoes to theater, dances and when visiting friends. At present most hospitals, fitness centers, and other organizations provide plastic socks (free of charge) to be put on top of your shoes. And all airports also offer plastic socks that you put on top of your socks so that you do not have to walk through security line barefoot.

Finally, there is a need to mention domashnie tapochki (home slippers, provided by hosts). This wide-spread phenomena had always been in homes of Russians and had been considered one of the hospitality gestures of an excellent host. Typically, these are slippers, very often really worn out. A guest who did not consider bringing smenka might feel awkward when faced with a request to wear somebody else's slippers. The best recipe is – bring smenka to any place you visit in Russia! That is a part of being a good guest!

P.S. If you are a girl, never ever bring stilettos to house parties as your smenka. They might look impressive but hosts of the party will hate you for wearing them since sharp heels leave dents on wooden floors. Nobody will tell you not to wear stilettos, out of hospitality, but you may never be invited to this house again.

5.2. Balkon, Dacha, Pomoika (Balcony, Country House, Garbage Can) or the Lifecycle of Things

This phrase will instantly cause a smile on any Russian's face. And will not be understood by a foreigner.

Soviet times of deficit of everything forced people to be frugal. Any old, out-of-fashion or not used for a long time, unbroken or broken thing could easily have a second life one day. No idea when, but when that day comes – you would be happy you have not thrown it away.

However, apartments are small and do not have a lot of storage space. Now, at least in Moscow, paid storage facilities (very similar to ones in the US) have become available (although still not used by vast majority of people). But back then no storages existed. A typical 3-room apartment had an "entresol" – a small storage unit, located under the ceiling above the corridor from the apartment entrance to the kitchen. Typically, people stored valuable season-related things there – ice-skates, camping tents, etc. It was about 3 meters long and had two doors, one on each side. When you needed to extract something from there, you had to guess whether the object is closer to one side or another. It was a project to find something there.

However, that storage unit was never enough, and there were no other storage units inside an apartment and no shared storages in a building. So, people used the next available option – balcony. The climate here, as you know, is quite harsh and it snows a lot. Most balconies were non-glazed, therefore they could serve as storage only in summer. Things that got to the balcony during summer were in danger of getting wet, frozen and spoiled during winter. So, people moved them to a "dacha" (country house). Because one day, when you will really need these things – you will be happy you have them, and it will be no trouble to drive to your dacha and bring the treasure back.

And only when there was no hope (or no place at tiny dachas) – the thing was moved to a garbage can. Quite often it was disassembled before thrown away, and the most valuable parts were kept.

What is interesting – times of total deficit of everything ended almost 20 years ago. But even now generations of 30- or 40 – year-olds have troubles when dealing with clutter. Sometimes we just cannot throw away old things. I wonder whether people in their twenties have this problem as well or they are free from it…

5.3. Apartments or Houses? How Urban Russians Live?

Most Russians (74%) live in the cities. What are the urban homes like? Are these apartments or private houses? Do people prefer to live in the center or in the suburbs? Let's explore.

Downtown vs. Suburbs

Foreigners do not realize that the tourist photos they associate Moscow with, do not show what the majority of Muscovites see out of their windows every morning. Moscow's historical center is cozy and beautiful, Moscow "sleeping districts" are rather dull. The city always needed more residential housing, so the approach to construction outside the city center was mostly functional. Buildings that could fit as many inhabitants as possible, standing close to each other plus a necessary infrastructure such as a kindergarten, a school, a medical clinic, a couple of stores, a playground for kids and maybe a park (if you are lucky).

Moscow is a huge city (~14 million people), and traffic in the city is terrible. So, living closer to the center is convenient, since that way you lose less time for commuting. Living in the historical center is considered to be prestigious, but the poor quality of air, the traffic situation, exorbitant prices and the prevalence of commercial buildings make living in the center a questionable win. Still, there are several charming streets where most people would love to live.

Close to the city center, mainly at the South-West of the city, and also at some Northern districts, there are several nice residential areas, where you have those "Stalin buildings" (built during Stalin's time) with thick brick walls and high ceilings, large apartments, beautiful views of the river and big parks nearby.

And, here and there are new residential buildings, which have indoor parking, gyms, private security and other benefits.

However, the majority of people in Moscow live in the sleeping districts, in the Soviet-style identical buildings.

How about living in the suburbs? Some people do indeed live at their dachas if those have heating, but there is no such thing as suburbia in the "American way of thinking." People do not move to suburbs when they start families and want to raise kids. People want to have an apartment in the city as a permanent home and dacha as a summer-house for weekends. And those people, who do live outside of the city, but work in the center are heavily penalized for the opportunity to have fresh air by staying in traffic jams on their way to and from work for many hours every day.

So, 99% of Russians, living in the city, live in apartments. To have a private house within the city limits is super rare. There are just several townhouse communities in Moscow, and all of them were established in the recent decade or two.

What Is the Typical Apartment Like?

The way one describes apartments in Russia differs from the US way of describing apartments. We do not count bedrooms, we count rooms. So, we have one, two or three-room apartments. In the rare case – 4-room apartments. Studios are rare – there will typically be a separate kitchen and one room in a 1-room apartment. Most standard apartments will have one bathroom, so having a master bathroom and a guest bathroom is considered to be chic. Apartments lack dedicated storage spaces, so the balcony usually serves as a storage for everything – from winter tires to skis, strollers, and other items.

There are several types of apartment buildings in Moscow. The least prestigious are 5 store buildings, built in the 50s-70s. Apartments there are super small – the goal of the government at that time was to get rid of "communal housing" (several families, sharing one apartment), so these were never meant to be permanent and still greatly improved the quality of life for young families. These apartment buildings are named "khruschevki" after Nikita Khrushchev, who ruled the country at that time or "pyatietazhki" – five-story buildings. Now, most of these buildings have been demolished, and their former residents got apartments in the new modern buildings.

One level up from "pyatietazhka" is "devyatietazhka" – a nine-story building, also made of big building blocks. A typical 9-story building of the 60s-80s will have about 300 apartments. However, apartments are still small – a 3-room apartment could be around 60 square meters, which means that the biggest room is about 18 sq.m, the smallest 12 sq.m, and the kitchen could be as tiny as 5-6 sq.m.

A more modern residential building may have up to 21 floors, but they are also built of panels (the house is assembled quickly, as from Lego blocks). Apartments in such buildings are bigger and may have a better plan, but in general, they are not that much different from the earlier versions. People strongly prefer to live in brick houses or houses built under the more modern technology, called "monolith" (when the skeleton of the house is filled with concrete).

"Stalin buildings," which have solid, thick walls, big rooms, and high ceilings are also quite popular but have their own disadvantages. These buildings are quite old, and a lot of them need serious renovation. New modern buildings are out of the reach of most people, but some of them are nice, have non-standard apartment plans, gyms in the building and indoor garages.

Rent or Own?

To have an apartment in Moscow is a dream for most of 143 M residents of Russia. Very few are lucky enough to have an apartment in ownership, many take an overpriced mortgage (15-20% interest rate!) to own a place once they pay back in 20-30 years. For the rest – it is a dream that may never come true.

Still, having an option to get a mortgage is a relatively new thing, and even the exorbitant interest rates do not stop people from buying since it is a way to get an apartment right away. Before people had to wait until they save enough money to buy the condo and that was really difficult. There are two options if you want to buy – either buy a "second-hand" apartment and do whatever renovation it needs. Or buy an apartment in a new building. What is hugely different from the US – if you buy an apartment in the new building – be ready that the apartment will have only grey concrete walls. No floors, no paint on the walls, no electricity, no bathtub and of course – no kitchen. You are buying an unfinished "cave" and let your own team of construction workers install all the wires, smooth the concrete walls, do the floors and later do all the renovation – from floor to ceiling. So, whatever you paid for a square meter (be it $5k or $10K or more), add at least $1-2K for the construction work per each square meter.

Rental prices vary by the city and the district within the town. With the recent exchange rate fluctuations, it is difficult to give exact prices, but in general, a one-room apartment in a sleeping district of Moscow will cost you around $700/month+electricity and water charges. For people, who own their apartment, communal charges, gas, electricity, etc. typically amount to $70-150 a month, which is really low compared to the US, but relatively high, compared to the average salaries and pensions.

Renting apartments is not a good business since there are no laws, that protect a landlord from tenants destroying the apartment and there are no fixed leases. Basically – your tenant may leave when he or she wants, and the only thing they will lose is a one-month deposit for the flat (which may not cover the costs of renovation).

5.4. "Euroremont – Interior Design of Post-Soviet Russia

What happened to Soviet-style apartments after Perestroika? In one word – what happened was "EuroRemont" – "Western kind of renovation." Let's see why I have put these words in quotes and what do they mean.

Cornucopia of Options and Deficit of Design Skills

For 70 years of Soviet time, there was a deficit of nice furniture and home decor. One basically needed to hunt for Western-made furniture, and even then, a selection was limited.

Such absence of choice led to a deficit of interior design skills and fantasy. So, when markets opened, and an avalanche of products came to the country, people we not ready. Too much choice confused consumers, and they started to look for inspiration and best examples of home interior design where they could find them.

Euroremont – Inspiration from Movies and TV Series

At first, there were very few interior design magazines, and there were no professional interior designers. Thus, the inspiration came from movies and TV series. And that did create a particular style, which was called EuroRemont – Western Renovation. What was it like? First of all – white walls, preferably painted white walls.

One can argue that people were tired from the ornaments of the Soviet-style wallpaper and wanted to start their life from a clean slate. That may be one of the drivers. But the primary driver was in soap operas – such as Slave Izaura and in the beloved Santa Barbara TV series.

The popularity of the first soap operas was beyond imaginable. There were no crimes reported at the streets of Moscow during the time of new episode broadcasts. Gangsters are also people, and they wanted to know how the saga develops, will Cruz and Eden marry, will Izaura get free from her sleazy boss, etc. And all the villas and fazendas from these TV series had white walls, so white walls immediately became the standard of a modern Russian interior design. That is quite funny – in warmer countries, white walls serve their purpose – it is too hot, so you do not want your walls to absorb any heat. Here in Russia, it is almost always cold. I bet that if we had Jeeves&Wooster series on TV at that time – we would've opted for the British colonial design with dark green walls and wooden panels instead. But it was what it was.

In addition to white walls, villas, and houses of California, Mexico and South America countries often have light-colored furniture or really bright furniture, especially sofas. In the movies sometimes couches were made of white leather, and white leather couches have become incredibly popular. James Bond movies also often had leather couches and armchairs, which only supported the idea. Also, Bond's style included a lot of technical gadgets – TV sets which emerged from the walls, as well as aquariums and other "luxury items."

That was the time, when a) home entertainment (video players) was on the rise, and b) restaurant business did not emerge yet. So, people mostly entertained guests at home and having a white living room with a white leather sofa, modern home theater, and some unusual interior design items (such as an aquarium or sophisticated lights in the ceiling) was considered super cool.

Influence of Asian Luxury and Tsar Luxury

You would suspect that the white walls, modern gadgets, and furniture would lead us to minimalist interior design – sleek, modern and stylish. But you forget two things: a) we are in between Europe and Asia, therefore we have a penchant for Asian luxury – gold, carpets, ornaments and b) we have had Tsar dynasties and still can see how Tsars lived in the numerous palaces, especially nearby St. Petersburg.

People who started to earn money wanted to incorporate part of that luxury in their interiors. Most of the time the result was a bit bizarre – a typical "EuroRemont" apartment of the post-Perestroika time had white walls, gadgets and some modern furniture. But it could also include Persian carpets on the floor (and walls), lots of elaborate decorations and even furniture à la Ludvig the 15th – chairs with the gold-plated curved legs and armrests. "Expensive and rich" – that was the motto.

Dealing with Limited Space

One of the most frequent issues was a lack of space. Typical Soviet apartments did not get any bigger after Perestroika, so people had to deal with areas ranging from 33 square meters to a maximum of 70-80 square meters. As we know from the earlier posts – Soviet apartments were designed so that they accommodate as many family members as possible – sometimes several generations. So, even if one person was buying a relatively large apartment for his/her own use, it was still divided into small rooms. That did not fit the "movie-style living" of vast open spaces.

An answer to that was often simple – just break the unnecessary walls. Quite often that was the wrong answer – since some walls do serve a purpose of holding the house together. There were a lot of questions, for example, when a large jacuzzi (another element of "luxury life") fell onto the floor of the apartment below.

An Era of Interior Designers and Interior Design Magazines

Of course, such a significant market niche could not stay empty for long. At the beginning of the 2000s, magazines and designers mushroomed and flourished. I have some interior design magazines of that time – some of their advice was useful and professional, but a lot of them were far from perfect. Same thing – for interior designers. Not many designers had professional education and experience – they often wanted to create pompous and unusual projects for their portfolios rather than create comfortable living spaces for their clients. Often such projects included elaborate decoration, cascades of lights, hanging from the ceiling, a mixture of styles, too much glass and other cold materials. But still having designers and magazines was a big help for people.

How Is It Now?

It really depends on the family and their taste, but I would say that things have improved. Interior design magazines and TV shows, designers, IKEA stores and worldwide travel did make a positive impact. Also, the interiors of public places (cafes and such) gave people ideas. A lot of residential interiors are still eclectic, but at least they reflect the taste of owners. It is ok to have an eclectic space if the owner feels comfortable in it.

Now it is more about the cost. Renovations are costly since most of the materials are imported. But even an average income city family can do something in their apartment to make it cozier. It takes some time to develop a good taste for interior design, but as people experiment, their skills get better.

5.5. What's Behind the Russian Steel Door Culture?

We have a saying – My house is my fortress. And fortresses should be equipped with safe doors.

Speaking seriously, although Moscow is indeed quite a safe city, apartment robberies do happen. That is why almost all apartments have fortified metal doors and sophisticated locks. People, who live on the first floor, usually also have metal bars on windows.

How Do Thieves Know When to Rob?

Thieves know that the majority of people in apartment buildings will be at their "dachas" (country houses) during holiday seasons and weekends. A thief can see who is absent by looking at the mailboxes. If a mailbox is packed with bills and other papers – most likely a person is away. Some people even go to the post office before a long trip and ask to hold their correspondence at the post office or ask neighbors or friends to pick up mail.

Thieves are quite resourceful – they can also find out landline numbers and make phone calls to make sure nobody is in the apartment. If they suspect that residence is a good target, they watch inhabitants to understand their daily schedule. A week is usually enough to get a picture. Finally, they always ring the doorbell before starting any actions.

What Kind of Valuables Are Stored at Home?

In addition to the usual possessions, such as computers, electronics, fur coats and art objects, Russians do store cash and jewelry at home.

And by cash I do not mean the equivalent of $100. Many people do not trust banks and keep all their savings at home in cash. That would sound weird to most Western people and especially to Americans, but Russians have a good reason not to trust banks. There were many instances when banks collapsed or when there was a sudden money reform, and people lost all their savings. Now the bank system is much more stable, and there are state guarantees for the sums up to $20K, but people still have trust issues.

Of course, people try to hide cash. But professional thieves know all the typical hiding places. They make sure to check the pantry for jars with flour and grains, look inside the freezer and inside the toilet tank, between bed linen in a closet, shake up books in the library and look under table covers and matrasses.

Having a safe box at home or renting one in a bank is also rare. All Russian women do love jewelry and usually keep their impressive collection in a special box on a bedroom table. That is an easy target.

How Do Thieves Operate

Thieves, who specialize in apartment robberies, know how to open almost any lock or how to drill the lock out without making much noise. However, opening a steel door takes much more time and is noisy, so thieves try to open steel doors only if they are sure that's worth it.

People, who live on the top floor, also are at risk since a thief can enter the apartment from the roof, especially if the apartment has an open balcony. Before, a lot of windows were constructed so that they had "fortochka" – a small window, which people often left open when going away. There were thieves, specializing on getting inside the apartment through these windows – usually, they used kids to climb in the window, get inside and then open the door. Now that type of robbery is almost obsolete since modern windows do not have "fortochka".

There is also a type of thieves, called "vorovka na doverie" (thieves, operating on trust). These thieves ring the bell when inhabitants actually are at home and talk them into giving their money for some cause or steal something while a senior apartment owner goes in the kitchen to bring them a glass of water.

What Could Be Done to Protect Your Property

Best way to protect your apartment is a combination of a steel door and a security system.

Price range for steel doors in Moscow is within $250-$5000. The cheapest option will include a thin steel door with a 2-3-prong lock. The most expensive option will provide you with a lock good enough for a Swiss bank, an insulated steel door, covered with an expensive wooden panel and will even have some metal or glass decorations.

I actually have two doors in my apartment, the first one is a thin metal door with an excellent 3-prong lock and the second one is the original wooden door. That combination provides both security and noise insulation. I do not mind opening several locks every time I get inside my home.

I also have a security system, provided by the city police, which I find very efficient. They install equipment that is sensitive to a door or window opening and movements inside the apartment. Usually you turn the alarm system on or off, using a key fob; however, I still have the old system, which requires me to make a phone call each time I need to switch the alarm on or off. I tell my personal numeric code, and the operator tells me a password for the day. She also tells me her operator number. If the alarm goes off – police is at my door within 3-5 minutes. Even if a thief managed to open a door within that time, he will not be able to steal much and will be caught. There are usually two policemen, carrying Kalashnikov machine guns and wearing bulletproof vests. How do I know that? From several times of forgetting to switch off the alarm…

By the way, that security service is really inexpensive – it costs only $15-20/month. And since you can see that the security system is installed from outside (a red light near the door) – chances are a thief will not even attempt to break the door.

There is also a video surveillance system at the entrance of most apartment buildings and inside the lobby. Most buildings do not have concierges, so video surveillance prevents crimes or helps to catch criminals afterward.

Finally, all apartment building entrances are equipped with either a code lock or a key fob lock. If you do not know the code or do not have a key fob to open the door, you call the apartment, and your host buzzes you in.

What Do the Statistics Say?

I bet that after reading all that, you are scared about even setting your foot in the Moscow city. So, how bad is the apartment robbery situation from a stats point? We have about 6000-9000 incidents of apartment robberies/year. The total number of apartments in Moscow is 3 million apartments, which makes a tiny probability of your apartment getting robbed. If you compare those statistics with statistics for the major US metro areas – you will see that Moscow is a very safe city indeed. Maybe the reason behind that is the presence of those steel doors? Apartment robberies percentage goes down every year. So, the city gets safer each day.

5.6. Dacha – More Than a Country House, Rather a Passion

The word "dacha" comes from a verb – "dat'" – to give and the noun "dar" – gift. For many years, receiving a plot of land for personal usage was an excellent and very much appreciated gift – whether it came from Tsar government or Soviet government. But the way people used that land did differ significantly in different times. One cannot fully understand Russia without understanding the cultural context behind Russian dacha.

Dacha – Before the Revolution of 1917

First dachas in Russia appeared at the beginning of 18th century under Peter the Great. He wanted his subordinates to stay close to him even on vacations, so he granted them plots of land near St. Petersburg. These plots of land were strategically positioned on the way to Peterhof, Tsar's residence, so he could always stop and see how his people are spending their free time.

In 1803 the famous Russian historian Karamzin wrote that in Summer Moscow gets empty since people go to dachas. And by the mid 19th century, dachas became a favorite place to rest and to have fun for all aristocrats, who could afford such a pastime. Dachas were often simple wooden houses, but always had a terrace, where the inhabitants could dine, drink tea and entertain in the long summer evenings. Not all people owned dachas, some did rent them for summer and usually traveled to dacha together with an entire family and servants. Read Anton Chekhov if you want to learn more about dacha stories of that time!

Dacha – Soviet Time

October Revolution of 1917 brought with it a law, which forbade private ownership of land in Russia "forever." The idea behind it was that all citizens of the country will be able to use all the country resources, all people will be equal, and none would be able to exploit other people or be richer than others. The new Soviet Republic values were mainly collectivistic. And instead of individually owned dachas, general population got access to group recreational facilities such as sanatoriums. A popular Soviet phrase was: "All around me belongs to the people, all around me belongs to me."

There was, however, another saying – "everybody is equal, but some are more equal than others." Josef Stalin, who ruled the country from

1924 till 1953, was fond of a good countryside recreation himself. He had many dachas in the most picturesque parts of Russia – from Moscow region to the Black Sea. These were huge mansions, fully staffed and ready to welcome him any time he decided to show up.

Stalin figured that granting such privilege as summer dacha to his closest people in the government and to the VIP people from culture and science élite will be very motivating for them. These dachas did not belong to their inhabitants, furniture and lamps had itinerary numbers on them, but these dachas were a big luxury and getting one was considered to be a tremendous privilege. To simplify things, dachas were grouped by the occupation – that is how we still have "villages" of writers, composers, artists, scientists, etc. At that time all dachas were a place to rest, fish, collect berries and mushrooms, play sports and entertain with friends.

After the WW II, limited food resources in the country forced the government to allow people to get plots of land and support families by growing veggies there. However, building a house on that plot was strictly forbidden. In the 60s, during Nikita Khrushchev's time at power – ordinary people were finally allowed to build dachas. But it was so not easy to get one. Distribution was merit-based, one needed to fully comply with the ideology and wait in a long line, sometimes for many years.

These dachas were not as luxurious – it was usually just a tiny plot of land with permission to build a small one-floor house there. Inhabitants still did not own it but could use it for growing produce strictly for family consumption (not for sale). Still, people felt as if it were their own land, so getting a dacha became one the dreams of Soviet people, in the same line as getting an apartment and a car. There were many manipulations – how to get dacha quicker. In Russia law and rules were always particularistic, so if you knew somebody, you could get the desired dacha much faster.

Building a house was not easy as well. There was a deficit of construction materials. It is difficult to imagine that now, but one could not just go to a store and buy wood or bricks or anything else, one needed to "get" the required materials somehow through his network of contacts or pay triple at the black market.

This was the time when the function of dacha started to morph – it became a place of hard work in the field rather than a place to rest and entertain. That function of dacha came in very handy in the turbulent times of the 90s, when food was scarce in the stores and people really supported their families by growing potatoes, fresh produce, berries and apples at their land. A lot of home-grown produce was conserved for winter in either pickled or salted form or as homemade jams.

Dacha – Modern Time

In the 90s it was finally allowed to own property. That is another big and interesting story, but the outcome was that people started to buy dachas if they had money. Or, if they already had dachas, they could privatize them. Restrictions on the size of the land or number of floors in the house were also lifted. Finally, you could do whatever you want on your own property. Curious what happened next?

People, who were always deprived of such an array of choices started to experiment. Wealthy "New Russians" immediately began building huge mansions at their small plots of land. A lot of these houses lacked taste or style. Generations of local people had never seen beautiful country houses, and commercial industry in this area was not developed yet. The tradition of building wooden houses was replaced by making brick or stone ones. Dachas used to be just summer houses, but now many people started to build all year round houses.

Now, finally, the industry works as well as in any other country and if you want to have a beautiful house of any style – it will be built for you. But it will be pricey. As with any commercial goods and services in Russia – from clothes to manicures, you pay a premium for good stuff!

So, how do people spend time at dachas now? That does vary. A lot of people still work all day, growing potatoes, cucumbers, strawberries, etc. The majority of these people have full-time jobs in the city, they are not agricultural workers, but every Friday evening from April to September they leave the city to have a weekend of arduous work in the field. Needless to say – they have to cope with massive traffic jams on the way to dacha and back. Sometimes getting to a dacha which is 50-100 km from the city can take 3-4 hours. It is not possible to give a rational explanation of why they still continue growing potatoes, although they can easily buy them in any store. Economically it does not make sense, but people are irrational. For some growing produce is a habit, some (mostly older people) enjoy to cultivate land with their own hands, some like the idea of organic food or say that potatoes, grown in your private garden just taste better.

Still, many people do think of dacha as a place to have fun. These people mow their lawns and plant flowers, so they still have to do their share of field work to make their dacha look presentable. But instead of spending all the time in the garden, they invite friends and entertain them, grill meat, eat strawberries sitting in gazebos, play sports and enjoy other recreational activities. Hopefully, this will become a mass trend, and more people will enjoy resting at dacha rather than working there!

5.7. Spring Cleaning in Russia

A time before Easter and/or May Holidays is time to do Spring cleaning, both at home and in the city. Here is how we, Russians, approach this task.

Spring Cleaning at Home

We do not call it Spring Cleaning – we call it General Cleaning. The difference from everyday cleaning is that it typically involves washing curtains, windows, lamps, crystal ware and comprehensive cleaning of everything at home.

Window cleaning in Moscow and other big cities (in apartment buildings) is done by people, who live in the apartments, not by the building maintenance, like in the US cities. Our windows open inside, so it is possible to clean them. It is usually a project in itself, especially if you have an old type of windows and have to unscrew and open them and clean two sets of glass. Now it is easier to do though, the modern cleaning products make this process go faster. In Soviet times window cleaning was done with soap and water. To get rid of soap stains on the glass after the glass dried, we used crumbled newspaper sheets, which squeaked terribly. Also, now we can call professional cleaners, who charge $7-10 per window. That really saves time!

Washing curtains usually happens at home (unless the curtains need to be dry cleaned). Again, unlike in the US, most urban households have a washing machine in the apartment. Laundromats in the building is a very foreign concept for us. We do not have dryers though. To dry washed garments, we use special hangers. In a case of curtains, we often just hang the wet curtains and let them dry naturally. That works really well if the curtains do not need ironing.

Washing carpets is often done without water. Having a carpeted floor is very rare here as we prefer wooden floors, so carpets could be lifted and brought outside to be "cleaned" by beating the carpet with a special stick. That is a "Summer" way of cleaning the carpet, the "Winter" way is to clean the carpet outside, using the fresh snow. Of course, many households just use vacuum cleaners, and some have washing vacuum cleaners now, so cleaning carpets outdoors is not seen as often as before.

Apartment cleaning during spring cleaning means that you may move furniture and clean in places, which are not cleaned at the everyday cleaning. You also wash ceiling lamps, which could be a big project if lamps are made from crystal. You dust in the places, which you usually do not get to, such as a top of the cupboards.

By the time you are done with the cleaning, you feel like "angels are flying in your apartment," as my grandmother used to say. But there is another way to strengthen that feeling. De-cluttering your space – that is what really makes the angels fly!

De-Cluttering and Storages

In general, de-cluttering is a very foreign concept for us, Russians. Years of the deficit in the stores in the Soviet Union made Russian people extraordinarily frugal and stimulated hoarding mentality. Anything, even if it is old or broken, could have a second life at dacha or could wait until it could be used for spare parts. Thankfully there is no deficit of anything now, so people slowly started to value free space and de-clutter their homes.

We are far from achieving zen, described in Marie Kondo books, we are still sending old clothes to dachas, but we did start throwing away things. I see that from the old TVs at the garbage, from the stacks of books and toys in the entrance of my building and from the changes that are happening in my own apartment. We definitely want to see less clutter in our homes!

Storages, very similar to the ones in the US, are mushrooming in the big cities. People use storages to keep seasonal clothes and sports equipment, and also to store things they no longer use (like the sets of china, etc.) but are not ready to part with. I am not an exception – my winter coats go to dry cleaning and then in storage in Spring, together with skis and boots. And, I am thinking that one day I should probably do the de-cluttering of the stuff I have in those 3 square meters of the storage space.

Spring Cleaning at Dacha

Once you are done with the Spring cleaning of your home, you can go play, right? No, not at all. May holidays are all about dacha. Thousands of cars stand in traffic jams, going from the city. There are seas of work and mountains of work there – from the Spring cleaning of the house to the agricultural work in the garden.

Most people do not mind that work though. After sitting in dusty offices, being outside and cultivating your own plot of land is something that Russians really enjoy. Work in the field is hard, but rewards will soon come in shape of berries, fruit, and vegetables. People also enjoy May holidays at dachas because of the warm weather and the first BBQ event of the year, called "shashlyki".

Spring Cleaning in the City – Subbotnik

But wait – we forgot to mention the Spring cleaning of the city! That happens even before you start cleaning your own home, in the last decade of April. And, again, it is not called "Spring cleaning." It is also not called General cleaning! It is called – "Subbotnik", from the word subbota (Saturday).

Subbotnik is a volunteer day of work for public goodwill. This initiative originated in 1919 and is one of the positive legacies of the Soviet Union. When it started, the Soviet Republic was very young and poor and could really use the free workforce. Leaders of the country also participated in that work and, the image of Lenin, carrying a wooden log with comrades at one of those events, was used later in propaganda hundreds of thousands of times. By the 70s subbotniki became mandatory, which kind of took the fun out of the game. Anyway, these initiatives were always good for the cities.

I very much like the modern trend – in Moscow subbotniki are viral now. All the parks invite young people to participate via social media. Organizers not only provide all the tools but also create fun ambiance with live music, snacks, and beverages. The city is almost spotless now at any time, but it is good that citizens can spend one day a year making the city more beautiful as it creates a stronger bond between the city and people.

5.8. If You Are Invited to a Russian Home – Russian Hospitality

What to expect if your Russian friends invited you to their place? How to prepare for your visit? First of all – prepare to enjoy the Russian hospitality and arrive being hungry.

How Often Do Russians Invite Friends Over?

In Soviet time there were few restaurants, it was difficult to book a table in a restaurant and going out was expensive for most people. So, people invited friends to their places all the time. Actually, friends could just pop in without invitation, and that was considered normal. People really enjoyed home visits. On regular days that was usually an informal gathering, around a kitchen table. On big holidays – people gathered around a big table in a living room. I still remember that my parents had a convertible dining table, that was used only for special occasions. These are good memories – mom cooking in a kitchen, dad setting up a dining table in a living room. Then guests arrive, sit around the table and I sit with them for some time, and then play nearby.

Russians still very much like both visiting friends and inviting friends over. In the recent years the pace of life and heavy traffic in big cities and thousands of cafes and restaurants have made going out more accessible, but people still enjoy relaxing time at friends' places a lot.

What to Expect If You Are Invited to a Russian Home?

Expect to eat a lot! For us, hospitality equals good food and plenty of it. If you are a foreigner – you should expect even more food. You are a special guest, so your local friends will make a lot of effort to make sure you enjoy the evening. To be a good guest – please be hungry, when you visit us. Nothing can make us more upset than a guest, who does not have a good appetite. We will think that you did not like the food.

At the same time that does not mean that you have to finish everything on your plate. We will not be offended by that. So, if you do not like an unusual dish – just pretend you tried it and leave the rest on your plate.

What kind of food to expect? Nowadays a lot of Russians are good at cooking international meals, but knowing that you are a foreigner, most will probably prepare dishes from the Soviet past.

You would be invited for dinner. Breakfast or lunch meetings at people's homes are not typical. It would be a seated dinner with "zakuski" or appetizers, which are enough to feed you hunger, but there might be soup, and there certainly will be the main course and tea and cakes at the end of the evening. Make sure you have enough room in your stomach for all that!

What Should You Bring?

A good guest might bring flowers for the lady of the house, and a bottle of wine or something sweet for dessert (a cake or a box of chocolates). Or you can bring something that is popular in your country – that will be much appreciated. Choose the most typical thing – what your country is famous for. If you are Swiss – bring some cheese or chocolate, if you are French – bring some wine, if you are from Scandinavia – bring some salmon, etc. Whatever you bring with you does not have to be expensive at all, your Russian hosts will enjoy the story you tell about the gift. Carrying a small souvenir for the house instead of wine or sweets is also a good option. Most Russians love "good luck" souvenirs, since we are quite superstitious, or will be happy to receive a small handcrafted item – a decorative plate or a textile souvenir. Actually, the value of the present is not important – we appreciate the time you spent selecting a gift for us and your thoughtfulness.

Home Etiquette

Russians do not wear street shoes at home. You need to know that. Although your hosts may be shy to ask the foreigner to take the boots off, it is the custom you should be aware of. In many cases, you will be offered "home shoes to wear." Those home shoes may be old, generations of guests wore them already. You have three options – a) accept the offer, b) tell that you will walk in socks (the place is spotless, they cleaned it thoroughly before your visit) and c) that you have your own "change shoes" with you. I do recommend the latter option, but please make sure you do not bring stilettos since they damage wooden floors.

After you give your coats to the host, change into "home shoes" and give your gifts – your host will show "where you can wash hands" It will be a long evening, so it is useful to know where the bathroom is right away.

After that, you will be offered a drink. By the way, we do not say "Na Zdorovye," only people in movies say that. When raising a glass – just say what you think – that you are happy to be here, that you are delighted to have found Russian friends, that you enjoy their hospitality and wish them happiness, prosperity, luck, love, etc. If you have to say that in Russian – here is the formula – [Let's drink] for – Za… vstrechu (for our meeting), za uspeh (for success), za hozyaev (for the hosts), za hozyaiku (for the lady of the house, who spent hours preparing the meal), etc.

Since you are a foreigner, your hosts will most likely give you a tour of their place. It will be interesting for you – a chance to see the entire apartment of a real Russian family. You may be surprised to see that the place is smaller than your home abroad. But you can always say that it is very cozy. That will be very appropriate and will make the hosts happy.

The official part is over, congratulations! You have done everything right and are a great guest. Most likely you already noticed a dinner table, with an overwhelming amount of food on it. That is your destination for the next 4-6 hours. Relax, enjoy, eat, drink and be yourself!

What Might Surprise You at the Dinner Table?

If you are new to the Russian food – food may be your primary concern. What if hosts offer something that you never tried before and do not want to try? For foreigners that could be such items as meat jelly, "herring under a fur coat" (mayo salad with lots of ingredients and salted herring) and some other dishes. As I said – be yourself. It is ok to say that you will taste just a little. Try it – you might be surprised that it tastes great! But if you are a vegetarian or vegan or have other dietary needs – it is better to tell your hosts about that when you accept the invitation, so that they adjust the menu accordingly.

You will have no problems announcing that you are a vegetarian. People do get that. Gluten-free is more tricky. Russians do not believe in gluten-free, this condition is unheard of and the majority of Russians eat everything with bread (and add flour and grains in the food). You will need to explain to your hosts that you have a medical condition that prevents you from eating a long list of ingredients in advance. Be careful about mixed dishes, they may still contain gluten, since local people are not trained to cook gluten-free meals.

Be ready to talk and listen a lot. Russians love telling stories. Also, be prepared to engage in a deep conversation. Russians like to talk about serious matters at the dinner table, they will want to hear your opinion on politics, economy, science and other subjects. And they will care about what you say.

If you are friends with the hosts – it is likely that you already know them quite well and know their political views. If you do not – given the current events it may be better to avoid political topics. Ask your hosts questions about their life, and you will learn a lot. Share your stories – they will be listened to with a lot of attention. Do not be afraid to sound silly or to ask too many questions, being yourself, being open and honest is the best strategy.

You may be offered to drink a lot. Good hospitality means that the guest's glass should never be empty. But if you are not used to drinking much or you are offered vodka, and you are not used to drinking vodka – it is absolutely ok to say that as a foreigner you did not have enough training and you will take it easy. You will be surprised to see that most young Russians do not drink vodka themselves. If you do not drink at all – my suggestion – just say that you have a medical condition that prevents you from drinking. That should be respected.

I hope you enjoy the evening! Friends in Russia are friends forever. That is very valuable. You can be very open with Russian friends, you can speak about any topics (aside from politics), you can complain about your hard life, you can be yourself. Bond with Russians, you will never regret that!

6. FOOD

6.1. What Russians Eat for Breakfast

Typical daily eating habits vary by region; I will be writing about an urban population of Moscow. Check out whether your eating habits are similar to the eating habits of Russians!

Russian Breakfast

Although most Russians believe that eating a full breakfast is a good habit, many people skip breakfast. In winter night is long, so most people wake up to go to work when it is still dark, and there is always a temptation to snooze. As a result, some people opt for additional minutes of sleep and just have a cup of coffee or tea as they hurry to get to work on time.

Russia was traditionally a tea drinking country. During the Soviet Union time, most people were choosing black tea as their preferred hot beverage for breakfast, lunch or dinner. Tea was usually consumed with two teaspoons of sugar and lemon. Some people preferred to add milk to their tea instead of lemon. However, even then, there were some coffee lovers, who could not imagine a morning without a cup of coffee. At that time, it was usually a Turkish style coffee. Later, multinational FMCG companies brought instant coffee to the market and spent a lot on marketing to promote it. Now, most people drink coffee for breakfast, and even though consumption of instant coffee is still high, more and more people have coffee machines, French presses and other equipment to prepare a perfect cup of morning coffee. Most people drink coffee with milk and sugar.

Typical fast breakfast is a pair of sandwiches with cheese or sausage (kolbasa). Russian sandwiches differ from US sandwiches a lot – it is usually a slice of bread, often some butter and a slice or two of cheese or sausage.

If you have a bit more time, you can cook eggs, porridge, pancakes or cheese dumplings, called "syrniki." We almost never eat scrambled eggs – typically that would be sunny-side-up eggs or easy over eggs or an omelet. Ingredients to add are kolbasa (the sausage), tomatoes and bell pepper.

Porridge does not necessarily mean oatmeal. It could be oatmeal, but it could also be cream of wheat (semolina) or rice or buckwheat, usually cooked with milk. Cream of wheat is the most controversial – kids typically hate it, because there could be clumps inside. My sister prepared the best cream of wheat for me when I was little – she made it really thick, as a pudding and made it jelly in the form of a dessert. Then she poured home-made raspberry jam over. That was tasty (and the only way one could feed semolina to me). Most kids do not like porridge and prefer pancakes.

Preparing pancakes for breakfast takes time, so for most people that treat is reserved for weekends. Pancakes are typically eaten with jam or sweet condensed milk or honey or sour cream. A good life hack is to prepare pancakes with fillings (usually meat or cottage cheese, sometimes cabbage) in advance and just reheat them in the morning. Pancakes with minced meat with sour cream on top make a perfect breakfast for any Russian!

"Syrniki" (cottage cheese dumplings) are almost as popular as pancakes. Easy to prepare (cottage cheese, an egg, some flour and salt/sugar to taste) – they make a perfect and tasty breakfast, more nutritious and high in protein than pancakes. Needless to say – we eat them with either jam or sour cream or both.

Cereals and muesli are not as popular, although in the last 10-20 years advertising budgets of multinational companies have made them a breakfast option as well. Juices have not been part of breakfast routine before (mainly because there were no juices in stores), but now people buy them.

Of course, those types of breakfasts are more typical for somebody, who works in the office, rather than has a day of physical activity ahead. And now, quite often, people go out to have breakfast and have early breakfast meetings before work. People, who have to work in the field or in a mine eat much more substantial breakfast, which could include meat and potatoes. But for a typical urban office worker, breakfast is a small meal.

6.2. What Russians Eat for Lunch and Dinner

Lunch is the main meal of the day in Russia. In old times workers were evaluated by their appetite – how you eat was supposed to show how you work. That is a legend of course, but Russian lunches require good appetite. Let's explore.

Russian Lunch at Home

Russians typically eat lunch between 1 and 2 pm. The typical lunch menu includes soup, main course, and fruit drink and ends with tea and something sweet. Soup is a must-have for lunch and, depending on the season it could be either a cold soup in Summer or one of the traditional hot soups. Variety of hot soups vs. scarcity of cold soups clearly demonstrates how much longer the cold season here is.

The most typical main dish would be a combination of meat and potatoes or grains but could also be chicken or fish. In the recent years, people started to eat more salads and vegetables, but potatoes are still the most typical side dish. Here are some recipes:

Kotlety (meatballs)

Take the minced meat (beef or beef & pork or chicken), add a piece of white bread, soaked in milk, one egg, some minced onion, salt, and pepper and mix that well. Roll meatballs in bread crumbs or flour and fry on both sides in a saucepan until the meat is well done. To make the meatballs juicier, you can add some sour cream in the process. Mashed potatoes are the ideal side dish for meatballs. Our mashed potatoes differ from the US version – it never has potato peel in it and is not chunky at all. Fried potatoes are also a typical side dish. Mushrooms also go well with this dish – fry chopped mushrooms and onion, add some sour cream, salt, and pepper and serve as a sauce. Another typical variation of minced meatballs – "teftelki" are very similar, but you can add garlic and sauté them in tomato sauce after frying over.

Beef Stroganoff

This famous restaurant dish is often cooked in the Russian homes. It is easy to prepare – fry some chopped beef (meat is usually cut in stripes) and onion, add sour cream and sauté until the meat is ready. I know, it is funny how much sour cream we use. Beef Stroganoff is also typically served with potatoes – either boiled or mashed. Another traditional side dish is buckwheat, it is healthier than potatoes and goes well with meat. If the main course is accompanied by salad – it will most often be a tomato/cucumber/onion/dill salad (with sour cream of course). Salads made of green leaves are not typical at all – green salad leaves could be added to tomato/cucumber salad but will not be served alone. Other vegetables could include boiled or roasted cauliflower or green beans in winter or sauté from squash, carrots, and tomatoes in Summer.

Pelmeni (Russian ravioli)

It is interesting that although pasta is not part of the traditional Russian cuisine, there is one really Russian dish – pelmeni – ravioli with meat. Now you can buy excellent pelmeni in the store, but the best pelmeni still are the home-cooked ones. Usually, people make dozens if not hundreds of them and freeze them (in former times, when winters were colder, people kept frozen pelmeny at the balconies).

Golubtsy (stuffed cabbage leaves)

Golubtsy is oversized dolma, but instead of a grape leaf – we use cabbage leaves. Stuffing is usually just minced beef but could be beef and rice. I do not need to say, that the best sauce is sour cream, right?

Interestingly, most Russian meat dishes are made of minced meat. I guess that the quality of meat is quite average; therefore, it is better to mince it. Of course, these are just some of the dishes that people eat for lunch in Russia. And people also eat fried meat, chicken and fish.

Kompot and Kisel' – Traditional Russian Alcohol-free Beverages

Typical Russian lunch will include either kompot or kisel'. Kompot is usually made from the season or frozen berries and fruits. You basically boil berries and/or fruits in water, add sugar to taste and enjoy it hot or cold. The key to making kompot delicious – use a lot of berries/fruit. The more, the better. You cannot go wrong with that tip. My grandma lived to 101 and most of her life she had kompot, made of berries daily. Not sure if kompot was the secret of her longevity, but it may have added to it since berries are the natural anti-oxidants. In any case, kompot is a healthy drink, unlike the sodas.

Kisel is a version of kompot, but you have to filter out the berries, dissolve some starch in the cold water and slowly add the mix to kompot, stirring the drink all the time. Starch makes kompot thicker – like a melted jelly. I really like kisel, it is a delicious beverage.

Lunch in the Office

Most cafes and restaurants in Moscow have a "business lunch" daily deal. Of course, a lot of people bring lunch from home, but going out for lunch with colleagues is much more fun. It is not only about food, but also about socializing with colleagues.

What you eat for lunch in that case depends on the location of your office. If you are fortunate – your office may be located next to a big shopping mall, where options for lunch are almost endless. We start discussing lunch plans around noon and figure out how much time we have before the afternoon meetings and conference calls, what we are in the mood for and how hungry we are. Depending on all the parameters – lunch could be as simple as a takeaway soup and salad to be eaten together in the office kitchen lounge to a really big and long meal in a steakhouse. Middle options include Asian, Mediterranean, Middle East cuisines, quality burgers, quiche, etc. Traditional Russian food is a more rare option on our lunch menu.

In the last couple of years, food delivery services changed how people lunch. Ordering food to the office has become one click away, and you are no longer limited to the nearby restaurants. There was even one startup, called Golod (hunger), which had two sets of simple lunches and brought them to you in 5-10 minutes. Unfortunately, that business model could not be sustainable, and the business closed.

Russian Dinner

I initially planned a separate post about the Russian dinner, but quickly understood that Russian dinner is very similar to the Russian lunch minus the soup. It is usually the main dish and tea with sweets or cakes instead of kompot or kisel'. Now it is difficult to say what is a typical time for a Russian, living in Moscow to eat dinner. I would say that it used to be 7-8 pm, but the traffic jams in the city are terrible, so for many people dinner is when they get home. Most people believe that it is unhealthy to eat after 6 pm, but often eat dinner at 9 pm and then have tea and cakes in front of the TV.

6.3. From Russia with Love – Pie Recipe!

About Pies in General

Pies are comfort food in so many cultures, it is insane. I guess – all cultures have some sort of pastry. Dough may be different, a filling may be different, but it is all – a comfort food. Nothing is better than a homemade pie, be it in Russia or Argentina or the US or any other country.

Here, in Russia, we are serious about pies. We make both the filling and the dough from scratch. And, it is easy if you follow my recipe. Let's start!

Recipe of the Pie

1) Dough (universal for sweet and savory pies)

- Mix powder yeast and 2 tablespoons of sugar in water that is 36°-38°C, not more; otherwise yeast may die. Wait to see the yeast rise
- Melt 80-100 grams of butter and add 3 cups of milk and some salt
- Wait until the milk-butter cools down to 36°-38°C, add yeast mixture and flour. I usually add just some flour and let the dough rise for 40 min. And only then I add more flour
- The dough will double or triple in size so you will have a lot of it

2) Filling

You can use any filling you like with that dough – apples, spring onions and boiled eggs, cabbage, meat, fish, you name it. My signature pie is a cabbage pie. So, let's proceed with it.

Chop the cabbage in big chunks and onion in small pieces. Fry cabbage and onion in different pans. I like to fry onions until they are brown, and cabbage should be half-cooked. Don't forget salt and pepper.

Once you have the dough risen up and the filling cooled down, assemble the pie. Butter the pan before placing a sheet of dough on it. Use the fork to make many holes on the top layer, so that the dough rises evenly. To add some color to the pie, brush the top of the pie with either a mixture of egg yolk and water or even with a strong coffee or tea.

Bake at 150-180C and visit your pie from time to time to not let it burn!

ENJOY! And if you happen to have some dough left, you can make cinnamon buns or apple pastry.

6.4. Russian Soups – Comfort Food for Cold Weather

When it gets darker and colder, hot soup is the best comfort food for both body and soul. Let's talk about traditional Russian soups, look at some recipes and cook those dishes at home!

Soup has been a staple of Russian cuisine since ancient times. It is an easy-to-cook hot meal and an inexpensive way to feed the entire family. Ingredients are interchangeable. During fasting periods of the year, meat could be replaced with fish or mushrooms. There is a wide variety of Russian soups. Let me tell you about the ones that we cook most often in Russia now.

Schi – the Most Traditional Russian Soup

Unlike the popular myth – it is not borsch, but schi, which is the most traditional Russian soup, made of meat and cabbage. Schi became popular in Russia in the IX century, when cabbage was brought into the country.

Schi Recipe

The basic recipe, which people use at home now is to cook a beef bouillon (put a piece of beef, preferably with a bone in cold water, add one whole peeled onion and chunks of peeled carrot, cook for ~30 min (taking away the meat foam from time to time). Take the onion out. Then add diced cabbage and continue to cook for 15 more minutes, add diced potatoes and cook until potatoes are ready. You can also add some tomatoes – either blended or diced and sautéed in a sauce-pan with diced carrots. Several minutes before the soup is ready, add bay leaf, peppercorns, and salt. Or you can add the salt and pepper at the earlier stage as I do. After turning the heat off, let the soup stay on the stove for 30 min and serve with sour cream and diced dill and parsley.

That is a basic recipe, and there are many variations to it. First of all – in old times cabbage was not available all year round. So, people preserved cabbage as a sour cabbage and added it to the soup instead of fresh cabbage. Sour cabbage adds more flavor to schi, so even now many Russians believe that proper schi should be made with sour cabbage. In Spring, when people ran out of both fresh and sour cabbage, they used nettle to replace cabbage in the soup. Nettle has a lot of Vitamin C, and when boiled, it loses the "biting qualities."

Most people did eat meat in old times, but during religious fasts, meat was not allowed, so it was either replaced by mushrooms or fish or was omitted. Russian people have a tradition of mushroom picking and have excellent knowledge of mushrooms. We collect mushrooms in Summer and use fresh mushrooms in our cuisine and use dried mushrooms in winter. Porcini is the best type of mushroom for the soup. Champignons will not work as they do not have enough flavor.

Borsch – the Schi with Beets

Borsch – soup that is believed to be Russian, actually has Ukrainian roots. But Russia was really good at adopting great dishes from the USSR countries, so by now even we do consider borsch to be our traditional soup and cook it often at home.

Borsch Recipe

There are as many if not more varieties of borsch as they are of schi. But the great news is that since you already know how to make schi – learning how to make borsch will be easy for you. Follow the same process, just add beets with cabbage. I like beets to be diced really thin and usually make a mixture of diced beets, carrots, tomatoes without skin and either let the mix marinate in the vinegar or lemon juice for some time or steer-fry the mix for a couple of minutes. Adding vinegar or lemon juice is a necessary step since acid helps to preserve the red color of the beets.

I strongly prefer borsch over schi. I think that beets add the taste and color. Even though the best borsch is the one made with meat, a vegetarian option is also tasty. Make sure you have a lot of veggies in the soup – it should be quite thick. We believe that borsch should be served with sour cream. I do not drink vodka, but I understand when people like to have a shot of ice-cold vodka with their borsch. Also – great addition is "pampushki" – small round pastries polished with garlic. And I usually add minced garlic either with dill when I serve the soup or add cloves of garlic to the soup when I turn off the heat and let it sit.

Mushroom Soup

Russians are crazy about picking mushrooms – it is a national sport! We go to the woods for this adventure – the goal is to collect edible mushrooms, which calls for a lot of skills – finding mushrooms in the forest, using your knowledge to understand which ones are not poisonous, cutting them the right way (so that they continue to grow after your harvest) and knowing how to peel and cook them! If everything is done right – all your family and friends are alive and happy.

The soup made of forest mushrooms is a fantastic dish! We do not make cream soups if we take the traditional recipes – we peel the mushrooms, make a bouillon, add potatoes, and the soup is ready. Of course, make sure you add the sour cream before serving the soup – otherwise, the experience will be incomplete!

You can also replace forest mushrooms with champignons. Not the best choice, but if you do not have forest mushrooms – that is still a viable option.

Fish Soup – Famous Russian "Ukha"

Best recipe for a traditional Russian fish soup "Ukha" – take several types of freshly-caught fish, a lot of it, clean it, cut into rather big pieces, make a fish bouillon and add potatoes (and carrots if you like). Make sure that soup is thick from fish, and preferably cook it near the lake, at the open fire. No need to add sour cream to this soup when serving!

Solyanka – the Strangest Winter Soup in Russia

Solyanka – the most bizarre Russian winter soup, since in addition to meat and vegetables, you use pickled cucumbers and black olives.

I am not a big fan of this soup myself, so I never prepare it at home. But I found the most traditional recipe for you. Millions of people love it, so give it a try.

Solyanka Recipe

Take lean beef and fatty pork, chop in small pieces and stir-fry with diced onion and garlic. Add diced pickled cucumbers and sauté for 3-4 minutes. Chop capers and tomatoes, add them to the mix and sauté for another 3-4 min. Place everything in a sauce-pan, add some chopped sausages and bouillon and cook for 20 min at a low heat. Add parsley and dill and lemon, cook couple more minutes. Turn off the heat, let the soup sit for 30 min and serve. Black olives are not present in this recipe, so I am not exactly sure at which point you are supposed to add them. (sauté them with pickles or add when serving the soup?)

Hot Milk Soups – Second Contender for Strange Soup Nomination

If sautéing pickles did sound ok to you – here is another invention that may make you wonder. Hot milk soup with noodles!

It is mostly cooked for kids though. Maybe because it is a good way to make kids drink milk. Or maybe because kids really like it for some reason. I also used to like it, when I was a child. A recipe is pretty straightforward – heat up some milk, add salt and sugar and noodles and cook until noodles are ready.

Chicken Soup – Loved in All Countries

There is something about this soup. Every country has its version of chicken soup – from spicy Sopa de Lima or Sopa de Pollo in Mexico to Avgolemono in Greece to Chihirtma in Georgia. Russia is no exception – we also like chicken soup and cook it often. And we also cook chicken soup when we feel sick since it really helps to get better.

Russian chicken soup is usually just a clear chicken broth. Sometimes we add noodles or rice to it. And we almost always add minced dill for the flavor and presentation.

6.5. Okroshka – the Most Bizarre Summer Soup

Everybody knows gazpacho. But people, who eat herring under the fur coat, meat jelly and other bizarre food are bound to have the weirdest summer soup in the world, right? Right. We do have such soup. It is called Okroshka, and I am going to tell you about it now.

What Is Okroshka?

Imagine you decided to make a bowl of soup with Coca-Cola! What would you add to Coca-Cola in such an unlikely event? Maybe some Russian salad? That is the closest description of Okroshka. And, yes, we find it very tasty and eat a lot of this soup in Summer!

Kvas Is What We Use in Okroshka Instead of Coca-Cola

Kvas is a fantastic non-alcoholic beverage, invented about a thousand years ago. It is a fermented beverage, made of rye bread. Since it is a fermented beverage, it has traces of alcohol (about 1%), but you cannot really get drunk on kvas. Kvas is natural and healthy – it is great for metabolism, cardiovascular system, hair, and skin. It is also a fantastic thirst-quenching beverage for hot weather.

In old times people typically produced kvas at home, in Soviet times it was produced industrially but was not bottled. If you wanted to buy kvas, you bought it from a street vendor with a massive cistern on wheels. You could drink it on the spot, from a provided glass mug, but you needed your own reservoir to carry it home. A typical tank was a metal one, called "bidon." Now there are plenty of brands of kvas sold in supermarkets – in bottles and cans.

Recipe of Okroshka

Chop cucumbers, radish, cooked meat or kolbasa (bologna kind sausage), boiled eggs, scallion, dill and boiled potatoes until you have a fine-cut salad. Put the mixture in a soup bowl, pour kvas over, add a dollop of sour cream, stir and enjoy the soup! Yes, kvas is a bit sweet, but it does not spoil the taste. If you want to make it a bit spicier, you either add more onions or you add a bit of horseradish (now in Moscow we have a special variety of kvas for okroshka, which already has the horseradish added).

How to Make Kvas at Home

I never made kvas myself, as it is available in any grocery store in Russia and is available in most Russian grocery stores abroad. But for those of you who do not have a Russian grocery store nearby – here is a recipe:

- Cut rye bread in small chunks, toast it in the oven until bread turns dark brown. Put 2-3 handfuls of bread chunks in a glass jar, add 2 tablespoons of sugar, pour over boiling water so that bread is covered and let the mix cool down until it is warm, but not hot (you will add yeast, they will die if the mix is too hot)
- Add a pack of dried yeast, stir and leave in the warm room for 2 days (fermentation process is always not pretty, but remember – it is just bread and yeast, so it is good even if it looks a bit strange)
- Take a big glass jar, put the rest of bread, more sugar (2-3 tablespoons) and pour boiling water over bread (carefully! so that the jar does not splinter. Let it cool down and add the leaven (filtered water from the bread mix from a small jar). You may also add raisins. Keep the mix in a warm room for another 24 hours
- Filter. Kvas is ready to serve

6.6. Festive USSR Style Dinner

Nowadays in Moscow, you really do not know what the hosts of the dinner party will prepare for you. It can be anything – from oysters to Beijing duck, from carpaccio to crème brûlée. But in Soviet time – there was one menu, which was favorite in all households.

Here are the main dishes of the festive Soviet dinner:

Olivier Salad (Russian salad)

That salad really showed up in 100% of households, 100% of the time. Most people still serve it even though it is not in line with healthy eating because of mayo and too many ingredients.

Actually, in Soviet time it was somewhat challenging to assemble all the ingredients in the situation of the deficit. It will sound crazy, but people did have to do careful planning and stay in lines to get mayo, canned peas, marinated cucumbers, etc. So even this salad alone was quite a project!

Mimosa Salad

Another salad, rich on mayo, but beloved by Russians. For any Russian still living in the country the first association which comes to mind with the word mimosa is not a drink that you have at Sunday brunch, but that salad.

The recipe is pretty simple: you lay out layers of canned pink salmon (in brine), diced boiled potatoes, diced boiled carrots, diced egg whites and diced egg yolks. A layer of mayo in between each of the layers is obligatory, a layer of diced fresh onions is optional. Served as a cake.

Herring Under the Fur Coat

I do not personally see why this particular salad is more frightening than the other mayo salads. Same idea of layers: potatoes, carrot, fresh apple, salted herring, beets, onions, eggs. Obligatory mayo.

I guess what scares foreigners is the salted herring, and the combination of herring and the other ingredients. To our taste – it is an interesting dish since it combines sweet and salty and sour.

Holodets (Meat Jelly)

Ok, if I did not manage to freak you out with herring under the fur coat – I have a good chance to freak you out now. How about having some meat jelly?

That dish is hugely popular and being a meat lover – I really like it. You cook meat on bones for a very long time, then take the meat off the bones, put it in a bowl, pour the broth over and put the thing in the fridge. It has natural gelatin, so you do not have to add artificial jelly.

That dish is especially useful if you have a broken leg or any problems with joints. It is basically just lean meat and collagen, and we eat it with horseradish to add some spice.

Julienne (Mushroom/Chicken stew)

That dish surprisingly does not include mayo, but it contains sour cream – the other staple of Soviet cuisine. You fry mushrooms (and/or chicken) with onions, add sour cream, then put the mix in the small pots, add diced cheese on top and put the pots in the oven for couple minutes to let the cheese melt. To be eaten with a spoon while still hot.

Pies (Pirogi)

Here is how it works in Russia – you are supposed to eat all your meals with bread. But on festive occasions, bread gets replaced with pies. Russian pies are really state-of-the-art. A filling can be sweet or savory, most typical savory fillings are minced meat, cabbage, fish, boiled eggs with scallions, etc. Typical sweet fillings are apples, cottage cheese and all kinds of seasonal berries. If the pie is big, it is called "pirog", small pies are called "pirozhki."

Other 'zakuski" (appetizers)

Other appetizers can include a variety of pickles (including pickled garlic), slices of ham&cheese, smoked or salted salmon, sandwiches with caviar and fish preserves (among which the two most favorite are shproty – tiny smoked fishes and cod liver).

Main Course

Yes, there is a main course. The most typical for Soviet era would be oven-roasted chicken, but some people opted for roasted duck or roasted goose or meat. The chicken was typically accompanied with roasted potatoes and since in Soviet times chickens were raised without hormones – they did taste good.

Drinks

As you have probably guessed from the heaviness of appetizers and presence of pickles main alcohol drink used to be vodka. At least for men, women could opt for sparkling or regular wine. As sodas were not present at that time – non-alcohol drinks would be mineral water with gas and home-made beverages made of berries.

Dessert

Dessert was never light as well. Proper dessert was a cake, and in addition to that, you may be offered ice cream, fruit, and chocolate. And of course, tea.

Cakes of the Soviet time were of limited variety. Therefore, women baked cakes themselves, so festive Russian dinner usually included a home-made cake.

6.7. How Spicy Is Russian Food?

Traditional Russian dishes are not spicy at all. There are two main reasons for that:

a) We live in a cold part of the world. Spicy dishes are more typical for tropical than for cold northern countries, where there is no need to use antimicrobial properties of spices.
b) Another reason Russian food is not spicy is that Russia does not grow most spices on its territory, so they always had to be imported. Russia was mainly an agricultural country, the peasants did not have access to imported spices, and their food was quite simple.

Since Russians do not like spicy food, most ethnic restaurants in Moscow go light on the spices or the waiter will ask you, how spicy you want your dishes to be. I usually opt for spicy, but it will still never be too hot. From my personal example – I think that tolerance to spices is something you acquire in your childhood. Food in our house was not spicy when I grew up, but when I was a kid, we lived in Kenya where there was a big Indian population and, as a result, I could enjoy spicy samosas and curry. Since I had been exposed to spicy Indian food, now I can eat even a very spicy Indian dishes. But most people did not have spicy food as kids, so they are not accustomed to it.

A traditional way of preparing food in ancient Russia was to cook dishes in a clay oven (which usually was the center of the house and served as a heater). Food was prepared in "gorshki" (clay pots), the main dish was a soup (most typical – schi – made of meat and cabbage and grains or potatoes). Pies were also very popular and baked in the oven.

The most popular condiments used for making food less bland in Russia are salt and black pepper (always used in moderation). Salt is also widely used for conserving food for winter – mushrooms, cucumbers, tomatoes, etc. Almost any Russian kitchen will have a bay leaf, no soup goes without it. Russians like to use a lot of herbs, the most popular one is dill. Dill is part of the salads, dill is on top of boiled potatoes, dill is added to the soups. We love dill and add it to so many dishes, it drives foreigners mad. We also use parsley and cilantro, but not as much.

Our food is rich on onions and garlic. However, we do not have any traditional recipes, where onion or garlic would be the main ingredient (like in French onion soup or Czech garlic soup). Onions are typically minced and fried and added to dishes and garlic is used either diced and raw as part of salads or to enhance a flavor of meat or vegetable stews.

6.8. Why Russians Love Sour Cream and Mayo?

Sour cream was used in Russia since ancient times. Sour cream is a product, made from cream. It has a lot of fat but is quite healthy despite that and is easily digested even by the lactose intolerant people. Why do we need to add more fats to our dishes? Living in a cold country calls for more nutritious food. Sour cream is definitely healthier than butter. Sour cream is typically used as a sauce for salads, it makes all traditional soups, such as schi, borsch, okroshka, mushroom soup taste better, it is added to boiled potatoes and million other dishes.

When it comes to mayo – things get more complicated. Mayonnaise is a sauce that came to Russia from French cuisine. It all makes sense. Our most "Russian" salad was designed by the French Chef Olivier. Fresh mayonnaise is made from olive oil and yolks, it is very high on fat content, but in the French cuisine, it was not meant to be eaten in large quantities.

How Russians Use Mayo?

Here is where things get scary. Russians use mayo in industrial quantities. Usually, this sauce is not prepared at home, people use store-brands. Most typical variety is Mayonnaise Provençal, 67% fat content. Mayo used to be expensive a long time ago, then it was part of deficit products during Soviet times, now it is really cheap and widely available.

Russians add mayo to most salads, a lot of people use mayo as a sauce for main courses and even instead of sour cream for soups.

But the scariest use is when meat, fish, chicken or veggies are baked under the coat of mayo. One of the most popular main courses of the 90s was "Meat French style" – meat, roasted under the layers of mayo and cheese.

There are several hugely popular local food blogs, devoted to cooking with mayo. Any ingredient that you could think of is represented there. And the presentation of the dishes is often very elaborate.

But the apotheosis of mayo-related cuisine is… fried mayo! Yes, you can fry that stuff! Just freeze it, make a ball, using an ice-cream spoon, coat with breadcrumbs and deep-fry in heated oil!

6.9. Do Russians Eat Fish?

At some point during the development of the young Soviet republic, it became obvious that the country can no longer satisfy the population's demand for meat. Poor harvest led to a decrease of livestock population, food distribution was uneven among the cities and the regions. The Soviet government understood the importance of protein in people's diet and decided to introduce fish as a good source of protein.

To make fish more popular, the so-called "Fish Day" was invented. From the 12th of September 1932, all canteens in the country served only fish on Thursdays. Why Thursday? Not sure whether these are rumors or truth – but they could not choose Monday, because it is a start of a week and people needed meat to be productive. And they could not select weekends since attendance of canteens on weekends is low. Wednesday and Friday are days when you are not supposed to eat meat, according to the Russian Orthodox Church (and the Soviet government did not want to support any religious habits). Between Tuesday and Thursday – they might have just flipped a coin.

As an idea, promoting the consumption of fish was a good thing. Eating fish at least once a week is a healthy habit; fish is an excellent source of omega fatty acids, protein, and many useful minerals and vitamins. However, as always, the devil is in execution. Fish burgers and fish soup, served in Soviet canteens, were horrible therefore people hated fish. In stores, fish was usually available, but it was frozen and did not look as attractive as the fish we see in supermarkets now.

I was amazed one day when I attended an expensive seafood restaurant in Minneapolis to celebrate a birthday of my close friend. That was a place that had a saying "Good fish cannot be cheap, cheap fish cannot be good" written in chalk on a black board. I ordered pollock and wondered what kind of fish I am about to consume. I was stunned when I found a translation. Fancy pollock happened to be an ordinary "mintai," fish that we always considered good only for a cat. It was delicious though, and I still do not understand why we never got fond of it in Russia in the Soviet times.

In the 70s promotion of fish also resulted in the development of seafood chain stores, named Ocean. Some types of fish became more or less popular, such as live carp, which was fished out from a large aquarium and you were supposed to put it in a bathtub at home before you cook it. But fish still never made it to the hearts of city consumers. Even now, from time to time, you can see social ads and billboards with the slogan – "Fish awaits you" and great mouth-watering photos, but although fish restaurants became quite popular since that time – most people will still prefer meat to fish any time.

Except for the fish that you caught yourself of course – that is another story and a sport. Freshly caught fish is usually cooked on the spot and consumed as fish soup "Ukha."

When talking about fish, it is also absolutely necessary to mention fish preserves. For some reasons canned fish had a much better fate than raw frozen fish. Number one fish preserves were smoked sprats. Flat oblong tins with these tiny fishes were welcome at any festive meal. They were hard to get, they were distributed to VIP people first. Now you can buy them in any supermarket – but they are of a different quality. Manufacturers use chemicals to achieve taste and texture of smoked fish instead of dealing with the proper process of smoking the fish, using aspen sawdust.

Russians also love herring. Now we mostly buy canned herring, already cut into pieces and floating in some sauce. But in Soviet times it was usually the whole herring, which you put on a newspaper, trim the inside parts and cut. Herring can be consumed with rye bread and fresh onion rings or as a part of a salad. This salad, called "herring under the fur coat" often appears in lists of Russian curiosities, but it is in fact quite tasty. It consists of layers of diced potatoes, beets, carrots, apples, eggs and onions and is saturated with mayo.

Another beloved and hard to find delicacy was cod liver. Chunks of the cod liver had a consistency of a pâté, people ate them as a part of a salad or spread them on bread.

Less difficult to find, but also popular canned fish was salmon in brine. It served as a base for two very popular salads – Mimosa (layers of fish, boiled carrots, boiled potatoes or rice, grated cheese and diced eggs, saturated with mayo) and Fish salad – a mix of canned salmon, cooked rice, diced boiled eggs and minced onion + mayo.

Finally – at that time people consumed more vodka and a great snack to go with vodka were sprats in tomato sauce. There were also canned sayra, sardines and other canned fish, but they were much less popular.

6.10. Do Russians Really Eat Russian Salad?

"Russian Salad," served in the restaurants outside of Russia, is usually just a bleak copy of the most popular salad in the country. In most cases, Russian salad abroad is a plain potato salad, which has only several ingredients, cut in large chunks. Our version has 6-7 components, all finely chopped in small cubes. We love it, but we never call it Russian salad here.

Russian salad in Russia is called Olivier, by the name of its creator – French chef Lucien Olivier, who had a chic Parisian-style restaurant "Hermitage" in Moscow at the end of 19th century. This salad was one of the magnets, which attracted people to his restaurant.

Chef Olivier kept the recipe in such secret that researchers still argue about the original composition of ingredients. Main ingredients of his version of this dish are thought to be: hazel hen, black caviar, veal tongue, crayfish tails, lettuce, cucumbers, capers, olives and boiled eggs. Provencal sauce was prepared from French vinegar, olive oil, and egg yolks.

Soviet time corrected the recipe of Olivier salad almost beyond recognition. Chicken (or bologna sausage) replaced hazel hen, caviar was eliminated, and potatoes and carrots were added. To the credit of Soviet chefs though – they changed the name of the salad to "Stolichny" (from "Stolitsa" – Capital). But all Russians still call that salad – Olivier.

And we do love it! Olivier salad is always present at the festive meals, especially at the New Year meal. To us, Olivier is a symbol of festivity and abundance.

Here is the recipe of the Olivier or Russian Salad – Soviet style:

Ingredients: 5-6 boiled potatoes, 3 boiled carrots, 2-3 boiled eggs, sausage or meat or chicken (200 gr), can of green peas, 1-2 salted cucumbers, 1 -2 fresh cucumbers, 0,5 -1 apple, small onion + mayo

This proportion of ingredients is approximate – you may experiment to your taste. You may even omit some ingredients – for example not everybody likes the sweetness of apple in this salad.

The main secret is the fine cut of the ingredients. All cubes should be equal to the peas or smaller. You may make mayo from scratch if you have time, if not – try to buy the provencal variety. Russian salad requires a lot of mayo. If you are weight and health conscious – use low-calorie mayo. The salad would taste best if you let it sit in the fridge for a couple of hours.

6.11. Do Russians Have a Sweet Tooth?

Russians do indeed have a sweet tooth. One of the reasons for that could be our climate. Sweets are high in calories. People who live in cold weather tend to consume more of the sweet food, which can be metabolized in energy quickly. In addition to that – lack of sun in winter affects the mood, and sugar and chocolate are instant mood boosters. Russians especially love cakes.

Soviet Style Cakes

In Soviet time a selection of cakes in stores was limited. At that time cakes were sold in Kulinariya (deli – prepared food stores). In a typical Kulinariya, around the corner, one could find 2 or 3 types of cakes and 2-3 types of small cakes.

A popular one was Praga – quite a tasty chocolate cake made of biscuit with butter-based cream filling and chocolate glaze. This cake is actually a simplified Sacher cake.

Another cake was Leningradsky tort – a short crust pastry with butter-based cream as a middle layer and decorations made of cream and chocolates.

Another, less popular but usually present in stores cake was Vatslavsky tort – biscuit dough, butter-based cream, decorated with nuts and one dried fruit of unknown origin on the top.

Small cakes usually included Eklery (puff pastry filed with butter-based cream, covered by sugar glaze) or Oreshki (puff pastry with custard, sugar glazing and nuts on the top), almond cookies and short crust pastry filled with egg white cream and jam. Big cakes cost 3 Rubles, and small cakes cost 15-20 kopecks in the 80s (average salary was 120 rubles).

Soviet cake industry was capable of producing more cakes, but it was not easy to buy the most popular ones, such as Polet (cake made of meringue, nuts and cream) or Napoleon (layers of puff pastry and custard).

And the most sought-after cake was Ptichye Moloko (Bird's milk) – a very light soufflé style cake with just a thin layer of biscuit at the bottom and chocolate glazing on the top. Bird's milk is something that does not exist, something that exists only in fairy tales. Similar to that – the Bird's milk cake was a rare guest at people's dinner tables.

As for other sweets that you could buy in stores – a variety of biscuits was quite limited, and cookies were not very popular. Best chocolate sweets were "in deficit." Deficit foods were distributed in "zakazy." A direct translation of Zakazy is orders or requests. But you could not just request chocolate sweets – they were given to a small part of the population before big holidays, such as New Year, Revolution day, Victory day, etc. My grandparents received chocolate sweets in Zakazy, but the quantity was always limited. Btw, typical Zakaz contained chocolates, salami, shproty (canned smoked fish), buckwheat, canned peas, mayonnaise, butter and marmalade in metal tins.

Home Made Cakes

Since there wasn't a big variety of cakes and sweets in stores – Russian women of all ages baked terrific cakes at home. It was like a sport and recipes were exchanged among close friends and relatives. Russian people did not have a habit of going out for coffee and cake at that time since there was also a scarcity of cafes. Therefore, cakes and other sweets were mostly for home consumption with tea in the evening after dinner.

Most women born in the 50s-80s can still bake a Napoleon cake from scratch (18 layers of dough and custard cream between layers) and have 30-50 other recipes of sweet stuff in handwritten books in their kitchens.

One of the cakes that I still bake from time to time is called Drunken Cherry. It takes 5 hours to bake and 3 days for preparation. You take fresh or frozen cherries, soak them in vodka for 3 days, and then you make a cake that will surprise your guests. Guests always wonder how you achieved putting fresh vodka-soaked cherries inside the pie – the trick is to cut the pie in half horizontally while it is still hot, scramble the pie content out, mix it with cherries and fill the new mix back in. After that, you assemble the cake, as usual, put the cream layer inside and glaze the cake.

Cakes in Modern Russia

Needless to say – when the market economy came to Russia, cakes became ubiquitous in stores. Russian consumers loved that. Now it is possible to buy anything – from traditional cakes to cakes with exotic fruit, low-calorie cakes, fancy looking cakes.

Ready-made cakes save a lot of time for women every year. However, sometimes I think that it is a pity that most 20-year-old girls now do not have a clue about baking anymore. And those recipes are sitting in the kitchen cabinets and collecting dust.

6.12. All You Need to Know About Russian Blinis

There are probably as many recipes of pancakes – blinis in Russia, as there are recipes of pasta in Italy. That often confuses foreigners. Here is a brief guide to Russian Blinis.

Shape and Size

Russian blinis are always round, but the size varies and basically represents all the available sizes of the frying pans. The average blin (singular from blinis) would be about 20 cm (~ 8 inches).

Blinis are always very thin, so they are more similar to French crepes, than to American pancakes. However, you might have also seen tiny and very fat pancakes. What is that? Those are from the "same family," but they are called – Oladyi (or Oladushki, using the diminutive suffix). The main difference is in ingredients – blinis are usually milk-based, and oladushki are typically kefir-based (or you can use buttermilk).

Whatever you cook though – you cook a lot. Russians never bake 2 blinis for each member of the household – you bake a stake of blinis or a mountain of oladushki. The same thing is with other traditional dishes – we like the abundance.

Recipe of Blinis

As I said – there are thousands of recipes. You can use different types of flour and either make blinis in a fast way – without yeast or in a slow way, using yeast. I believe that the most traditional recipe is yeast-based, using buckwheat flour. But I always use the fast method and a regular baking flour. This recipe is for 6-8 blinis, if you want more, just double or triple the ingredients:

1 egg
1 cup of milk
1 cup of water
a pinch of salt
1 tablespoon of sugar
flour (in quantities to make the dough liquid, but not too watery – sorry I do not have the exact recipe, I always do it as we say "by the eye")

You just mix all the ingredients with a fork or mixer, so that you do not have any lumps of flour. Then you heat a frying pan really well, add some oil and pour batter on the frying pan, in the same time moving the frying pan so that the batter distributes evenly on the surface. When a blin is done on one side, you turn it over.

However, I should warn you that it is easier said than done. I looked at my mom, making blinis, all my childhood. But when I tried to replicate that – it took me almost a year until I got edible results! And in any case – the first pancake is always not the prettiest. We even have a saying – "The first blin is a lump." But if you master that skill – you will be pleased, since they taste delicious and are so fast to make. Those Russian blinis are an ideal Sunday breakfast!

If you are lactose or gluten intolerant – you can still make blinis, but you have to use soy milk or almond milk and choose the gluten-free flour.

Best Blinis Fillings

Blinis are so universal that you can add almost any good stuff to them, be it sweet or savory. Here are the most popular toppings for blinis in Russia – raspberry jam, honey, condensed sweet milk, sour cream. In addition to that, we also love the following fillings:

- minced meat with fried onions
- fried cabbage & onions (sounds horrible, but it actually is delicious with blinis – try it!)
- mushroom & onion sauté in sour cream
- smoked or marinated salmon
- marinated herring
- sweetened cottage cheese with raisins
- apple sauté

6.13. What Are Some Favorite Junk Foods in Russia?

One could argue that the most favorite junk food in Russia is blinis, but actually it is McDonald's. McDonald's came to Russia in the 90s, opening a store in the heart of the city. That was a time of shortage of basic food in grocery stores, but it was also a time of great interest to everything Western and especially everything American.

What Are Some Favorite Junk Foods in Russia?

People were standing in line for 3 hours during winter to get into McDonald's and buy a BigMac, fries, and cola. This food was expensive but so tasty. Many people took plastic boxes from BigMacs home and put them on display in cupboards, next to expensive crystal and china. Now, when I write about it, I feel shame. Why have we been so barbaric and hungry for everything Western?

A BigMac at that time was much more than a piece of meat in a bun. It was a taste of freedom, of all the new opportunities, a feeling of change. Even now, when grocery stores are packed with any kind of food you wish, and restaurants are omnipresent, McDonald's is still crowded.

Once I was on a road trip with my mom across the States. I wanted to show her the variety of food in the country, so when we were driving through California, I made sure we stopped at In-and-Out burger joint. My mom said those burgers were quite tasty, but McDonald's is still better.

As for traditional junk foods in Russia – it is interesting that this question has puzzled me. In general – street food, snacks and junk food were never part of the traditional food culture. People had a healthy habit of eating proper meals at home – breakfast, lunch and dinner. Working people usually had lunch at a canteen at their workplace. Snacking was never part of our culture except for tea drinking, usually accompanied by candies, biscuits or cakes. Partially, that was caused by poor quality and limited offer of street food.

The only high-quality street food available was ice cream. Russians were always proud of their ice cream, and they had a right to be proud: ice cream was made of pure cream, butter, and other natural ingredients. It melted in your mouth, and it tasted great. In Soviet times there was never a wide variety of ice cream. Typically, you could find an eskimo – milk ice cream brick, covered with chocolate glaze on a wooden stick for 15 kopeks, waffle cups with creamy ice-cream, called plombir for 20 kopeks and bricks of plombir ice cream to be eaten at home for 48 kopeks. Ice cream is considered to be a summer treat all over the world, but in Russia we eat ice cream in any weather. It could be minus 20°C (minus 4°F), but people will savor ice cream outside. Now there is a vast variety of ice cream, but quality has gone down: milk, cream, and butter are being substituted with artificial fats, which affects taste. Only a couple of factories in the country produce real ice cream, but the habit of eating ice cream as a tasty snack on the go is still there.

Another favorite junk food of Soviet times – ponchiki(donuts). They were usually sold in grocery stores cafeterias. They were sold not piece-by-piece, but rather by weight. Frying oil was used over and over, so those donuts were really unhealthy. Now we have both Krispy Cream and Dunkin Donuts stores, and those Soviet donuts disappeared.

A less favorite treat was belyash – a non-sweet donut with meat filling. People joked that they are made out of kitten meat and tried to avoid them if possible. A more safe and tasty variety of beef stuffed pastry was cheburek – meat-filled oil fried samosa. In Moscow, there were just several places where one could get them.

When business came to Russia, street food became an excellent business opportunity. Kiosks, selling food on the streets started to mushroom. One popular chain sold hot dogs, another one sold blinis. Kroshka-kartoshka – "baby potatoes," the size of a baby head is still making a lot of money selling stuffed baked potatoes with variety of fillings – fried mushrooms, meat, salads with mayo, fish, etc.

However, the most universal were Shaurma (shawarma) kiosks – Gyros. Meat particles, carved from a large chunk of meat, combined with salad and sauce in pita bread, have won hearts of Muscovites. It is a fast, tasty and inexpensive street meal. Not very safe though, food poisonings from shaurma have happened often.

Now in Moscow, one can find most Western fast food chains – McDonald's, KFC, Wendy's in addition to a range of local fast food chains. And some really upscale fast food joints, where you can get expensive burgers with shaved truffles or other exotic ingredients. And, there is also a recent movement towards healthy food, so salad bars and healthy food stores started to emerge as well.

6.14. How the Self-Imposed Food Embargo Impacts Russia

Several years ago, our government decided to give an asymmetrical response to the sanctions, imposed by Western countries. Russia banned the import of food from countries, which supported sanctions. French cheese, Spanish jamón, Polish apples and many other products were not allowed to be imported to Russia anymore.

Attitude to Food Became a "Patriotic Test"

"Patriots" or rather people, who watch Russian TV a lot, welcomed these news. They said that we do not need a foreign mozzarella and it was never good anyway. They claimed that Europe and other countries sent us food of poor quality – as told to them by the State Propaganda machine. They also said that the absence of foreign-made products will give a chance to local farmers to grow their business. And while the farmers are working on that – we can import food from the "friendly countries." Happy cows at local lands – that is how patriots envisioned future. Not bad, but it takes time to grow cows.

"Non-patriots" were unhappy about the sanctions. They wondered how their favorite restaurants would deal with that; they started to ask friends to bring them a piece of Parmesan or other delicacies from vacations abroad.

The rest of the world was speechless and was curious to see how the situation develops.

I must make a disclaimer here – food embargo did impact mostly high-income people, who live in Moscow and other big cities. Percentage of population, who had French Brie cheese, Spanish jamón or New Zealand beef in their diet was tiny. Most people, who live in Russia, have low income and their menu is skewed towards locally grown potatoes, grains, processed food and other inexpensive options. So, I do understand why they did not care about the food embargo and were annoyed when hipsters said that they will "suffer" without some exotic food.

Real Pros and Cons of the Food Embargo

It was indeed interesting to observe, how that situation unfolded.

The first week after the announcement, grocery stores noticed a significant spike in sales. Russia experienced many instances of food shortages in the past, so people are used to stock on essential items, such as salt, buckwheat, sugar, matches, etc. However, this time rush was seen mostly in the grocery stores, which sell expensive imported food. Consumers were stocking on cheese, jamón, olives, olive oil and other "luxury items." I admit that I also bought some olive oil, just in case (btw, olive oil is still available – for some reason it was not included in the list of banned food).

At that time food embargo became one of the most popular media topics. One story was about a young entrepreneur, cheese aficionado, who used all his savings on opening a small cheese store just one month before the food embargo. A year after, I was wondering whether he had to close his business or had found a way to survive, so I found him in social media and arranged the interview. Talking with Alexander Krupetskov was a such a pleasure, and I am happy that Alexander is still running his Cheese Sommelier business and even opened the additional cheese stores, started to conduct cheese master classes and his company is doing well. How he managed that? Alexander quickly figured out that the only European cheesemaking country that was not subject of food embargo was Switzerland, so focused on Swiss cheese first. But he also started to explore import from other countries and made deals with local manufacturers of cheese.

Most stories in media though still focus on the potentially positive side of the food embargo – how our farmers will create better cheese and other food. Some of that is seen indeed – but on an insufficient scale. Agriculture is not something that could be built in several months or even several years. It is a "culture," that needs decades of hard work, dedication, modern technologies, best practices and support from the government in the form of lower taxation, better laws, low-interest credits, etc. The previous decade of high oil prices and relative stability was wasted; there was no support to the small business and insufficient level of support to the local business in general. There were also a lot of speculations about "grey import" from Belarus, which did happen to some extent. "Grey import" means that products are first entering Belarus and then documents are changed. That's how you get Belarus, a country which does not have the sea, to import oysters into Russia.

Restaurants did suffer too. Replacing Black Angus with the local beef was difficult. The Moscow restaurant scene was dependent on imported food products – chefs were competing in making their menus unique, outstanding, extravagant and exotic.

In general, there might be some positive consequences of the food embargo in Moscow restaurants. Chefs started to experiment with local ingredients and apply fusion and molecular cuisine techniques to the traditional recipes. Or, took international recipes and replaced missing components with local ones. Sometimes it leads to funny results – I still do prefer veal carpaccio to a beetroot carpaccio, but I like that chefs are becoming more creative. Russian traditional dishes suddenly came in fashion as well. One of the most popular restaurants – Dr. Zhivago, located steps from Kremlin on the first floor of a luxury hotel National offers only Russian cuisine and waitlist to get a table is at least a week long.

Many restaurants now work with the local farmers. It is easier for farmers to deliver a limited amount of produce or dairy or meat to a restaurant, than to a retail chain. For retail, they need to have a proper packaging, appealing brand and – a lot of money to pay for the place on the shelf that all retail chains charge. With the restaurants – they just need to deliver refrigerated products if the buyer agrees to buy from them.

So, What Is the Summary of All of the Above?

There is no summary – just some facts and observations. My education tells me that it is never good when the government regulates the market. But it is fascinating to see how things develop when a government starts to do that. And it is interesting to observe such a situation from several angles – economic, political, sociological, psychological, marketing.

6.15. Serving Food – the Russian Way

A big help for me in writing Understand Russia blog and this book have always been questions from my readers:

> *"In the UK, people would have separate courses – appetizer, main course, dessert – with the main course being a protein and side dishes. But I can't work out how a meal like that would be served in Russia. Can you help? I was thinking of the Olivier Salad as the appetizer."*

We do not have such a thing as one single appetizer in Russia. Appetizers (zakuski) are always plural and sometimes cover the entire table. If that is too much for your guests, you may think of ways to create abundance (i.e., big plates and small portions on them). It would not be very authentic but will help your guests to save the space for the main course.

> *"I would like to do pirozhki and/or pelmeni, but I can't work out if they are served as separate courses or as part of a course. Or what side dishes would be served with them. If at all!"*

Pelmeni is a separate dish, the main course, so you do not need to serve a garnish with them, just the sour cream and/or butter and lemon or vinegar.

> *"I would like to avoid stroganoff as being too obvious."*

Beef stroganoff is never among the festive dishes, it is considered to be a day-to-day dish, something I would cook myself as a quick dinner at my Moscow kitchen. Best with mashed potatoes, sometimes I also add mushrooms.

"How is pirozhki eaten – with hands or fork and knife? Do you have any flavorings with them? A dip or something or just melted butter over them?"

Pirozhki basically replace bread, so they are eaten with hands. No dips. Classic pirozhki will have cabbage or meat or spring onion & eggs as a filling. Pirozhki are small, and there are also pirogi – big pies.

"Could you give some guidance? And place settings? And general etiquette? I got the point about the shoes, not refusing food and the mild alcoholism though!!!"

Modern serving is not different to how you would serve food at your home dinners. But if you would like to recreate the atmosphere of the Soviet Union, you can serve salads in the crystal bowls.

"But are there are any traditional dishes that would be considered vegetarian? I am aware that the Lenten period would suggest a vegetarian diet but what sort of dishes would be served? Is it observed? Are there any customs?"

Lent is observed in Russia by many people nowadays. Usually during lent meat is substituted with mushrooms, or just omitted. On some days of the lent it is allowed to eat fish.

Priyatnogo appetita! (Bon appetit in Russian)!

7. HEALTH/WELLBEING

7.1. How Do People Keep in Shape in Moscow? Part I – Fitness

Being in shape in Russia is more or less valued by men and is absolutely crucial for women. Why it is optional for a man to be fit – men are judged more on their income than on their appearance, but women are expected to be in great shape all the time.

Fitness in Moscow is more than just going to a gym. It is a status symbol. Many people occasionally enjoy ice-skating or cross-country skiing, but they do not engage in dedicated workouts at the gym. That is a thing for people who are well off. Such people spend most of their days sitting – in their cars (2-3 hours on a typical day) and offices. Sedentary lifestyle calls for either dieting or exercise.

And they pay a premium. A typical gym membership in Moscow costs $1000 or more per year. That includes access to machines and free weights, unlimited group classes, access to a swimming pool/sauna and small freebies such as water coolers and towels. Annual membership in a gym often includes one or several private classes with instructors, but that is mostly a marketing thing – a way to sell private sessions (which cost from 30 to 50 USD per hour). Gym facilities that cost over $1K are nice, modern and clean but they are very similar to an average US gym, which is much cheaper. Why do people pay so much?

The majority really pays for staying in shape, or at least have the intent to work out often. The abundance of food, daily business meetings in restaurants and sitting for 12 hours a day do call for additional exercise. During most of the year, Moscow weather is nasty, which makes outdoor runs either impossible or unpleasant. And even when it is warm and sunny, finding the right place for outdoor sports is not so easy. There are free cross-fit and yoga classes in a couple of parks in the center, but most people do not have access to a public tennis court or a park in walking distance of their homes. Air is quite polluted. Hence – having a gym membership is valuable – it is a place where specially qualified people and ambiance make you move and burn those calories or gain muscles.

The minority does buy gym memberships for other reasons. For some, that is the club – you go there with your buddies. You do not spend too much time really working out but have a great time nevertheless – drinking smoothies or fresh juices in a club café or chatting with friends. Some people go to a gym with the goal of finding a date and although that strategy is fruitless all over the world (people in the gym are too focused on fitness), many guys and girls still give it a try.

It is necessary to mention that there has been growth in an affordable fitness segment over the last couple of years. Now it is possible to find gym memberships for $300-400/year and sometimes that could be a good value for money. Yes, there will be no free water coolers and gym will most likely be located in a dingy basement and will be overcrowded. But if you know what to do with weights and other equipment and you actually visit the gym regularly – you will get fit. Another popular trend is dance studios of any kind. That is pure cardio, but it is fun and people like it. Yoga has also become super popular in the last 5 years. Finally, there is a lot of interest in tennis, skiing, snowboarding as well as such unusual sports as snow kiting, kite surfing, curling, etc.

7.2. How Do People Keep in Shape in Moscow? Part II – Diets

Russia has long and cold winters. People tend to eat more in cold climate. Layers of clothes make it easy to hide a few extra pounds.

How Do People Keep in Shape in Moscow? Part II – Diets

Traditional food includes a lot of potatoes and fatty dishes. The cumulative effect of that is that many people have a few or quite a few extra pounds, which they want to shave off. After all – magazine stands here are identical to magazine stands in the West and Cosmo, Vogue and Marie Claire still have skinny models on their covers.

Exercising is the best way to keep in shape, but in Moscow or other big cities, exercising could be unaffordable or hard to incorporate in an everyday lifestyle. Our famous ballerina Maya Plisetskaya once said – if I want to lose weight – I stop eating. That is the best recipe, but it is way too hard to follow. Food is one of the pleasures in life; eating less requires a lot of willpower. Ancient people never had the luxury to forgo food, since it was scarce. Now food is abundant, but our body is still not wired for limiting food.

But from time to time we notice that skinny jeans do not fit anymore, or we need to look extra good for that special event. Or we just do not like what we see in a mirror or on the scales. And that is when we start to "sit on a diet" as we say it in Russia. Businesses all over the world have extracted zillions of dollars out of that habit. So, in many ways, dieting habits of Russians do not differ from the dieting habits of people from other countries. But it is still interesting to overview which weight-loss plans are most popular here.

There are many approaches to losing weight, but in essence your body functions exactly like a machine – you put inside X amount of fuel (calories) and burn Y number of calories every day. If $X=Y$, your weight stays the same, if $X>Y$, you gradually gain weight, if $X<Y$ – you lose weight. But people do not like to acknowledge these simple facts, what they really want is magic. Ideally – it should be a magical tablet – you take it and continue eating but become slimmer.

And such tablets do exist. In the last 2 decades in Moscow, there were many rumors that pop stars lose weight with the help of some magical Thai pills. These pills were 100% chemical, they dehydrated bodies and added artificial energy so that people did not want to eat as much but stayed super active. No wonders that slim victims of those pills often ended in a hospital and had to deal with kidney and heart problems. There were also some pills that had a placebo effect. Typically, these pills contained bromelain – extract from pineapple. There is no scientific proof that pineapples have a significant slimming impact on human bodies, but people believe in magic.

Another approach was trendy due to sci-fi novels. Astronauts on other planets rarely eat chicken tenders; they usually eat a protein soufflé. How about consuming pills and cocktails instead of typical meals? It sounds especially great since you do not have to worry about nutrition – all this food is always "developed in secret laboratories of NASA" and has all the nutrients needed by human bodies. Herbalife and other concoctions such as vanilla, banana and strawberry protein cocktails that one had to take instead of meals were super popular in the 90s until people understood that they do not work and are also potentially harmful.

Finally – the old proven diet. Dieting was popular in the Soviet Union, and it is equally popular in modern Russia. Among the most famous – Atkins diet (protein diet), soup diet (you are supposed to cook a large bowl of soup and eat it for breakfast, lunch and dinner), mono diets (you eat only cucumbers or boiled eggs or kefir or apples in unlimited quantity but only one product daily). Some other diets are more balanced, but most of them consist of really dull food, such as buckwheat without salt or butter, boiled chicken fillets, one apple, one boiled egg and some vegetables a day. Some diets claim that magic happens if you eat half of the grapefruit with every meal (another magical fruit) or drink tea with milk or drink water with lemon, pepper, and honey.

However, in general diets do not work and many young beautiful Russian girls turn into big women by 30-40 and lose their grace, while simultaneously gaining health issues.

Why do we talk about females only? Most men in Russia could not care less how they look. There is a saying – a man should be just a little bit more handsome than an ape. Staying fit is a social norm for the girls and women, but not for the guys. Society is very mild to them in that sense.

7.3. Preventing Colds – the Russian Way

Most Russians believe that "colds come from a cold," not from infection. Here are some of the most common advice that you will hear in Russia about avoiding colds and flu.

Dress well and dress your children extra well! Children have to wear hats and mittens and scarfs from the beginning of Fall to the end of Spring. Moms usually especially control wearing hats! Young kids comply with that, but older kids and teens consider wearing hats uncool. If a kid decides to trick mom, agreeing on wearing a hat and takes it off while taking the elevator down, that is what she will hear from the window: "Tanya put the hat back on!!!". Smart kids learn fast to take the hat off only after they are out of mom's sight.

Adults should dress well too. Warm coat, hat, gloves, and scarf, plus – a lot of women wear tights under jeans or pants! That is very uncomfortable, but a lot of women believe that it is essential in cold weather. And in former times women used to wear wool tights, called reituzy, on top of regular tights (those were to be taken off indoors).

There is an opposite school of thought though – cold water treatment to train your body to cold. This involves cold showers, so in practice, not many people do that. But a lot of adults do swim in ice-cold water in winter. How does that fit with the previous concept? Easily. People only swim in the ice-cold water on a particular church holiday, when they believe that cold cannot do any harm.

For all other times – opening windows and even sitting near a closed window is believed to be a harmful practice, leading to catching a cold. Turning the AC on is considered to be even more harmful.

But nothing is worse, than sitting on the cold stone (even in Summer)! Any Russian will tell you never to do that!

And if you start to feel under the weather – you better not eat or drink anything cold. Even though eating ice-cream outdoors in Winter is a standard practice – when you catch a cold – your parents will allow you to eat only melted ice-cream!

Other than that – Russian people do not differ from Western people in how to prevent cold. We also take vitamins and know that sport makes you more healthy. And from time to time you start seeing people, wearing masks in the subway, but that is still very rare!

However, if you are unlucky and you caught a cold, see how to treat colds and flu using Russian home remedies!

7.4. Home Remedies in Russia

Winter is the season of colds, sore throats, cough, and flu. Drugstores are bursting with anti-cold remedies of all kinds, pharma companies are investing millions in TV advertising. But Russians still do not trust flu shots, prefer self-treatment and go to the doctor only in extreme cases. Here are the most typical recipes (think twice before trying some of them at home!)

Belief in Self-Treatment Starts in Childhood

When you are a kid – stuff happens. You fall a lot and often have scratched knees. Every Russian kid knows how to heal that fast – you take a leaf of a goosegrass and apply it to the damaged skin. Goosegrass is a part of the urban flora, and it magically heals small wounds. Some pharma companies already sell band-aids with the extract of the goosegrass!

Self-treatment with goosegrass is usually the first home remedy experience in a kid's life. Kids also experience a variety of other more or less effective home remedies, typically administered by moms and grandmas. By the time kids grow up, they believe that it is possible to treat almost anything with the right home remedy.

Home-remedies Against Cold

The typical treatment of any cold starts with hot tea with home-made raspberry jam before going to bed. Raspberry has the anti-inflammatory and heating effect and works like aspirin but is much tastier. Best to have 2 cups of tea and only then have a cup of tea with raspberry, so that you are not dehydrated when you sweat. That is especially important for kids.

Healing with food is quite typical – people use lemon, garlic, onion. Lemon provides Vit C. Garlic and onion have phytoncides – volatile organic compounds, which have anti-microbial effect. One does not need to eat onion and garlic to get the effect – you can mince them and inhale for 5 -10 min. Another very popular inhalation, when you have a cough – to breathe over boiled peeled potatoes. Boil some potatoes, drain the water, cover the pan with a towel and breathe underneath the towel for 10 -15 min. Be careful to control how hot is the steam so that you do not burn the throat and bronchus.

Honey is also a popular home remedy. Some people use honey for their tea instead of raspberry jam, some have milk with honey and butter, some put honey in the center of black radish and then have a teaspoon of honey a day (honey + phytoncides). And of course, Russians, like any other people, have chicken soup (usually a clear bouillon), when they feel sick.

Finally – if you have a nasal cold – in Russia you usually use natural remedies instead of a chemical nasal drops. We have a saying though that if you have a runny nose and do not treat it – it will go away in one week if you do treat it – it will go away in 7 days. People use warm salt in a cloth bag to warm the area (be cautious with that one – could help, but could also do harm, depending on your case). People rinse the nose with warm water (sometimes with added sea salt), use aloe juice (many people grow aloe at home) as nasal drops and inhale pine oil. Some people also use pine oil as nasal drops, but it is a bad idea to use undiluted pine oil for that purpose – you can burn the epithelium, and it will be painful. One somewhat effective "home remedy" that Russians use a lot is "zvezdochka" (little star). It is a Vietnamese balm with a robust menthol aroma. It was exported to the USSR, so all Russian people know it and believe that it has only natural ingredients such as oils, etc. Zvezdochka does not cure a running nose faster, but it certainly helps to breathe. The smell is so strong that one jar (of the size of a large coin) usually lasts for years.

Weird Home Remedies in Russia

I guess the above-mentioned home remedies are more or less typical for other countries as well. But there are also some unusual home remedies!

Let's start with the scratched knees. Most Russian households have a tiny bottle with the emerald color liquid in their medicine cabinets. This green stuff is called "zelyonka" (from the Russian word – "zelenyi" – green). Zelyonka is an antibacterial treatment that you are supposed to apply in small doses on scratches. It does not exist in the US, and I doubt it exists elsewhere in the world, except Russia. It is even banned in most countries since it contains a chemical aniline coloring which, according to some research, might be cancerogenic. If you ever come into contact with zelyonka (for example if you rent a flat in Russia and have found zelyonka in the medicine cabinet) – be super careful with this liquid. You can stain the entire apartment with one drop of zelyonka, and you will never be able to wash it off from clothes and furniture.

The other weird, but the very popular home remedy is to draw iodine nets on your body. People usually do that when they have back pain (and against 100 other illnesses – from bruises to colds). It is believed that such treatment stimulates blood circulation and replenishes the need for iodine in the body.

Stimulating blood circulation and heating the body is usually central to most treatments in Russia. That is understandable – we live in a cold country! And living right to the stereotypes – quite a few people believe that vodka with black grounded pepper is precisely what you need before going to bed if you are sick. Sometimes that gets replaced with vodka compresses.

Or if you want, you can put some dry mustard in your socks before going to bed. Dry mustard is supposed to keep your feet warm. Not sure if that could cure a cold, but probably would not do any harm. And if you are really adventurous, you can try hot mustard applications. That does not involve spreading real mustard (the one you put on your hot dog) on your body though! Compresses are made of real mustard, but this mustard is attached to the sheets of paper. In Russian, it is called "gorchichniki" (from the Russian word "gorchitsa" – mustard).

Putting mustard applications on calves is the most typical. Place "gorchichnik" in warm water, then apply on the skin for 5-10 min and cover the area (or the entire body) with a blanket. You should feel a hot sensation, but it should be pleasant, not burning. Do not use mustard applications if you have a fever.

If you are even more adventurous – you can try "banki" (glass jars). I never tried this method myself, but many people say it is very effective. This home remedy came from ancient China. Jars are relatively small. A person, who administers the treatment, heats each jar with a big match and places it on the skin on the back of a patient. A jar is supposed to stick to the surface very tightly and pull in some of the skin inside. The idea behind that is in stimulating blood circulation. Beware – it leaves your skin bruised!

Wishing you a great and healthy year! Take care!

7.5. Healthy Lifestyle – a New Trend in Russia

Russians are well-known for their love for vodka and festive dinners, which include lots of pies and salads with mayo. Being in a cold country, that is understandable. But guess what – the current trend is against all that! It is all about a healthy lifestyle now!

Planking Is a Thing Here

One of my colleagues does planking in the office every day! I am not kidding! And she has a special app for planking on her phone, which tells her how long she has to plank on a particular day!

Yoga Craziness

I first heard about yoga as a kid. At that point, this topic was as relevant as building colonies on Mars. Yogi were people, who walk on burning coal, do headstands and other crazy things. In recent years, most of my friends started to do yoga and claimed that they actually enjoy the peace of mind and the flexibility of the body that comes with that practice. It actually did not take them long to convince me to buy a yoga mat and sign up for yoga classes as well. And it does feel good.

Marathons and Fitness/Sport Festivals

Most of my friends run. More than that – they sign up for running in other world cities and get excited if they win a chance to run… and an opportunity to pay a significant fee for doing that. Some of my friends also bike and not just a bike, they bike in winter, in Russian Winter, and bike for hours!

You should go to the parks in Moscow in the Summer too. Hundreds of people are biking, rollerblading, running and participating in various sport/fitness festivals. That is crazy but good crazy!

Farm Products

To be fair – Russia is lagging several years behind the US. Kale is just entering the market, organic is still in talks (no proper legislation, governing that topic). Farm products have become mainstream though, and farmers markets are in fashion. Best markets also offer ready-made food, and have become a cool place to hang out, have brunch or lunch on the weekend.

Food Delivery of All Kinds

What changed too is how we get our lunches at work. Earlier we were limited to whatever cafes or canteens are around the office. Now choices are endless because of the food delivery apps. It is also possible to order "food constructors," which allows you to save time on shopping and thinking about the menu. Carefully measured ingredients for your breakfast, lunch, and dinner will arrive at your door in craft bags filled with smaller containers and recipes. Or, if you want to outsource cooking altogether, you can order ready-made food for the entire week or month. Companies that provide such service will interview you first to find out your goals and food preferences and restrictions and will build your menu based on that.

Still a Long Way Although we are moving towards a healthy lifestyle, the most happiness I see in the office is when we order burgers.

8. TRANSPORT

8.1. Ways to Entertain Yourself in Moscow Traffic Jams?

People living in other cities will not be able to relate to that. Most people consider an everyday commute of 30-40 minutes each way as long. But guess what? For your Moscow peers, the one-way commute can be anything from 1.5 to 4 hours. Why is it so and what do people do in traffic jams?

Why Are Traffic Jams in Moscow so Bad?

First of all – the city is huge! Official data says there are 12 M people, who live in Moscow. But we have to add at least 2-3 M of visitors and non-registered residents to that number. 4 million cars are registered in the city, and an unknown number of vehicles come from elsewhere – either Moscow region or other regions to Moscow daily. Moscow takes more than 1000 square km of land.

Secondly and most importantly – Moscow was founded in the year 1147, and radial ring planning was the most typical for ancient Russian cities. Now Moscow has 4 rings – Boulevard, Garden, Third and City Limit rings and many radial roads. What worked in ancient times does not work well now – the closer you are to the center, the more dense traffic becomes.

In addition to that, the city government only recently has started to regulate parking in the city, introducing paid parking in the center. Before you could park wherever you find a spot of land big enough to land your car. People parked cars in several lanes on each side of small roads and even on sidewalks. Fines and towing now prevent that. Also, large trucks are now banned from entering the city limits during the daytime. But there is still no fee to enter the central area or other economic, regulatory measures.

Finally, Russian drivers do not like to abide rules, and that creates many accidents and contributes to traffic jams, especially in winter time.

So, one hour of commute each way to and from work is considered to be great, 1.5 hours is supposed to be normal, 2 and more hours – a valid reason to complain about it to friends.

Why Not Use Public Transport Instead?

Valid question, especially given all the accolades to the beauty of the Moscow metro system! The Moscow subway is indeed one of the treasures of the city, which evokes genuinely patriotic feelings in any Muscovite. Each station is different, and most stations in the center are veneered with marble, granite, have murals, sculptures and other amazing decorations.

Although Moscow metro stations do look amazing, they get incredibly overcrowded during rush hours. And there is no air-conditioning in most trains. In addition to that, for most people, the nearest subway station is within 10-30 min walk, which is not convenient in the winter time. Of course, there are buses, but buses also get crowded during rush hours.

If you look at the Moscow metro map, you will see that it repeats the radial ring road plan but has fewer rings. As a result, all people have to first travel to the center if they need to change lines. That explains traffic jams in the metro during rush hours and length of commute time. To give you an idea of how big is the city – travel from one end to the other end on any of the radial lines takes more than an hour.

What Do People Do in Traffic Jams?

So how do people spend time in traffic jams? There are lots of activities:

Listen to the radio, mostly music stations. There is an abundance of those – from pop music to Russian music, from mellow jazz radio to brutal prison songs on Shanson radio. Radio mix typically includes songs, DJ talks, advertising intermissions, and contests. Some people like to call a radio station from traffic to take part in games. They sing songs, answer quests, tell their stories, congratulate their friends with birthdays and other events. Many people listen to audiobooks, some also study languages.

But audio is not enough to entertain us for 3-4 hours every day. We do a lot more in traffic.

Drink coffee/Eat. Fast food outlets have drive-through windows and people also take food from home to snack during the long drive. That is a relatively new behavior, even 10 years ago drinking coffee in a car while driving was almost unseen.

Do Makeup. Morning traffic is so slow, and there are many lights, so it is possible to do the full makeup while driving to work and even refresh nail polish

Use our smartphones. We do that a lot. Mostly for talking on the phone, using a headset since holding a phone can easily result in a significant fine now. These hours of driving are a great time to have long chats with friends and relatives. People text, email and play games too, even though that is not a safe practice

Flirt. A lot of relationships have started in traffic jams and rumors are that some of them resulted in long-time relationships and families.

We complain about traffic a lot. And always use traffic as a valid excuse for being late, even if the real reason has nothing to do with it. Our president often uses a helicopter to get to work from his residence in the Moscow suburbs, which tells you something about the traffic situation.

However, most drivers still find driving more comfortable than using public transport. We spend so much time in our cars that they become mini-versions of our homes. A typical Moscow girl has a spare pair of shoes, food, a change of clothes, reading materials, an umbrella, makeup kit and so many other things in her car. We are trained to survive in traffic every day. We have everything we need here.

8.2. Why Russians Are Crazy Drivers

"But, if Russians became safe drivers, what would YouTube do for content? Well, there will always be cats..."

The entire world looks at YouTube videos of how people drive in Russia and questions the sanity of people here. Why are Russian drivers that crazy? They do not care for their life? What is going on? Let's explore.

What Is "Being a Good Driver"?

When I just started to drive a car, the answer to that question was obvious to me. Great drivers drive really fast! At that time, I was not one of them, I was moving slowly in the right lane, totally scared of the moving objects around me and the moving object I am sitting inside. But I wanted to become the fast and fearless driver. My silly 20-year-old-self thought that cutting the lanes and speeding is a really cool adult behavior.

I was fortunate to have three conversations with really wise adults at that time. One was with a Canadian lawyer, who told me, that good driver is not somebody, who can drive fast, but the one, who can anticipate the situation on the road, predict how other cars will be moving and drive safe. The other conversation was with a British friend. That one was particularly funny. I asked him: "What would they do to a driver, who speeds up in the oncoming traffic lane?" That was typical behavior of drivers in Moscow at that time – to avoid a traffic jam, cars would go into the oncoming lane and really speed up. I was interested in learning how big is the fine for that in the UK. His answer was: "That guy will be probably brought to a mental hospital." The third conversation was with my Russian friend – he said that smoothly adjusting the gears is a key to a great experience of my passengers. These conversations were timely and shaped my attitude towards driving.

But Why Many Other Drivers Seem to Be Insane?

There are several reasons for that:

Bought their drivers licenses – you would be scared to know that a lot of drivers out there would've never passed the test if they did not pay a bribe. I am not sure if that practice still stands now, but some time ago it was typical

Fatalist's approach to safety – "it is what it is, if it is meant to be, it will happen. We are not the masters of our fortune". Usually, those people will tell you that "you never know what is going to happen to you 10 min from now. A brick could fall at your head from a roof of a building". Consequences of being a fatalist in Russia – you stop caring about safety at all. If you believe that fate is in God's hands – why buckle up, why be careful, why follow the rules? That pattern of thought is the one that spurs crazy driving behavior most

Competitiveness – "Oh, that guy wants to show off? He thinks he is the fastest one on the road? He thinks I cannot beat him? Challenge accepted!"

Bribes that can get you out of almost any situation. That is diminishing now with the video cameras on the roads in Moscow. But before those cameras were installed, people knew that any behavior on the street is acceptable if you can afford it. Literally. If you have enough money – you could drive drunk, pass red lights and even bail yourself out of a terrible car accident.

Are There Any Objective Obstacles to Safe Driving in Russia?

Yes, there are. Roads in Moscow are great, but if you go just 100 km outside of Moscow, roads are pretty bad, and in many cases really narrow. That is a real obstacle to the safe driving even if you are a good driver. If you plan to travel far in Russia – taking a train or a plane is a more reliable option.

Also, some road rules are strange, and traffic density in Moscow is crazy. It is objectively difficult to drive here even if you have best intentions.

Do Russians Use Insurance, Safety Belts, and Other Safety Measures?

Basic insurance is mandatory now, which is great, since it eases some of the tension, when road accidents happen. Full insurance is expensive, so it is bought mostly by owners of expensive cars.

Russians do not believe in safety belts. I recently listened to a radio program about Volvo. They are close to inventing the car, that will be 100% safe (no deaths even in significant road accidents). That is big, really big. But that system would never work in Russia. Because Russian drivers feel that seat belts are a) uncomfortable and b) there is an urban legend that tells about that case when a person's life was actually saved because he was not buckled up, and in the event of an accident was thrown through a window and just had a couple of scratches

Other safety measures? Yes. A Lot of Russian drivers have tiny icons, glued to the car panel, and people believe that those icons can protect from bad luck. And if the driver is not Christian, that function could be delegated to a string of beads. Or even to an amulet/charm. That makes perfect sense if you think about it – if your fate is in God's hands, what could protect you more than a piece of God?

Russians also believe in the power of dash cams! And indeed, dash cams often help to prove the case. Even if the case is a meteor, falling from the sky!

Is There Anything Good You Can Report on the Subject?

In fact, yes, there is. Drivers in Moscow started to obey many of the rules after fines became bigger. Also, surprisingly, in the last couple of years, drivers became more courteous to each other on the roads. What I like especially is the following habit: if you let another car to change lanes in front of you – that car will most certainly blink emergence lights to you two or three times. That means Thank You.

Aren't Things Bad in Other Countries Too? Why Are You Always So Critical of Russia?

There are a lot of problems in other countries too. Some countries even have earthquakes. But most well-developed nations do not have crazy drivers, because they have good roads and rules and policemen that are not corrupted.

Why is that? Because policemen in Western countries make a good salary and would not want to risk that salary and the benefits. But I think Russia is moving in that direction too, and things are improving, at least in Moscow.

8.3. Why Dash Cams Are Popular in Russia

Driving in Russia has always been an adventure. Lots of traffic, poor road conditions, crazy and impolite drivers on the streets. Having a dashboard video camera in such jungle is useful. And once in a while, it can record a meteorite fall as a bonus.

In the past several years roads in Moscow have drastically improved, and drivers have become much more careful. One especially lovely new habit is to signal a couple of times with emergency lights to say thank you to drivers who pause to let you change lanes. But the traffic density in the city has increased and is increasing every year, which inevitably leads to an increase in the number of accidents.

And when you have a car accident in Russia – things can get ugly and violent very fast. Liability insurance has become mandatory only recently, and full (two-way) coverage is optional and very costly, therefore not affordable for many people. Hit and runs are frequent too.

My first car accident was about a month after I started driving (it was at the end of the 90s). It happened right in front of the Kremlin. In a dense traffic jam, my car had lightly hit a car in front of me. I do not think the other vehicle was even damaged, but the driver was mad at me. He shouted at me and called his personal security. They arrived in 5 min or so, a black jeep with sporty-looking bouncers. He wanted them to scare me, which, to their credit, they refused to do. They looked at me and saw a young girl already scared, sitting in her car, talked to him and got back in their black SUV. But that was good luck – for years after Perestroika, and up to this moment, many car accidents do become scenes of violence. A dash cam in the car can help you in court, since Russian court system accepts videos from dash cams as evidence, or even help you at the moment if you refer to it during the dispute.

However, when you are liable for the accident and a car owner is mad at you – it is half trouble. In Moscow and other cities, there are groups of people, which do accident-staging and extract money from drivers by provoking accidents. Having a camera in the car is an excellent way to deter these criminals.

Another significant danger of Russian roads is the road police. At present in Moscow, if you obey the rules, they almost never stop you. If you violate the traffic rules, the bill with your fine will just arrive at your mailbox or email together with a photo of your car speeding or moving in the wrong lane, taken by a street camera. But in the past, small talk with police was not always a friendly one. Usually, it was a haggle between you and the police about the sum that will let you go away safe. That, however, did change in Moscow, because the road police now also have dash cams installed in their cars, so it is not so easy for them to demand money from drivers. But outside of Moscow, the situation has not changed yet.

So, having a dash cam in your car is a good idea if you drive in Russia. And after the fall of great Chelyabinsk meteorite, captured on thousands of dash cams – video cameras have become more than just functional gadgets. Now they are fancy accessories, and they offer insights not only to the craziness of Russian drivers but also to the stamina of Russians as we have seen from how local drivers kept their cool when seeing the meteorite!

8.4. The Advent of the Unofficial Taxi in Moscow

When I was writing a post in my blog about taxis in Moscow several years ago, Uber and other similar taxi services did not exist yet. But people in Moscow used private cars instead of the official taxi since the 90s, and a lot of people moonlighted as taxi drivers in their spare time. Basically – when you needed a car, you lifted your hand, and one of the nearby cars stopped. Foreigners always said that it is unsafe and strange to take a ride with a complete stranger.

That practice was called "bombing." Drivers who were not in a hurry and wanted to make some extra cash for gas gave rides to people. These cars were not equipped with a meter and did not have a special color or signs, you typically just negotiated the price before starting the journey. Sometimes a driver said: "Sorry, I am going to a different part of town." But in most cases, they took you.

Surprisingly, that practice was quite safe. Cases of robberies or other dangerous events associated with this "bombing" practice were rare. Drivers usually told you their life stories on the way, and, as taxi drivers everywhere, complained about city traffic jams, government, and gave their opinions on the important worldwide events.

On the top of my list is the story of one woman, which I heard more than 15 years ago. It was quite rare for women to work as unofficial cab driver. This woman, in particular, did not look like she belonged there. Here is her story. In Soviet times she used to work in a large state organization and held a significant position. That was the time when currency exchange was illegal, you could get imprisoned if caught when trying to buy US dollars at the black market. That was precisely what happened to her. She lost her job, went into jail, her husband vanished, her life was utterly destroyed. When she got released from prison, USSR did not exist, and currency exchange became a ubiquitous part of everybody's life (inflation was so bad that the only way to save your money was to convert it in foreign currency immediately upon receiving). When she was under trial – she was pressed for information about "other members of the criminal group." She stayed strong and did not succumb to an offer to reveal names, so when she was released from prison, people whom she saved from the same fate gave her that car as a present. And that present really helped her and eventually led to our meeting. I was stunned that this woman was not bitter about the unfair situation she got into. She said that one has to accept what life throws at us and think about the future rather than mull over the past. Russian women are incredibly strong!

One funny story involved a driver, who took me to the airport. A man in his late 50s. He asked me whether I was traveling to Turkey. I said that I am going to a different destination. But he kept saying that it is such a pity that I am not going to Turkey. I was curious and asked him why? He answered that he had been to Turkey many years ago and bought himself two pairs of great pants, but now they got worn off. If I were traveling to Turkey, he would've asked me to buy him those pants. Oh, and btw, there was already no deficit of pants in Russia at that time. But he sincerely thought that the best pants are sold in Antalya, and he was entirely sure I would help him if only I were flying there.

There were many other stories, big and small. A boy in his 20s, madly in love with his new girlfriend, bombing to earn cash to take her to movies and cafes. An old gentleman, whose granddaughters asked him to send them to relatives in Armenia for school holidays and he had already booked tickets but needed to pay for them before midnight. A guy who had a date that evening and ordered cooked shrimps from a fancy café and needed money to pay for them. We actually stopped by this café on our way, and the intense smell of shrimps accompanied us on the rest of the way.

And, now, people everywhere take rides with strangers. Taxi apps made our life so much easier! Car arrives in several minutes and you don't even need cash, as payment could be taken from a card, attached to the account. There are not many differences in how that works, comparing with the other countries. The main difference is that Uber is not the market leader, it is Yandex Taxi, followed by Gett. And, that a lot of people take the front passenger seat in the taxi, the same as they did when they used private cars.

8.5. How to Travel in Russia – by Car, Plane or Train?

Looking at the map of Russia, tourists often wonder which transport to choose for their travel – car, plane or train? Pros and cons, and an insider's view on experiences you will get may help you plan your trip.

Travel in Russia by Car

My American friends often ask me, why I do not explore Russia by car even though I have an SUV. Road trips are a very American thing. Indeed, in the US I did travel by car a lot and always enjoyed that. Traveling by car in Russia is however quite challenging. The poor road condition is the main obstacle. Technically it is possible to travel by car, but it would be a complicated affair unless you choose a newly build highways (Moscow – St. Pete, Moscow – Crimea).

Roads are narrow, have holes, a lot of drivers are crazy, there are lots of accidents, and traffic jams are horrible near main cities. On top of that, road police in the country like to make money on tourists. Of course, if you do not break the rules, you will not have to pay, but road signs aren't always straightforward or may be absent. So, there are very high chances that you would break the rules at some point, and road policemen will be there, waiting for you.

Another problem is navigation. Near big cities, you will, of course, have Yandex or Google maps, but unless you download the directions, you may get lost once you are out of the reception zone. Finally – the infrastructure of gas stations, hotels, places to eat and restrooms exists mostly in the well-developed parts of the country. If you travel by car, you have to be well-prepared and have everything you need – water, food, gas with you.

For the foreigners, I would not recommend renting a car and traveling in the country. Hiring a local driver may be an option, but that option is suitable for short-haul trips, such as trips along the Golden ring of picturesque towns, which are not far from Moscow.

Travel in Russia by Plane

If you plan to travel far away – to lake Baikal or Kamchatka or other destinations, planes will most likely be part of your itinerary. Each major city has an airport and our main airline Aeroflot is flying to all those destinations. There are also other airlines, some of which are discounters. But if you want to be on the safe side, I would recommend choosing Aeroflot as I believe that this airline has newer planes and better pilots.

If you travel from Moscow with Aeroflot, you will depart from the domestic terminal in Sheremetyevo. There is not much to say about air travel in Russia, it does not differ from air travel in other countries. Food will be served in-flight, but do not expect gourmet food, so if you are a picky eater, bring your own snacks. And, also, bring your own in-flight entertainment as not all planes are equipped with modern entertainment systems. Flights to many places take a long time, for example, a trip to Irkutsk (Lake Baikal) is 5,5 hours, flight from Moscow to Petropavlovsk-Kamchatsky (Kamchatka) is 8 hours long.

Travel in Russia by Train

Trains are the preferred method of travel for locals. Less expensive than planes. Less hassle than car travel. Efficient. And providing unique experiences and ambiance. Let's explore why we love traveling by train so much.

First of all, trains depart from the center of the city. And arrive to the center of the other city. Instead of spending 2 hours getting to the airport and another hour or more for airport procedures, you can come to the railway station minutes before the train departure and still make it.

Secondly, we just love the experience of traveling by train. I need to explain to you though, what that means. And there is a lot to be described here. But first, a brief crash course, which will help you to buy the tickets.

There are several types of trains in Russia:

High-speed trains are similar to Shinkansen in Japan. These are such trains as Sapsan (Moscow-St. Pete-Moscow) or Lastochka (Moscow-Nizhny Novgorod-Moscow) and several others. The entire trip between Moscow and St. Pete lasts 4 hours, it is very comfortable, you can use wifi and enjoy a meal or snacks.

Fast trains – for example, the famous Red Arrow train (train #1 or #2) between Moscow and St. Pete. This train departs at midnight and arrives around 8 am. It is a sleeping train, perfect if you are used to sleeping on a train.

Long-haul trains – slower, with more stops, you can also sleep on those trains.

"Electric trains" (electrichka) – short-haul train between the city and suburbs, basic comfort, seated cabins.

How to use this information? I usually suggest foreigners choose high-speed trains if they are available on their route. Several hours on those trains are a comfortable experience. Would high-speed trains be a preferred choice for Russians? It depends. A lot of Russians would prefer fast night trains. Sleeping on a train makes the trip seem much shorter. But before you book a trip on a night train, there are some things you need to know.

First of all, choose the train. I mentioned that trains #1 and 2 go between Moscow and St. Pete. Train numbers are important. The smaller is the number, the better is the train. I would advise against taking trains #100-300.

Next essential knowledge is carriage types. There are 4 main types of carriages:

An SV is a 2-people cabin, considered to be a luxury. You will have 2 bunk beds and a table in the cabin. Linen, pillows, and blankets will all be high quality. Some tickets may include meal and beverages

A coupe is a 4-people cabin with a table and 4 bunk beds (lower and upper levels). Bed linen is also provided. Most Russians like to choose this type of cabin. The only nuisance is that you never know, who will be your neighbors. They could drink alcohol and then snore all night or just be too loud. At some routes, you can buy tickets to the women-only cabin, but that is not typical. As one of my foreign friends said: "I could not sleep because I am not used to sleeping next to an unknown shirtless man, who is staring at me as I sleep." Also, when booking tickets for coupé, pay attention to whether you are getting upper or lower level beds. I prefer to choose an upper bed for myself, I usually sleep or read on a train. If you want the lower level bed, be ready that the person, who has an upper-level bed may sit next to you during the daytime

Platzcart – is like coupé, but cabins do not have doors, and there are two extra beds in the corridor. The cheapest of the sleeping options, but zero privacy and much less security. And security is important when you travel for an extended time with all your belongings. With SV or coupé, you can lock the door inside for the night. When you travel in platzcart, your best bet is to put your purse under the pillow and sleep lightly

Sitting cabin – not typical for extended travel. Sitting for 4-5 hours is ok, but it is impossible to travel that way for 2 or more days

Food on a Train

Having a meal, served to your carriage, is a very new option, only available on some trains and in the luxury type carriages. On all others, the only thing you can get is hot tea. Which is not bad at all – tea is served in a traditional "train-style," in the glasses with metal tea-glass holders. That is a unique experience in itself, so make sure you do not miss it.

So, where do people eat? Many trains have a restaurant carriage. It is an entire wagon, which looks like a restaurant, with tables, menu, and dishes, ranging from soups and salads to the main courses. Quality of food really varies. Better trains (the ones with the lower train numbers) usually also have better food.

Most locals though bring food with them on a train ride. A classical "train picnic" would include a boiled chicken, boiled eggs, boiled potatoes, cucumbers & tomatoes, bread and something sweet. There are no refrigerators on the train, so it is important to choose food that does not spoil fast. Just do not forget to bring some salt with you.

However, as time goes, food from home is eaten. What do people do then? It may be possible to buy snacks at the train station kiosks, but many people have missed their trains doing that. Demand always creates supply, so local people, who live near train stations, bring food for sale to the platforms. They sell snacks, and they also sell boiled potatoes, eggs, and chicken, home-made pies, etc. But you have to be adventurous and look what you are buying and from whom you are buying.

How About Taking the Trans-Siberian Train?

Making that trip is on a list of almost every foreigner, whoever planned to travel to Russia. And virtually no Russian would ever take this train unless you pay us a lot of money. Why?

First of all – it is a Very long train ride. We are ok with traveling 2-3 days by train, but more than a week is too much for us. Food is the smallest of our concerns. Number one concern is hygiene. Restrooms at trains are not the cleanest places on Earth. I heard that on a very long train ride, there would be a shower, but I do not believe it would be clean either. It is possible that the experience is different if you take a luxurious Trans-Siberian Express. Finally – after a day or two any train ride becomes boring. People think that they would be able to see the country from a train window, but the reality is that for most of the time you see the same landscape – hours of forests or fields.

The summary of all the above is that in such a big country like Russia, you may need more than one means of transportation. Knowing more about the pros and cons of each of them could help you plan the trip. For example, I hope that now you will choose a train instead of a plane for a Moscow – St. Pete – Moscow trip, you will hire a local driver with his car for a short excursion outside of the city, and you will take a plane to a far located destination.

8.6. Metro – the Underground Wonder

Moscow Metro is indeed one of the famous tourist attractions. Visitors from all over the world admire underground palaces, richly decorated with marble, bronze, mosaic, etc. How did the poor Soviet Republic manage to build such a luxury subway and, why did Bolsheviks decide to do that?

There is an obvious logic behind that. At that time ordinary people struggled – they lived in communal (shared) flats, worked hard at factories, did not eat well and did not have much entertainment. The government was promoting an idea of a "bright future" that will come once communism will be established. However, the government felt the need to show some improvement, that the country is heading in the right direction to this new and bright future. Creating something awe-inspiring and for the use of public would send a proper signal to the population. Before only rich people had access to palaces, now every worker would have underground palaces for everyday use.

Also, the Soviet government was always obsessed about showing off to the West. At that time both New York and London already had functional subways. However, Bolsheviks said that in other countries subway was built solely for extracting profit and in Soviet Republic metro was developed to make the life of citizens better. So, they decided to create such a subway that does not exist in other countries. What is interesting though, when metro construction started, they invited foreign specialists and used foreign tools and technologies. Building metro in Moscow wasn't easy – soil varies, there is water under the city and other complications. But they managed to succeed, and the first line of Moscow Metro opened on May 15th, 1935.

What is interesting – it was also the first time escalators have been installed in Moscow, so people needed to be educated about "moving staircases." Also, in general, people had to be taught about the concept of traveling under the surface. Having well-lit and gorgeous underground spaces certainly helped!

During the WWII Moscow Metro served as a bomb shelter, and even when I went to school, teachers told us that in the case of war we have to go to Metro, to find safety there. Surprisingly, this gorgeous space is rarely used for concerts or fashion shows. But what is excellent – trains run every minute, or even less and all public spaces in Metro are super clean and gorgeous.

9. EDUCATION/ENTERTAINMENT/CULTURE

9.1. Cultural Life I – Literature

In Soviet times Russians were consuming more books than any other nation. In a big part that was due to mandatory school education, so every person in the country learned to read early and did study literature in school. Also, TV of that time had only 3 channels, and broadcasting was far from 24/7. Even in the subway people were reading, and they were reading thick books. You could easily see Turgenev, Dostoevsky, Tolstoy, Pushkin and other editions of classics. Sci-fi was also very popular, especially among men.

At the time of total deficit of everything, good books were also hard to find in bookstores. Especially in demand were collected editions. These series were very well published, intellectual part of the population enjoyed them for reading, less intelligent people liked how pretty books looked when displayed on bookshelves at their homes. Blue, green, grey, dark red book covers indeed looked good on shelves.

About a year ago my cleaning lady, who comes to my place for more than 15 years, and always strives for improving my life, proposed to straighten out my home library, by sorting books by colors of book covers. I have politely declined this offer and managed to hide a smile.

So, collections of books were hard to get, bookstores had long waiting lists. One could improve chances for faster purchase by donating "makulatura," paper for recycling (old newspapers, paper, and books). Books for kids were in particular demand, kids at that time did read a lot since not much was going on TV and movies were a rare treat. Books developed the imagination of kids, kids learned stories and did plenty of role-playing with friends. A great thing about Soviet time was that real masters of the word, famous writers rather than translators translated favorite books for kids. Quite often translations were even better, and more entertaining than original stories.

A big part of book culture in Soviet times were "forbidden books" – books that the Soviet system did not approve, but people had typed versions of them and exchanged them in secret among friends. My parents had such books at home, hidden in our apartment. One example – Master and Margarita by Bulgakov with parts that were censored out in an official edition. These parts were highlighted in italic, and when reading, I kept wondering why this or that part had been wiped out by the official censorship. After Perestroika more and more books were officially published. Also, at that time literature magazines, such as Novy Mir or Literature Newspaper were hugely popular. These newspapers and magazines published Solzhenitsyn and other previously forbidden authors.

However, when publishing turned into a business, it not only provided availability of great books for Russian audience but also opened a channel for sub-par books of various genres. Fantasy and crime stories (easy-read literature) became widely popular. Fantasy was especially prevalent in the 90s when it served as an escape from reality. Grown-up men were reading fantasy fairy-tales, women read romance novels.

I do not have statistics about current reading habits of Russians, but I assume that people read less. You can still see people reading in the subway (now mostly on e-readers). I always wonder what they read, and if I have a chance to have a peak above the shoulder, I do that. I have not seen Turgenev or Dostoevsky on e-readers. And about half of the people holding gadgets in subway do not read – they play games or text friends. People who do not use public transport do not have a lot of free time – they work a lot and spend too much time in traffic jams. Discussing books among friends has become an anachronism. Kids definitely do not favor reading now – cartoons and video games are much more entertaining for small kids, and teenagers spend their time in social networks. Very often I find stacks of books near mailboxes in my apartment building – people get rid of them, and from time to time I adopt some of these books and bring them home. Finally, books now have become expensive, so although bookstores have a great selection of books – there are no lines for buying books anymore.

9.2. Stay Tuned to Music

Russia has solid traditions when it comes to music. From folk music to classical music, from ethnic music to modern styles. Many people receive an education in music and many play musical instruments. And everybody loves to listen to music! In Summer people especially like to listen to live music outdoors – at the multiple music festivals. Let me tell you about two festivals I went to some time ago:

Nashestvie Rock Festival

That is The Rock Festival of the year, the annual event since 1999. The year I went to the festival, it took place 120 km from Moscow at the place called Bolshoe Zavidovo, 60 km from Tver city. 153 K visitors attended the event, and most of them camped at the field near the stage.

It is impossible to describe how big is this festival. "Nashestvie" literally means "Invasion." A very accurate name for this particular event! Let's start with "getting there." How long do you think it can take you to drive 120 km (~ 100 miles)? It took me 7 hours! That was insane, especially given that a lot of festival visitors take a train instead of driving.

When you arrive at the festival, you hear the music and see the sea of cars, tents, and people. Organizing a music festival of that scale requires a lot of logistics. I was surprised to see how well it was managed. I guess that hosting a festival for so many years has led to perfection.

Now, who plays at Nashestvie? The line-up includes ALL the iconic bands of Russian Rock, such as Alisa, Aquarium, DDT, Bi-2, Neschastny sluchai and many more. Festival is 3 days long, all this time bands play non-stop to the enjoyment of visitors.

The audience is very diverse. Most people are in their 20s-30s. They dance, chill out in the sun, and many drink beer (local beer brand is sponsoring the festival). Very laid-back crowd. For some people though the festival is the opportunity to show themselves, so you can see people with all kinds of tattoos, haircuts and even people dressed up as film characters.

Usadba Jazz Festival

This event is at the other pole from Nashestvie Rock Festival. It started in 2004 as the first open-air jazz festival in Russia, uniting bands that play jazz, funk, world music, acid-jazz, lounge, jazz-rock, and blues. Usadba Jazz takes place at a beautiful venue – country estate Archangelskoe, built at the end of the 18th century. "Usadba" actually means "country estate."

At first, it was a relatively small event, now it has more than 40K visitors. Since 2008 Usadba Jazz first hosted bands from other countries, Festival received the status of an international event. Some of the famous jazz musicians, who played there in different years are: Marcus Miller, Avishai Cohen Trio, Branford Marsalis Quartet, Charlie Hunter Trio, The Brand New Heavies, Yusef Lateef & Belmondo Quintet, Nils Landgren, Aaron Parks, Jazzanova Live!, Trilok Gurtu, Zap Mama, Jimi Tenor, Lucky Peterson, John Scofield, Puppini Sisters, Oleg Lundstrem Orchestra, Igor Butman Big-Band.

There are other popular festivals and, a lot of famous artists and bands come to Russia to give concerts. Due to the recent anti-piracy regulations and convenience of music streaming services, more local people started to pay for music content.

9.3. Movies from Soviet Time and Now

Movies are always a good reflection of what is going on in society.

Early movies of the Soviet Republic were mostly about revolution, fighting, battles. The most famous film is "*The Battleship Potemkin*," by Sergey Eisenstein. Later, in the 1930s, movies were influenced a lot by Hollywood, so the most famous actress of that time, Lyubov Orlova, looked like a Hollywood star, and many movies ("*Circus*," "*Jolly Fellows*," etc.) were musicals.

For people of my age, Soviet movies are movies for children, movies about WWII and movies from the 70s-80s. I would divide movies for children further in two categories – movies about school kids and movies about adventures (pirates, musketeers, explorers). Films about WWII were showing the bravery of Soviet soldiers at war, and there were so many of them, that kids often played battle, and discussed how terrible the war is. Soviet movies of the 70s-80s were mostly kind and witty movies about the day-to-day life of ordinary people.

The most famous Soviet movie is "*Moscow Does Not Believe in Tears*," 1980 film, directed by Vladimir Menshov. It is the only Soviet film that got Oscar, and it shows the life of three young women, who came to Moscow from small towns. They share the same room but have very different personalities and goals in life – one wants to marry up, another one wants to have a traditional family, and the third one – to make a career. This epic movie shows the life of these three characters for 20 years, meanwhile giving almost an encyclopedia of life at that time.

Another great movie of the same director, "*Love and Pigeons*," tell the story of a family, living in a village. Main character's hobby is raising pigeons, he lives a simple life with his wife and kids, until he meets an eccentric urban lady and falls for her. He eventually returns back home, since he sees that they are not compatible, and he misses his wife.

A very famous director, Eldar Ryazanov, directed more than 10 iconic Soviet movies, among which are:

- *"Irony of Fate"* – a movie about a guy, who went to a sauna on the New Year's Eve with his friends, they all got drunk and forgot, who needs to fly to Leningrad (St. Pete) and sent him there. At that time all apartments were typical, and many street names were similar, so he takes a taxi from the airport, thinking that he is in Moscow, but ends up at the apartment of this lady, who is expecting her fiancé to celebrate New Year with. Typical situation comedy.
- *"Office Romance"* – a movie that shows life at one of the typical state organizations, where people pretended to do productive work, but in fact each day started with women doing make-up and continuing with lots of sidelines from work. There are several main characters in this film: an ordinary middle-aged man, who is raising two kids on his own, because his wife left him, and is scared by his boss – a smart, but a strict and unattractive woman. Suddenly, his old-time friend from school joins the organization. Since the time they last saw each other, his friend's career picked up, and now he has all the material attributes of success – nice car, apartment, expensive things, and also a family. It happens so that another of their classmates also works there, she was always in love with him, and now, seeing him successful and good-looking, she starts to chase the guy. And our first character is fighting with the boss half of the movie, but then ice begins to melt, and they get to like each other. One of everybody's favorite parts of this movie is the makeover of the boss, as a result of which, she transforms into an attractive woman. Needless to say – film ends well

I can go on and on with describing Soviet movies, but not sure how interesting that is in a format of the book (in my blog I could at least provide screenshots or movie clips). In general, those Soviet movies were more about human relationships than anything else, they were not action movies, and people loved them because they showed the everyday life of somebody like themselves very accurately. Censorship at that time was extreme, it was not possible to add any critique of the Soviet regime, and a lot of topics, such as sex or anything not approved by the government, were banned.

At the beginning of Perestroika at the end of the 80s, beginning of the 90s, things changed. Censorship was lifted, which had its pros and cons. A lot of mediocre movies, consisting almost solely of sex and violence were released since there was no censorship anymore. Of course, there were also high-quality films, but they too reflected the harsh reality of the 90s – showing prostitutes, bandits, etc.

Now the situation improved and there are some outstanding directors and actors, and more financing is available for the local movie industry.

9.4. Robots Among Us

The term "robot" was introduced by Czech playwright Karel Capek in his play about humanlike machines. In Czech, the original word "robota" means grunt work or hard labor. When we were kids, we all dreamed of a time in the future, when robots will live among us. Now in Moscow, we can all experience this future.

Robots Should Look like Us

Robots actually existed even, when we were kids. They worked at the factories and other industrial places, such as assembly lines, packing, sorting facilities, etc. But these were not the robots we wanted to see. And even robotic dogs and Roomba vacuum cleaner did not make us 100% happy. We wanted anthropomorphic robots – the ones who have legs, arms and, most importantly – eyes. Robots that look like us!

Several years we finally got that, when dozens of robots from all over the world came to Moscow to dance and play at the Robot's Ball!

EDUCATION/ENTERTAINMENT/CULTURE

Robot's Ball in Moscow

I did not expect it would be such a cool event! I ended up spending most of my Sunday, playing with robots and absolutely enjoyed that experience!

There were more than 20 robots from Russia, USA, Europe, Korea, and Japan. The biggest and most exciting robot Titan has traveled all over the world and worked along such superstars as Rihanna, Will Smith, Jackie Chan, and many others. Titan dances, signs, talks to the audience in many languages and even cries.

British robot Thespian was the most emotional robot at the Robot's Ball. Thespian can show a range of emotions – from happiness to shyness, he can blush and even fall in love. Of course, he can also sing, dance and read poetry.

French robot NAO is probably the cutest one because of its size.

There were even robots-animals, for example, a cute baby seal.

An additional attraction at the Robot's Ball was to look at the kids, playing with robots. For instance, robot NAO asked kids to choose a picture of a duck or other bird and show it to him and was happy if they have chosen the correct image.

Another moment that really melted my heart was a theater show of robots, which my friends, who organized the exhibition rehearsed for 2 months. That was a show of the smaller robots, and it was fabulous! But there were moments when things did not work out as planned. Like a moment, when a tiny robot, doing his best, performing in front of the large audience, slips and falls and a human being rushes to save him.

The Three Laws of Robotics

Seeing smart and playful robots is nice, but it also makes you wonder whether they are becoming too intelligent. Fears and concerns about robots have repeatedly been expressed in a range of books and films. A common theme is the development of a master race of conscious and highly intelligent robots, motivated to take over or destroy the human race.

Isaac Asimov had defined the three laws of robotics, which are often called Asimov's laws:

1) A robot may not injure a human being or, through inaction, allow a human being to come to harm.
2) A robot must obey the orders given to it by human beings, except where such orders would conflict with the First Law.
3) A robot must protect its own existence as long as such protection does not conflict with the First or Second Law.

9.5. Russian Language Is Difficult Even for Native Speakers

One of the top 5 questions I get in emails from my readers is "How to learn Russian?" Russian is indeed one of the most challenging languages to learn because of grammar, pronunciation, and exceptions to the rules. But guess what?! We, Russians, study our language for 10 years in school, yet very few people do not make grammar mistakes when they write or speak.

My Own Experience with the Russian Language

I am told that my Russian is really good, and I like to agree with those people. I think that is because my mom taught me how to read when I was 3.5 years old. Reading a lot helps because you remember how words are spelled on some subconscious level and have an excellent source to expand your active vocabulary. However, even after so much reading, I still do make punctuation errors every now and then.

Russian is very difficult for even the most deliberate speaker/writer of the language. Yet, it is sometimes painful to hear fellow Russians make "lazy" use of the language (not caring about declension, proper use or spelling of words). We do notice mistakes and, in general, are not tolerant of them. Some time ago one of my friends started a discussion on Facebook about errors we hate most and, it became the most extended discussion thread I have ever seen.

On the other hand, we are absolutely delighted to see non-native Russian speakers attempt to learn and practice the language. We are not only tolerant and forgive any mistakes in that case, but also try to help our foreign friends in any way we can.

How Russians Learn Russian?

Like any other people, we learn to speak from our parents at an early age and build the active vocabulary from books, TV and being immersed in the Russian-speaking environment.

But to write well, we need to study Russian in school for 10 years. First of all – these studies are to learn grammar rules. And to learn how to check your spelling, based on these rules. Secondly – we memorize numerous exceptions. The Russian language does have a lot of them. Finally, a good teacher will weed out "parasite words" and, improve pronunciation if needed.

I often get questions about pronunciation and accents. "Can you recognize which part of the country is somebody from?". I usually cannot, except for understanding whether a person is from Moscow or not (Muscovites reduce most "o" sounds to "a"(sounds like "u" in "under"). So, when I say "moloko" (milk), I actually pronounce it as "malako." That is considered a correct pronunciation. It is funny that now, learning Spanish, my correct pronunciation in Russian is a big problem – I have a heavy Russian accent when speaking Spanish precisely because I tend to reduce vowels.

Sometimes I can also say that a person is not from Moscow or is not from the same cultural strata as I am, judging by the words they use. It could be just one or two words and, you understand that you have a completely different background. These words serve as codes the other way too – people can recognize "their people," based on the vocabulary the same way people who are working in the same industry connect when they hear common professional slang.

How Does Russian Change with Time?

Like any language, it evolves. New words are being added. Some of these words are indeed brand new, such as "selfie," some have changed their meaning with time. Also, some words have become extinct because they are no longer needed.

In general, that is positive. Language is a living being and has to change. Business influenced a lot of changes. Many English words (such as "marketing") have now become part of the Russian vocabulary. Sometimes though, there is an entirely relevant Russian word, but people still use the English word instead. Critics are against that. Some critics even think that all English words should be replaced by Russian words in the language. I do not agree with such an extreme, but I also feel that people, who work in both Russian and in English could use less English words when they are speaking Russian. At one of my jobs, we even made a point of notifying each other about the usage of English words when it was not necessary.

Many people think that the Russian language is deteriorating in general, but that is not true. It is just that with the appearance of social media, more people started to write, and their writing is now public. So, we do see many more mistakes in written language. These mistakes do not affect middle-aged people, but they can influence young people. When you read a lot of incorrect text, you absorb the errors and may start to repeat them. What is also interesting about social media writing – although it is a written text, it is usually a conversation, so it is closer to oral speech than to a book text. And that is one of the reasons why people love to use smileys and other emojis. In a face-to-face conversation, you smile and use different facial expressions and body language. It is faster and easier to add an emoji to a phrase in social media rather than carefully select words so that they convey the emotion. But that happens in all languages now, not only in Russian.

What Are the Most Difficult Things for Foreigners, Who Learn Russian?

Pretty much everything. We really admire foreigners, who not only learn Russian, but master speaking fluently. To us, it shows that they are interested in our country and our culture and want to better connect with us.

Here are just some things that are difficult in my opinion:

Cyrillic alphabet and pronunciation. 33 characters, some of which look like characters in the English alphabet (but may, in fact, be a different letter, such as "p" which is our "r"), some look completely foreign. To make the situation worse, some characters are the ones we never pronounce. For example, we have a letter "ь," which is called a "soft character." We do not pronounce it, but it softens the pronunciation of the preceding consonant, similar to how in Spanish you say "manyana" when you see the word mañana. We also have a letter "ъ," which is called "hard character" and is not pronounced at all or a letter "й," which is quite rare, but it changes how the vowel that is after it is pronounced. "йо" would sound as "yo." As in "yogurt." But my favorite is "ы." Very few foreigners are able to pronounce that vowel!

An absence of articles. Unlike most Indo-European languages, we do not use articles, which can be confusing for the people, who are used to having them. Articles really haunt me in my English. As my blog readers may have noticed, I often omit "a" and "the" and a lot of my English-speaking friends tell me about that.

Genders. To make up for an absence of articles – we have genders. Each noun has its own gender, and it is important to memorize it. Most of that is quite logical – for example in Russian "a girl" is "девочка" and is feminine (contrary to German, where das Mädchen is for some reason neutral (which drove me crazy when I was learning German). But English does not have genders for nouns, so it must be difficult for the English-speaking people to memorize the gender of each noun.

Conjugation of adjectives. All adjectives conjugate according to nouns they belong to. That must be understandable for the Spanish-speaking people, but pretty difficult for English speakers.

Cases. We also have cases, and unlike German, which has 4, we have 6. One needs to understand which case to use, and make sure that the entire chain of verb, noun, and adjective have correct endings

Prefixes. Are the endings the biggest nuisance? No! Prefixes (part of the word that is before the root) are! Prefixes often take over the function of prepositions. For example, the verb "ехать" – go/drive changes its meaning when you use different prefixes. (приехать means arrive, поехать – start going, заехать – drive in, переехать – drive over, выехать – drive out, объехать – drive around, съехать – drive away/under, etc.)

Slang. A lot of words have double or triple meanings. Most of that is slang – for example, drive away/under – съехать is one meaning, but we can say съехать с темы – which literally means drive away from the topic. But you cannot say приехать к теме – drive to the topic. You would use придти к теме. (walk to the topic). No logic, just memory training.

9.6. Learning Foreign Languages... and Not Speaking Them

I often get questions – how many languages do Russians speak? Do all Russians speak English? Aside from English, would the next favorite foreign Western language for Russians be French? Do Russian students have an opportunity to study Latin in school? Are Russian students interested in learning Chinese? Let's explore.

Do Russians Speak English?

Most Russians do not speak other languages. Learning foreign languages has not been obligatory until a couple of years ago (now the curriculum of all schools should contain a foreign language). A lot of Russians did study a second language at school and even at the university but have an insufficient level of knowledge of the language they studied.

I was fortunate to live abroad with my parents and study English with native speakers. I found such note in a diary of my dad: "Tanya is 8 years old. She already speaks some English. She has a heavy Russian accent, but her English is anyway better than mine was after I studied in school, at the university and did my PhD.". According to the National census of 2010, only 6% of Russians wrote that they speak English. According to other research studies (English First etc.), the percentage is higher but still is around 10-15%. Discrepancies in numbers may be explained by the different samples – among urban population that percentage is higher than among the rural population.

Why is the language learning so poorly organized in schools? I guess that the main reason is the old and boring curriculum and lack of real language practice. Kids just do not see why they need to study the unnecessary subject. London is the capital of Great Britain. Ok. Making kids learn texts of songs, learning 100 useful phrases or even watching animated films would've been much more entertaining and productive.

Still, most foreigners know at least one Russian, who speaks English or another foreign language pretty well. Sometimes, really well. How did they master the language? Chances are most of them went to the specialized English-speaking schools, where they had many hours of English classes per week, professional tutors, specialized equipment to improve pronunciation and maybe even a chance to go on a study exchange program abroad. Some of the students later enhanced their language skills at the specialized linguistics institutes or at work or by taking the private classes. A lot of parents now make their kids study English with a private tutor in addition to the school curriculum, although that is possible only for families with above average income.

What About Other Languages?

English is indeed the most useful language to learn in the world now. If one speaks English, it is enough to travel and even work in the majority of the countries, so most people study English. However, historically that was not always the case. For a long time, French was the preferred second language in Russia. Not for everybody of course. The majority of the population did not speak French, only people from upper social circle did. They were usually taught French in childhood, by the native French speakers and spoke really well.

Now French is the third favorite language, German is the second and Spanish is the fourth. The language, which is on the rise, is Chinese. A lot of parents think about the current demographic trends and want their children to have an advantage in the workplaces of the future. So, their kids do study Chinese. Whether that will really give them an edge is questionable but learning a language which is so different from Russian is, of course, beneficial for the development of the brain. Still, in absolute numbers, the number of students who study Chinese is fractions of the percent.

How About Latin?

Unfortunately, Latin is not studied in schools. Very few people, such as medical students have studied Latin. Even the Biology departments of universities do not teach Latin as a separate subject. Students may have to learn parts of the body or botanical names in Latin, but they just learn the lists by heart, which is not productive. The idea of studying Latin is to understand the roots of the words and how the language is built. I did study Biology at the university for 5 years and learned those lists. Guess what the only Latin name of a plant that I still remember is? Ajuga Reptans or the carpenter's herb in English. Why did I remember it? Because the Russian name of this plant (живучка ползучая – something like "a crawling living being") does sound really funny!

Are There Language Schools in Russia?

Yes, plenty of them. But most are located in big cities and taking lessons is still quite costly. Of course, there are so many apps, sites, chats, and other free opportunities to learn languages. But learning a language takes a lot of hours, and it is difficult to motivate yourself, especially for people who do not travel abroad or interact with the foreigners. There are 143M people in Russia, all speak Russian, so a Russian person has many fellow citizens to talk to in a native language. Also, all foreign movies are dubbed, and most books eventually are translated into Russian.

9.7. Facts and Legends About Moscow State University

Moscow State University is named after Mikhail Lomonosov. He was an amazing self-made man. Born in a village near Archangelsk (North of Russia), he was so keen to study that he took what he could learn in his village and then left home and moved first to Moscow and St. Petersburg and later to Germany.

Lomonosov became a professor of Chemistry when he was 34. Founding of Moscow State University was done under his influence and according to his project.

Now MSU has 15 Scientific Institutes and 40 Schools. In total there are about 50 thousand students (35 thousand undergrads, 5 thousand PhDs (and other graduate majors) and 10 thousand students from prep departments. There are about 4 thousand professors and 5 thousand researchers. There are actually two campuses – the old one, located near the Kremlin and the new one (opened in 1954).

For me, University associates with the new campus and, in particular, with the gorgeous Stalin high-rise, the main building of the university. Campus territory is huge. The main building is the most interesting because, in addition to hosting several Schools (Math,

Geography, Geology, Medical School), it is a small city in itself. Students, who study at one of those schools and who live in dorms in the same building, do not need to go out of the building. It has libraries, canteens, hairstyling salons and even a museum of minerals. Other Schools – Biology, Chemistry, Physics, Economics, etc. have their own buildings, but the Main Building has always been the biggest magnet and the center of attraction.

This building was built by prisoners – in Stalin times that was usual practice. There is a sad legend, which may be true, that one of the prisoners decided to escape, like Ikar, but plywood wings did not hold him well enough, and he died.

There are also plenty of others, happier legends. We, students, really believed in them! Myths about the Main Building say that the building is too high for Moscow soil; therefore, there is large freezing equipment, located in the basement, which helps to hold the thing in place. There are also many rumors about ghosts in the basement of the building, and guys always used these rumors to scare girls. Massive revolving doors at the entrance are very heavy, you have to push them. People said that they are so heavy for a reason, that they are connected to power generators. Thousands of students, who go through these doors every day, help to produce electricity, which enables elevators. All elevators are equipped with phones, but from one of the phones, you can call any country in the world free of charge. Finally, there are many conspiracy theories about Moscow Subway system, and one of them says that there is a secret subway line going from Kremlin to the University and, if you are attentive, you can see it from one of the stations. I totally believe that the secret subway exists, but I think the line goes from the University to the outskirts of Moscow rather than to Kremlin (it makes much more sense – in case of emergency you may want to evacuate the best minds of the country).

Other buildings of the campus also have thematic legends. There might be a super-intelligent dolphin, living in the basement of Biology School. And Chemistry School certainly has an alcohol pipe, hidden among the water pipes at the labs.

9.8. 25th of January – Student's Day and Tatiana's Name Day

Do all Russians celebrate their name days as you do?

The short answer is no. Name day used to be celebrated by most people in the pre-Soviet time since this day coincided with people's birthdays. Actually, a name was chosen from the church books based on the date of birth. You have been born on the day of several saints, and your parents named you after one of them. After the Revolution, that custom vanished and parents started to name kids as they wished.

When I was born, my parents named me Tatiana – first of all, because they loved this name. Secondly, though – they both worked at the Moscow State University, and this school was the first university in Russia, founded on the 25th of January 1755 by Empress Elizabeth under the guidance of St. Tatiana. The Church of St. Tatiana still exists near the oldest campus of the University, in the heart of Moscow and some students ask St. Tatiana for better grades at that place. My parents were not religious, but the name Tatiana means a lot for any MSU alum or employee.

I am fortunate that my name day is celebrated nationwide as a holiday for alums of MSU and an official student day since nobody ever forgets my name day and I receive many congratulations. From the very start, it was a fun day for students. Festivities started at the University and later spread to streets and pubs. On that day police were officially not punishing drunken students, they were expected to drink on that day.

Tatiana's Day has also always coincided with the end of winter finals, so all students could finally relax and start the winter break. Any current or former student knows how nice it is to get done with finals, but in Russia, that is especially true! Having experienced both Western and Russian system of education in two reputable universities, I see many significant differences between both and would like to use this opportunity to expand on that topic.

The first notable difference is that in the US, college students do not choose their major upon enrollment. Here, you actually select the major when you are 15 and start preparing for entrance exams, and when you are 16-17 and graduate from high school, you get admitted either to Biology School (as in my case) or School of Math or Chemistry or any other school. And after less than a year you choose your concentration – in my case it was Microbiology, and it was quite a random choice. I think that nobody should make such decisions when they are 16-17 years old, so the Western system is better in that sense.

Another big difference – the US education system makes students work a lot during a quarter. You always have some homework or papers to submit. In Russia, we do not have that. During the quarter (or a semester, in our case), you are supposed to attend classes and study a lot on your own. Nobody controls you. Needless to say – you tend to skip studies most of the time. When finals approach – you are in trouble and have to digest the entire course in 2-3 days (that is a typical break between exams). The vast majority of students stay at home or in a dorm and really study only during these couple of weeks. But they study hard indeed! We have a joke about a student, who needs to pass an exam in Chinese, which he never studied. His only question is – when is the exam? The ability of Russian students to consume an immense amount of material within 2-3 days is insane. Most exams are oral, that is also a big difference between the systems. That means – the professor will ask additional questions and might recognize if you are not prepared.

So, how do students cope with the avalanche of knowledge twice a year? A – they study, B – they prepare cheat sheets, C – they ask for luck. Studying is the most tedious part – you sit at your desk for days and nights, you use tons of coffee, Red Bull, cola and special herbs to keep you awake. Sometimes when you go to an exam – you are so deprived of sleep and so high on stimulators that your hands tremble.

But very often it is not possible to put half of a textbook in your memory. And here comes the most significant difference in our educations system. Russian students do cheat, and it is considered to be normal by both professors and students. Students write cheat sheets before exams. That exercise is sometimes sufficient to remember the material, but if not – they use these cheat sheets. Before the era of cell phones cheat sheets usually looked like a thin pleated strip of paper 2-5 meters long. You had 20 of them – one for each exam questions and managed to flip it with one hand under the table while writing with the other hand. Another, less popular variety of cheat sheets was to prepare "bombs" – written answers to questions, which you skillfully replace when going to an exam table. However, although professors were ok with pleated cheat sheets, they hated bombs and often gave the stamped paper at the exam. In that case, your prepared bombs become useless.

However, 3 days of intense studies and cheat sheets do not guarantee success. You also need some luck. To lure luck, you take your report book, open the window and shout three times in the night – "Halyava pridi" while holding the report book open outside the window. "Halyava" is a word that does not have an exact translation into English. The closest translation will be – free ride or easy ride. "Halyava" is supposed to fly into your report book, attracted by your invitation, then you close the report book tightly and put it underneath a bed leg so that it does not get out during the night. Also, there was a widely accepted belief that you should not wash your hair before the exam; otherwise the newfound knowledge may wash out. Finally, you may try keeping a lucky coin in your shoe.

After stories like that, you may think that Russian education was mediocre and students only managed to graduate because of cheating. However, that is not true. I will only speak about Moscow State University – that school really gave analytical skills and the ability to see the Big Picture. Education at Moscow State University was very profound. By the way, Moscow State University was one of only two schools in Moscow, which were called universities (the second one was the University of People's Friendship). All other schools were named Institutes, but at the end of the 90s that limitation was taken off, and since then any institution could name itself as it wished.

9.9. How Tatiana Becomes Tanya – Russian Names Explained

Once, when I changed jobs, my new boss asked me whether I prefer to be called Tatiana or Tanya. He noticed that I use Tanya for this blog and Tatiana at work. I replied that I prefer Tatiana for work since I know that having several versions of the name confuses people in a Western work environment. But I thought that an explanation of how Russian names work would be useful!

Russian Names 101

Full name in Russia consists of a first name, a patronymic and a last name (my full name would be Tatiana Gennadievna Golubeva). A patronymic is a derivative from the father's name. All Russian names also have multiple diminutive versions.

The most tricky part for a foreigner is to learn in which situations it is proper to use just the first name, first name with the patronymic, only the last name or the diminutive version of the name.

I am going to give you a guide on how to address your Russian counterparts, but let's look at the origins of Russian names first as it is quite amusing. I must make a disclaimer first though – I am not a specialist in the subject of the etymology of names so there may be inaccuracies in this part of my text.

Origins of Russian Names

In pre-Christian times people named kids based on the season they were born in, the order of birth in the family or based on distinguishing features or personality traits. Most of these names, such as Tretyak (third child born in a family) or Molchoon (the quiet kid) or Vesna (Spring) do not exist now or exist as last names or their roots.

From the end of the 10th century and the adoption of Christianity, Russia started to use names from the church calendar. These names

EDUCATION/ENTERTAINMENT/CULTURE

have come from a variety of origins, but most Russian names came from Byzantine. For most names it is possible to trace the meaning and origin – such as my name, according to Google, comes from the Roman name Tatianus, a derivative of the Roman name Tatius. This was the name of a 3rd-century saint who was martyred in Rome under the emperor Alexander Severus. But most names have lost their initial meaning now and are just words, except for some, such as Vera (Faith), Nadezhda (Hope) and Lyubov (Love).

Up until the October Revolution of 1917, when a baby was born, the family typically looked into a church calendar for that day and chose the name of the Saint, whose day that was, so the name day usually coincided with the birthday, and people celebrated name days. The language is fluid, so the better sounding names (Olga, Elena, Ilya, Alexander, etc.) were more popular, and the names that were hard to pronounce were modified or eliminated from the language. Some names were used by noble people, some by peasants, so the name often reflected the social status.

To add the other level of complexity, some names were adopted from Western Europe, especially in the 17th-19th centuries. At that time a lot of French names came to Russia together with the French language. Later, at the beginning of Soviet times, many German names, such as Roza (after Roza Luxemburg) and Klara (after Klara Tsetkin) came to Russia.

In addition to that, political changes influenced kids' naming a lot. After the October revolution and for 70 years of the Soviet period, a church was banned. People still named their kids using traditional names, but a few new names were "invented." The example of such name – Vladlen, which is the abbreviation of Vladimir Lenin. Every 4 years there are more and more kids named after Olympics ("Olimpi-ada" would be a girls' name)

Despite all the multicultural roots and varieties of names origins, the pool of most popular names isn't big. 15-30 names top the lists and altogether – there are no more of 300-400 names which people use.

When I went to school, there were always several Tatianas, Natashas, Olgas, Annas, Elenas, Andreys, Alexanders in class.

Change to the free market economy in the 90s led to a new phenomenon – many parents wanted their kids to be "unique" and named them like Hollywood stars name their kids – by inventing new names. "The artist formerly known as Prince" really fades in comparison with such names as "Luka-Happiness-Somerset-Ocean" or "Viagra" (not what you thought – a popular Russian girl band) or "Nikita-Kit" (Nikita-whale). These are all the registered names, boys and girls who own them will have to carry these names at least until they are 16 years old and have a right to change them. Some names such as USDMX720 or similar were refused from registering for the benefit of a poor fellow.

Use of Diminutives in Russian Names

But although origins of names may be confusing, the most confusing part is in the usage of full vs. short (diminutive) forms of the Russian names.

Say – you meet me in the workplace. I say that I am Tatiana. You work with me for 2-3 months, we get along well. And suddenly I say that you can call me Tanya from now on. What??!! Did you just change your name? What happened? And if you did – why do some other people in the office still call you Tatiana?

It is confusing. But here is how it works. It is similar to how you first formally greet a new acquaintance, but later can address him or her with Hey and finish your message with Cheers. Or it is like calling your friend David – Dave.

In the US a person usually sticks to one name – you either like David or Dave and you go with the version you like most. Here – I will always be Tatiana for people I have just met in the formal setting, Tanya for my co-workers and most of my friends and, either Tanyusha or Tanechka for my spouse and other people I know for ages and who are really close to me.

It is incredibly hard for foreigners to understand this concept and guess when you switch and start calling a Russian person with a seemingly different name, which is just a more personal version of his/her name. To make matters even worse – I may call my colleague Alexander – Sasha in personal encounters but will refer to him as Alexander in the business meetings.

Is there a golden rule? Yes and no. The key is to see and accept "name changes." If a person offers you to call him/her a diminutive either in person or via business correspondence – accept it and call him/her with a shorter name (except for meetings with third parties). Once you start calling me Tanya – do not switch back and forth and stick to that name.

What about other 100+ diminutive versions of my name? Unless there is a possibility we may get married in future – avoid them (for native speakers it is easier to understand when to call a friend Katya and when to call her Katyusha (when you want to do something sweet to a friend or when it is a friend's birthday or when you both started using super-diminutives for each other etc.) But if unsure – stick with safe options – Tatiana – Tanya, Ekaterina – Katya, Olga – Olya, Alexander – Sasha, etc.

Some names might puzzle you – Alexander, Eugene and a couple of others are unisex, add the "a" in the end when addressing a female (Alexander – Alexandra, etc.)

Correspondence of Short and Long Versions of Russian Names

Ok, now you know that each Russian name has many diminutives (some names have 20-30 short versions). But what you do not know – some of the diminutives belong to different extended versions of the name. For example – my niece Asya loves her name. It is a diminutive from Anna, but she uses Asya even at work. But guess what – Asya is also a diminutive for Anastacia, and that is more common. I remember the day when I met Asya – she was a tiny newborn. My sister said – she is Asya, and hesitated for some days – what Asya's full name will be.

My sister went for Anna. But it is sometimes difficult to guess what a person's full name is based on the diminutive. Just ask if you need to fill out any legal papers.

Use of Patronymics

If you think the earlier chapters are crazy confusing – wait until the next level of complexity. My real full name consists of my first formal name and a derivative of my father's name – Gennady. So, if you want to be really formal with me or if I am much older than you or I am your doctor or your kids' teacher or have higher status (or we still live in the USSR)) – you have to call me Tatiana Gennadievna. Every time you address me in a conversation!

Things do get simplified now though, especially in the Western companies. The new formal for people under 40 working in such companies is to use the full version of the first name + formal "you" if you talk in Russian.

How Bad Is It if You Make a Mistake in Russian Names?

Well, as in the rest of the world – you better do not call Tatiana Olga and vice versa. But if you are a foreigner and you call Tatiana – Tanya or not use a patronymic or use the wrong version of the name – that is not the end of the world. When my foreign friends meet my mom – I tell them that her name is Irina. When my Russian friends meet my mom – I tell them that her name is Irina Ivanovna (with patronymic). It will be inappropriate for any of my Russian friends to address my mom with her first name only, but we do not expect the same from foreigners. It is similar to me not adding -san to my Japanese friends' names.

And in general – do not stress out too much about names. It is always good to have a sense of that subject, but for us, Russians, it is more important to see that you are open, sincere, like to spend time with us and are interested in things that matter to us.

EDUCATION/ENTERTAINMENT/CULTURE

9.10. Mushroom Picking – Russian Tradition and Passion

For most people, living on our planet, mushrooms are either champignon or shiitake mushrooms, and both are sold in a grocery store. For Russians – mushrooms are creatures that live in the forest, and you have to hunt for them. Mushroom picking is one of our favorite activities in Summer.

Which Mushrooms do Russians collect?

It is probably the first time when I had to google translate dozens of words when writing a post. Белые (porcini), подберезовики (birch bolete), подосиновики (red-capped bolete), маслята (slippery jack), лисички (chanterelle), рыжики (saffron milk cap), опята (honey mushroom), грузди (milk mushrooms), сыроежки (russula) etc. And I am not sure whether I selected correct translations – I never saw most of these mushrooms in grocery stores abroad, and my foreign friends do not gather mushrooms.

But for Russians – mushroom picking is a skill that we master since childhood and one of the favorite activities in the countryside. Any Russian can distinguish at least 15 edible mushrooms in the forest and, what is even more critical – not collect the poisoned ones, such as мухомор (toadstool) or бледная поганка (death angel). As a precaution, though we usually add a whole peeled onion when making mushroom bouillon – if it turns blue, that means that one of the mushrooms was not edible.

Why Do Russians Like Picking Mushrooms So Much?

Forest mushrooms have always been part of the Russian diet for several reasons. There are hundreds of edible mushroom species in our forests, mushrooms are nutritious, tasty and one can preserve them for winter either by drying or by marinating or salting. During lent mushrooms replace meat in traditional dishes, at all other times, they are a tasty addition to any meal. So, at first picking mushrooms was a necessity and a practical thing to do.

Now we do not have to pick mushrooms to survive the winter, but we still like that activity a lot. Mushroom picking is akin to a scavenger hunt. You have to be really alert to see mushrooms in the forest – a lot of times they are covered with leaves or grass or hide from you in shady places. Mushroom picking gives a purpose for a walk in the forest, and you can easily spend several hours walking and enjoying nature. Finally, nothing is better than a hot mushroom soup after spending a day outside.

What is the correct way to pick mushrooms?

- Early morning is the best time to gather mushrooms. You will see them better and will have a better chance to be the first mushroom picker in the forest
- Most mushrooms grow in "families," so if you find one, look around for others
- Experienced mushroom pickers will know which mushrooms to expect in a forest from the kind of trees that grow in that forest
- When you find a mushroom, you need to use a knife to cut it, so that the mycelium is not damaged. If you do not have a knife, you can carefully "screw the mushroom out," but if you went mushroom picking, a knife should be the first thing you take with you
- If you are not sure whether the mushroom is edible – do not pick it up. Also, avoid old or wormy mushrooms
- Avoid areas near roads, railroads and industrial plants. Mushrooms absorb dangerous chemicals so even edible mushrooms can become poisonous if they grow in such places
- Woven baskets are better than plastic bags for carrying mushrooms from the forest. You can put some grass on top to cover mushrooms from direct sunlight to prevent drying
- It is best to clean mushrooms right away when you get home. Mushrooms can survive a day in a fridge, but it is best to cook them when they are fresh

EDUCATION/ENTERTAINMENT/CULTURE

How to Cook Mushrooms?

There are multiple ways to cook mushrooms. Some are better for soups, some for frying, some for preserves. The king of mushrooms – porcini is great for any method of cooking.

Soup made of forest mushrooms is a fantastic dish! We do not cook cream soups if we take the traditional recipes – we peel the mushrooms, make a bouillon, add potatoes or pasta, and the soup is ready. Of course, make sure you add the sour cream before serving the soup – otherwise, the experience will be incomplete!

We also love fried mushrooms. For many mushrooms, the first step before frying is boiling them in water for 5-10 min. Then you can fry chanterelle with potatoes and add sour cream in the end. Or you can serve fried mushrooms with meat or chicken as a garnish or sauce. The primary approach to cooking mushrooms in Russian cuisine – not to add many spices, since mushrooms have their own distinct flavor.

9.11. Russian Pets

One topic that will undoubtedly unite my readers everywhere in the world – pets. We all love animals, whom we bring to our homes. Let's explore, what kind of pets live in Russian homes.

Pets in Russia

According to the various surveys from 55 to 75% of Russians have a pet at home. Cats are the most popular pets, with dogs following them, but people also have fish, birds, turtles and small mammals at home.

More exotic animals sometimes live in average Russian apartments as well. The most famous story was from the 80s when one family Berberovy had lions and puma at home. That went well for quite some time but ended in a tragedy. Keeping poisonous snakes and crocodiles also does not end well, so it is good that such cases are rare.

Pet products and grooming industry is still developing, most people take care of their pets themselves, including walking the dogs and giving them baths as well as grooming cats. However, in big cities it is possible to outsource pet grooming, order special ready-made pet food and leave your pet in a "pet hotel", when you are going on vacation.

Pets on Instagram

I do not know about you, but I follow several cats and dogs accounts on IG (@cat_bas, @starkythecat, @orlu_and_morgan, @boopthissnoot, @rufus_the_corgi). Some of them live in Russia, some abroad, and in general life of pets in all countries is wonderful.

Now a big trend is to adopt cats and dogs, which is wonderful! Social media greatly helps in promoting that by posting cute animals that are up for the adoption. And, from time to time there are fairs in the center of Moscow, at which potential pet owners can meet their future pet and take it home.

Every human needs a pet! And pets need their humans to live a good life!

9.12. Iron Madness or What Russian Tourists Want

I was booking some travel today and read reviews of hotels at my destination. At some point, I decided to filter Russian reviews and was stunned. Guess what is one thing any Russian traveler demands in his/her room? Iron Board It Is!

100% of Russian travelers mentioned the absence of an iron board in the hotel rooms. Hoteliers pay attention! Russians need an iron everywhere they travel! I actually looked through other travelers reviews out of curiosity – nobody mentioned the need to iron! So, that must be a particular Russian thing.

I thought – I am not that dependent on having an iron in a hotel room. But yes, it is nice when it is provided. And then I also remembered that I bought an iron board last week since mine broke down. Delivery of an iron board to the office made people laugh a bit, but everybody understood that it is a necessary purchase and even shared their "ironing stories" and tips for choosing both an iron and an iron board. So, why do we like to iron so much?

Absence of Dryers

That discussion brings us to the other topic – washers/dryers. My American readers, you would not believe what I will say now. Russian people do not know, what a laundromat is. We do not have any. Every urban Russian household has a washing machine at home. And now, guess what? No one has dryers! So, folding clothes is an unheard problem for us. We dry clothes old style, and then we iron them. All of them! Including the bed linen! And clothes for babies are ironed from both sides. Isn't that crazy?

Non-wrinkle Fabrics? Have Not Heard About Them

In general, Russian people prefer natural fabrics – cotton, linen, etc. All those need to be ironed to look good. Men shirts that do not need to be ironed are not popular here (even though it is a great invention).

Giving bed linen and shirts to a dry cleaner is not popular too – it is expensive, and quality is so-so.

10. HOLIDAYS

10.1. How Holidays Disrupt Business in Russia

One of the many things that surprise expats about Russia is the amount of holiday and vacation time. Understanding local time-off habits is crucial if you plan to do business in Russia.

Let's look at the situation month by month.

January

New Year's Eve is the most beloved holiday in the country. New Year's Eve is more significant than Christmas since Christmas was not celebrated for many decades during the Soviet time. By the way, our Christmas is celebrated on Jan 7th, not on Dec 25th (because the Russian Orthodox Church still lives according to the old Julian Calendar, which is 13 days behind the Gregorian Calendar).

It looks logical to have Jan 1st, maybe Jan 2nd and Jan 7th off. However, we typically have at least 8 official days off – Jan 1st-Jan 8th. That is a long holiday week at the beginning of the year. But in fact, most people have even longer holidays. We celebrate a bizarre unofficial holiday – Old New Year on the night from Jan 13th to Jan 14th. Do not plan any business meetings in the first 2 weeks of January – most people will be on vacation during this time. And it takes some time to get out of holiday mode, so the best bet is to plan business meetings sometime after Jan 20th.

February

There is just one official holiday in February – Day of the Defender of Motherland (or Men's Day), celebrated on Feb 23rd. How disruptive can one holiday be for business? Very disruptive.

In Russia, if the holiday falls on Saturday or Sunday – Monday is a day off. If it is on Tuesday – Monday will be the day off and although Saturday is supposed to be a workday in that case – most people will ignore that. So, any holiday turns into a long weekend, around which people tend to take several days off.

March

Similar to February – just one holiday – International Women's Day, celebrated on March 8th, but it turns into a several day vacation. Also, keep in mind that workday on the day before the holiday is 1 hour shorter (and since in most cases people will celebrate the holiday at work on that day, planning meetings for that day is risky).

End of February and beginning of March is also time for Maslenitsa – pancake week, which is loved and celebrated, however, does not bring more days off work.

April

April is a really good month to do business in Russia. No official holidays, since for some reason, there are no days off for Easter. People are energetic and welcome spring. Plan your business meetings for April.

But be careful on April 1st – that is a Fool's Day. Be prepared for pranks even in the business environment.

May

Forget about business at least for the first half of the month. There are 2 official holidays – May 1st (May Day) and May 9th (Victory Day), but in 2019 official holidays are May 1st-5th and May 9th– May 12th. Needless to say – people will take days off in between too.

May is one of the best months regarding weather, and it is also time to plant flowers and veggies at dachas (country houses). Most people will be at the countryside either working in the garden or doing barbeques. If you happen to stay in the city, you will enjoy no traffic jams.

Summer

Officially there is just one holiday – Day of Russia, which takes place on Jun 12th, but you already know how it works with one-day-holidays here, right?

Also, summer is traditionally the time when most people take long annual leaves. Russians have 28 vacation days a year, and some people have even more (if your work demands for long hours or unpredictable work schedule, you officially get 3 to 5 extra days of vacation a year).

In Soviet time people tended to take the entire month off and spend it in a sanatorium at the Black Sea or elsewhere. Now, most people take 2 weeks off in summer and divide the rest of the vacation time to add it to other holidays.

When you plan any meetings in summer – check the business partner's vacation schedule first.

September – October

These 2 months are great for doing business. First of all, most of your business partners will be in the city by September 1st since kids go back to school. Secondly, people treat September as a start of the new business year in some way, because it's the start of a new school year.

No holidays during these 2 months, business is in a productive mode. If you are looking for a job – also the best time to get hired.

November

In Soviet time November 7th was the day to celebrate the October Revolution. The reason the October Revolution was honored in November is again the discrepancy between old and new calendars.

We no longer celebrate the October Revolution, but since people are used to celebrating something in November – there is another new holiday – National Unity Day, celebrated on Nov 4th. Most people neither understand the roots of that holiday nor care. But November is the month when the weather gets really nasty, so it is a perfect time to take a week off and spend it in a warmer and sunnier place. Do not plan any business meetings for the first week of November.

December

Officially there are no holidays in Russia in December. But the last 2 weeks of the month are devoted to preparation for the New Year and companies have corporate events. That time is really unproductive for business.

Also, a lot of people take the last week off and add it to the January holidays. That happens especially often in the foreign companies since their international offices are closed for Christmas, and expats, who work in Russia also travel home. In short – forget about any business in Russia starting from Dec 15th.

I hope that this calendar of holidays will help you to plan your business schedule in Russia.

10.2. 8th of March – International Women's Day

International Women's Day is celebrated in some countries and is entirely unknown in the others. It is a big holiday in Russia, but the symbolic meaning has changed from the equal rights day to a day when all women get praise for being women.

History of the International Women's Day

The origins of that day are believed to go to 8th of March 1857, when female workers of the textile industry went on strike in New York, demanding better work conditions and higher salaries. In the spring of 1908 women of New York City went on another street meeting, demanding women's suffrage (the right of women to vote on the same terms as men).

In 1910 German communist Clara Zetkin offered to establish a special day in honor of fighting for equal rights for women. Since then women in different countries conducted meetings and went on strikes on the first week of spring to fight for their rights – to be treated equally, to vote and to receive equal pay and work benefits. International Women's Day was officially acknowledged by the United Nations in 1975.

Is IWD Celebrated Worldwide Now?

No, it is well known and celebrated in some countries and unheard of in the others. From my personal experience, I know that it is observed in Russia and other Eastern European countries, in Latin America and in Japan. I asked my friends on Facebook whether they celebrate IWD in their countries. I found interesting that the US women do not know about that event, although their ancestors have started the women equal rights movement.

I want to quote my friend, who lives in the Dominican Republic:

"In the Dominican Republic, they do make mention of it. A lot of women here are influential personalities in Communications and other fields like Medicine and Arts. It's more about women empowerment and how far we have come. It's not a holiday, everybody goes to work, and the country continues its regular schedule, but some places and institutions have special activities including art and music showcasing the works of women. And of course, it's a special commercial day to go shopping, spa treatments, beauty treatments, so any venue related to those appealing things for women will offer specials for the day".

I completely agree with such an approach and the wording. "Women empowerment and how far we have come" – that phrase captures the essence of the International Women's Day. It is a day to celebrate the successful fight of women from all over the world for their rights, full equality with men, democracy and peace.

However, in Russia, International Women's Day's meaning had altered entirely over the years. I think that you will be amused to read about that.

8th of March in Russia

International Women's Day in Russia has transformed in a day when every girl or woman is congratulated and praised for being a female. I personally find that extremely weird. I want to be commended for being an expert in marketing, a good skier, a good photographer or a good friend/spouse/daughter, etc. Being born as a girl was not my personal achievement – it was just a 49% probability.

Don't get me wrong – I love to hear compliments and receive flowers and nice gifts. But I would rather get all that when men genuinely feel like it, not on a particular day when they are obliged to do so.

Here in Russia, the 8th of March is an official holiday and a day off from work since 1965. So, the craziness actually begins on 7th of March, when male colleagues, congratulate all females in the office.

Women dress up for the occasion; men are on their best behavior and appear with flowers and chocolates. Director of the company will make a speech, saying how much all male employees value the presence of "the best half of the population" at the workplace and how our beauty decorates the office. Afterward, there will be an office party or a corporate event at one of the city restaurants.

On the 8th of March, any girl or woman is treated like a princess. She will be spared of any household chores; husband and sons will clean the house, cook breakfast and other meals and might even bake the cake. Why is that a big deal? All other 364 days Russian men typically abstain from household chores. So, that day is the day for a woman to relax, watch TV, go to a spa or do anything else she feels like doing.

Do People like 8th of March in Russia?

The majority of women adore that holiday. The majority of men hate it but understands that they have to comply with the rules.

That is the day when men have to congratulate all women they know – wife, mom, sister, grandmothers, aunts, all female colleagues and friends, teachers at the kids' school and any other women they meet during the day. Men are expected to give flowers (yellow mimosas or tulips) to most of them and give a good present to the wife or girlfriend. And they have to say – "Congratulations on the 8th of March" thousand times during that day.

Women are also expected to congratulate other women. Gifts and flowers are obligatory for close female relatives and optional for acquaintances. In the workplace, women do not bring flowers to the colleagues.

I think that partially the popularity of 8th of March could be explained – we don't have the Mother's Day in Russia, and St Valentine's is also not universally celebrated. So that is the day, which is highly romantic and at the same time, enhances family relations.

What If You Are a Boy? Is There a Special Day for You?

Yes, there is! That day is exactly 2 weeks before the 8th of March – on Feb 23rd. Initially, that was a Red Army Day, then it transformed into a Defender of the Fatherland Day. Army connotations were strong, so at first, congratulations were for men, who currently serve in the army or used to be on duty. But as time passed – that day transformed in a universal Men's Day. So, men do get their share of praise and love on that day!

Power to the Women of the World! Celebrate or not – but remember how far we have come!

10.3. Maslenitsa – Time to Eat Russian Blinis!

Do you guys eat blinis all the time or just on some special holidays?

Yes, we eat blinis (Russian pancakes) from time to time all year round. But this particular week is when all the Russians eat pancakes every day. This week is called Maslenitsa or Butter Week (from "maslo" – butter).

Maslenitsa has a dual origin – it is a pagan holiday, a farewell of winter. Most people believe that round pancakes symbolize the sun and the variety of fillings symbolize prosperity and fertility of the land. In the same time, Maslenitsa is tied to the Orthodox Christian calendar – it happens a week before the Great Lent. During this week church allows eating dairy products and fish.

Maslenitsa is a fun week. In addition to eating numerous pancakes, people play a lot. But this week is also highly structured – each day is supposed to be devoted to the specific activities and has its own meaning. Not all people follow these rules in modern times, but all Russians definitely celebrate Maslenitsa and pancakes are the center of attention every day:

Monday is the Welcoming – people build ice-hills, bazaar pavilions and Maslenitsa scarecrows (giant dolls made out of straw and old clothes).

Tuesday is the Playing – people engage in games and activities outdoors, single girls do fortune telling, matchmaking is going on

Wednesday is the Sweet-Tooth day. On that day sons-in-law are invited to enjoy pancakes, made by their mothers-in-law

Thursday is the day when the Wide Maslenitsa starts, and people should stop doing any household chores and just have fun for the rest of the week. That day is usually called Wide Thursday. People enjoy festive parties, visit bazaars, play games outdoors and do sledding. In old times that was also a day for fist-fighting tournaments

Friday is the day when sons-in-law should treat their mothers-in-law to pancakes

Saturday is the day when young wives invite their sisters-in-law to eat pancakes and give them presents

Finally, Sunday is the Forgiveness Day – you are supposed to ask everybody you know for forgiveness for any harm you might have done intentionally or unintentionally during the previous year. It is also a day when the Maslenitsa scarecrow is burnt, and its ashes are scattered at the fields to end the winter and bring the good harvest in the coming season.

I am a mind reader; I know what you are thinking now. How can people eat pancakes every day for an entire week?! Right? The answer is in the great variety of both pancakes and fillings. But of course, next week is when there are extra many people in gyms.

10.4. Back to School – Russia

September 1st is the day when we start the new school year in Russia. This day is significant for both students and for adults whether they are parents or not. We all went to school, and most of us still think of Sept 1st as the start "of a New Year." Let's have a look at school in the USSR time and now and also compare Soviet/Russian school to Western.

September 1st – Day of Knowledge

The distinct feature of September 1st in Russia – lots of kids, carrying large bouquets of flowers to school. Custom is to give flowers to teachers. Since the typical school class is 25-30 people – at the end of the day you can see teachers, carrying huge bunches of flowers home. For some reason, the most popular flowers for that day are red gladioluses (sword lilies).

The first school day in the secondary school starts with the gathering of all classes and teachers and parents in the schoolyard for an official welcoming ceremony. Then, the first graders (youngest kids) enter the school building, followed by older grades one by one. The first day at school is emotional, exciting and stressful for the newcomers. It is called – the Day of Knowledge, a holiday, but it is far from a holiday.

School in Soviet Time and Now

In Soviet time kids started school at 7 years old, and school lasted for 10 years, now they start at 6, so they go to school for 11 years. Attending school for 8 years was mandatory in Soviet time. If kids decided to end their school education after 8 years, they had to go to a professional technical college to get a blue-collar profession. If they chose to stay – they could apply to an institute or university after they complete 10 years of education (and study 5 more years to get an undergrad diploma).

Class sessions always last 45 minutes. First graders typically have 3-4 classes a day, for the graduating class, it could be up to 8 classes a day. Some subjects are taught throughout the entire duration of school (Russian, Math, etc.), some start from 4th or 5th or 6th grade (such as Chemistry or Physics or Biology) and are substantial new milestones.

Grading is done on a 1 to 5 scale, where 5 is the best mark ("A"), but 1 technically does not exist (teacher may give 1 once in a while, but more to express her or his emotions. So, the equivalent of Fail is 2). Behavior and willingness to study are also graded. Final grades are given each quarter, based on the average for that quarter. At the end of each year are exams. Up until recently, the graduating class had to sit through many exams first to get the certificate of matriculation and then go through a series of exams to apply to university. Now there are unified tests similar to SAT, which are called EGE. It is not an exact version of SAT though since there are still several exams – in Russian, Math, etc. but those are multiple-choice exams. Many people are against EGE partly because it is far from perfect yet, partly because they are not used to such a system. But at least kids do not have to take more exams when applying to undergrad.

Since parents work until late in the evening, there are after-school facilities to take care of the kids. Kids either do homework or learn extracurriculars. In the Soviet time that was free (sponsored by the state), now in most schools, parents have to pay for that service. It was quite usual though in Soviet time that kids (even 7-year-olds) just went home on their own after school, opened the door with their key, re-heated lunch and did homework or played with friends outdoors until parents come back from work. Russia still does not have laws, forbidding minors to be unattended, but now it is less safe on streets, so most parents either keep their kids in school or ask nannies or grandmothers to collect them from school.

School in Soviet time was saturated with Communist education – via the communities of October kids, pioneers and members of Komsomol. Some of the things from that time were not necessarily bad, such as summer camps and games. But overall school's mission was viewed not only to teach, but also to shape values. During Perestroika (the 90s), there was no time for values, so school just taught the subject.

Back to School – Comparing Russian and Western Education

It is difficult for me to compare Russian and Western secondary education. I have some brief experience of studying in a Swiss college, but it was not long enough to make proper comparisons. Probably the only thing that I would like to mention is that Soviet schools always had a mandatory school uniform. Of course, we hated it! For small kids uniform consisted of a brown wool dress and either white or black apron (white for special events, black for regular days) for girls and grey-blue pants and jacket for guys. Clothes made of wool were uncomfortable, and we had to change collar and cuffs pieces by stitching them to the dress. In the high school, both boys and girls had blue uniform suits – with pants for boys, with skirts for girls.

But I can compare Russian and American education at the University. The main differences are in the style of teaching (Russian style is drier, American is more entertaining) and in the distribution of the workload. In Russia, you are supposed to be responsible during the semester and be prepared well for exams, which sometimes could count as 100% of your grade. In the US, exam scores are only part of your grade, and you are forced to study hard during the quarter, which is facilitated via multiple homework assignments and class participation. In my opinion, the American system is more efficient.

Back to School – Experimental Schools

In the Soviet time, all kids in the country went through the same education in school. Curriculums, textbooks, teaching approach were identical in Moscow and Vladivostok. Hundreds of thousands of classrooms had the same topics written on the blackboard with chalk on any given day. Curriculum might have been different only in schools, which specialized in some subjects – foreign languages or math or science or sport.

In modern Russia, people are free to send their children to private schools, which use experimental methods of teaching. Some of those schools are fantastic, but some emphasize creativity more than learning the basics.

I recently met with a long-time friend. We went to University together, but unfortunately do not see each other as often as we both want to. He has 3 kids, so he and his wife are swamped. Last time I visited them; their oldest son was about to start school. They were ecstatic that he was accepted into a very famous experimental school in the center of Moscow.

That school was so picky that it did not accept kids from households, which had TV sets! And of course, kids had to go through an admission interview. I asked how they enjoy that school. And do they plan to send their daughter to the same school this year? The story I heard made me think that standardized education might be not such a bad idea.

Experimental School via Insider's Eyes

At first, things seemed to go well. Kids were doing a lot of handcrafting, semi-theatrical performances, playing and seemed happy. It was a lot of work for the parents since homework was usually both creative and demanding. Sometimes parents even had to take their part in school theatrical performances and multiple other activities. My friend, a really tall and bearded guy got to play a role of a little hare. But there is nothing you would not do for your kid, right?

Teachers at that school are evangelists of the experimental methods. They do not believe in textbooks, they use their own teaching materials and approaches.

But the first real red flag appeared when my friend's son was sick, so the father came to school to collect the homework assignments. Being a professional mathematician himself, he was excited when the teacher offered to give him math homework for his son. Finally, he could help his kid learn a subject that he knows so well! However, he soon found out that his profound knowledge of math is severely outdated. Instead of expected sheets of paper full of numbers, the teacher gave him something that vaguely reminded clocks made of paper, drawn with color pencils (only natural pigments used in school). He got puzzled and asked: "So this is the math homework?". The teacher replied: "Yes, your son will understand what to do with these items." And surprisingly he really did!

Long story short. When my friend started to evaluate his son's level of math (and also other subjects, which were supposed to be taught in the first grade) – he understood that the situation is pathetic. The boy did not know how to write, solve basic equations, etc.

My friends were lucky to find a place for their son in an "ordinary" school for the next year. But he was accepted only under a promise that they will teach him the entire curriculum of the first grade during summer.

11. DOING BUSINESS IN RUSSIA

11.1. What Are the Do's and Don'ts in Russian Business Meetings

Knowing business etiquette is vital for successful cross-cultural communication anywhere in the world. The business environment in Russia is becoming less and less unique and more similar to the business environment in the large companies elsewhere. But it is still useful to understand the local differences. Learn the dos and don'ts of meeting Russian business people.

Being late

In general – being more than 15 min late is not good, but not a crime at all. If you are in a big city and are late because of any reason (you overslept) – traffic jam is your friend. Apologize for being late and blame it on the heavy traffic in the city. You will always be understood and forgiven. Or, say you got lost in a Moscow subway (foreigners who are brave enough to take the Metro on their own melt our hearts). But make sure you mention how gorgeous our subway is. We, Russians have strong patriotic feelings about Metro, ballet, caviar, Gagarin, chocolates, and several other things.

Handshakes

You will undoubtedly notice that men greet each other with handshakes, but often do not greet women in the same way. My Western colleagues see terrible discrimination in that, and Russian people, who work in Western companies would agree with them. But far from Moscow or in a very "Russian-style" company, women themselves might be not used to handshakes.

Business cards

As for the business cards exchange – no rituals here. Most likely people at the meeting will just pass you their business cards, and you should do the same. Nobody will pay attention to how you handle business cards (with one hand or both hands). Business cards are just a convenient way to exchange contact info. Some people will not even have cards with them because of various reasons (new to the company/no longer use business cards, etc.)

Smalltalk and hospitality during the meeting

You will be offered tea or coffee at the office meeting. Choose what you want and accept with brief thanks. If you do not drink instant coffee and are outside of the capital – choosing tea is your best bet – it will be a well-brewed tea since tea culture is prominent here.

When served tea or coffee, it is a good time to mention how much you value Russian hospitality. You can tell a story of how your host of the trip cooked a festive meal for you or showed you the city the night before. We love it when foreigners appreciate our hospitality and love to hear good stories. If you have learned even 1-2 words in Russian and will use these, we will be delighted! You can also tell that you are in our city for the first time and it is gorgeous. Or, that you are in our town for the tenth time, but it continues to amaze you. Or, if you are visiting a small town and nothing really surprised you – say how good it is to get out of a big city, how calm and pleasant it is here. If that city reminds you of your home city – make sure you talk about that. Or say that you have never been in such cold weather. Russians like when foreigners are curious and explore.

But at the same time – make sure that the small talk lasts no longer than 5-10 min. We do not like useless chitchat. Move to the core of your subject fast. Say – I thank you for welcoming me here, our meeting is very important, let's talk business. Russians are very direct, so you can speak freely about your goals and expectations.

Smiling in the Business Environment

You better stay serious, when talking business. Russians tend to approach business meetings seriously, too many smiles may ruin their perception of you and make them wonder whether you have serious intentions.

At the same time – even if people do not smile at you at the first meeting – never forget you are meeting with human beings. If you are able to connect to them on the emotional level – next time they see you – they will smile because they know you and like you and that will be a sign of appreciation, not the smile "out of custom." So, try to make an emotional connection with your audience. To do that well – observe what you see around.

Useful clues

It is quite likely that the meeting will be in a managing director's office (you are a foreigner, so you are treated with profound respect, and the CEO might personally welcome you).

If you have a tête-à-tête meeting with the CEO in his/her office – that is the best chance to build a connection. If your host has a photo with the President (or Montserrat Caballe or Pamela Anderson), proudly displayed in the office – make sure you show your appreciation. Do not hesitate to ask about the story behind the photo. There will be a story, make sure you listen well!

If you see some fancy diplomas – that might also be a good conversation starter, although displaying diplomas in Russia is not as popular as in the US. If the diploma is in English and you recognize its value

– positively speak about that. If the diploma is in Russian – just ask about it.

Some people give out clues on their life by displaying hunting trophies (worst scenario) or their miscellaneous collections (of ceramic frogs for example). If you also happen to collect ceramic frogs or have in-depth knowledge on the subject or your cousin collects ceramic frogs – talk about that to create connection.

Finally – photos of the family. In most cases, you will not see them in the offices of Russian people since people do not like to mix business and personal life. If you see western kind photos of wife and kids, proudly displayed – that instantly gives out a clue that the director has studied abroad. Again – if you also have kids – talk about them, doing that connects people everywhere in the world.

After hours

After the business is done, you will see that your hosts are more prone to chat than before. That is a great time to talk about almost any subject. It is entirely possible that your host will invite you for lunch or dinner after the meeting. Agree! You will have a great time and will be able to get to know these people. Relax about not being allowed to pay for your meal and drinks. Hosts will always pay, it is part of our hospitality, so do not insist. Try to avoid business talks at the dinner table (talking about business at lunch is acceptable).

You do not have to drink vodka or drink any alcohol if you do not wish to do so. Just say that you cannot drink due to some health issues and there will be no questions asked.

Be a good listener, most stories will be long, bear with that. If your host tells a joke – laugh or smile even if it does not sound funny (we have a good sense of humor, but very often our humor is "insiders jokes," based on Russian books or cartoons or movies, so not all foreigners understand it). Tell your own long stories, your host will listen to you attentively. And, what is most important – relax and have fun! Russian people may look unapproachable from a first glance, but if you make a connection with them, especially if you share a meal – you might be surprised how warm we are.

11.2. Are Russians Good Public Speakers?

The short answer is NO. Most Russians are terrible public speakers. Now, let's try to understand – why.

No Public Speaking Training at School

In the US, kids start doing presentations in school from a very early age. There are multiple opportunities to speak in front of an audience – both in classes and at science fairs and other events.

In Russia kids also have to speak – mostly when answering homework assignment at the blackboard in class. But in Russia, it is the substance (how well you know the material) that gets good grades. In the US – it is both the substance AND how well you present it.

In the absence of training and rewards for good public speaking skills, only those, who have real talent, do shine. And usually, get penalized by a teacher since that was labeled as clownishness.

Not Many Good Examples

After studying for 5 years in the Moscow State University, which is #1 school in the country – I can say that I have seen maximum several professors, whose lectures were entertaining. I studied Biology, Chemistry, Math, and Physics. One might argue that science is a serious subject and should not be fun. But watch the Discovery Channel or BBC or National Geographic!

Also, in the business school at the University of Chicago, I did study some dry subjects, such as statistics, corporate finance or accounting, but professors there managed to make every lecture entertaining.

Now you may see a good or even great speaker on Russian TV occasionally, but during Soviet time TV programming was also rigid, official and lacked the entertaining part. An absence of good examples of public speaking does not make you want to improve your own performance.

Why Being Entertaining Is Important in School and Beyond

When the material is delivered in a fun and exciting way – the audience is more engaged, less sleepy and remembers more from the lectures. Also, if something you hear is impressive, there are more chances you will actually read the textbook and assigned readings to learn more about the subject.

Emerging market reality has shown that people, who speak well – sell well, are listened to and have influence. But for people, who never trained to speak – change is difficult. Public speaking courses are popular in Russia now, but it will take a while until we see the real difference.

But How Come Russians Are Good Storytellers?

Anyone who read novels, written by famous Russian writers such as Tolstoy or Chekhov would definitely remember the vividness of details and the greatness of story. Also, foreigners who have Russian friends know how much Russians love to tell stories.

Next chapter is about storytelling. We will explore why Russians like to tell stories, what is the cultural meaning of the stories. We will also talk about why Russian stories often remind War and Peace in their length and the number of primary and secondary characters.

11.3. Storytelling in Russia from Tolstoy to Modern Days

Russians love to tell stories. Narrative styles do show intercultural differences in the most vivid way. So, how do Russian stories differ from stories from other countries? Let's explore!

Fairy-Tales and Fables

These are the stories that shape our thinking and way we see the world. Main learnings are that Russians are superficial and believe in fate and luck, are more motivated by challenging projects rather than every-day hard work and that country's turbulent history made a significant influence on the folklore.

Personal Life Stories

As I learned from the class of "Understanding Russians: Contexts of Intercultural Communications", personal life stories are not only shaped by stories people listened to as kids but also are greatly influenced by the historical period everyone lived in throughout his/her life and country specifics.

Most Russian people, who witnessed World War II will name it as the main event of their life. People, who were born after the war will name Perestroika and the challenges of the 90s as the main events that shaped their life. In addition to that, all people living in Russia are influenced by the geographic location (cold and big country), the multi-ethnicity of the country and other factors.

Stories of Daily Events – Russian and the US Way

However, the topic I am most interested in – how does storytelling differ among cultures when it comes to stories, which describe everyday events. I have not found any significant research papers on that subject, so here is my utterly unscientific view of the insider in Russian culture and the frequent visitor to the West.

I will use the US for comparison for two reasons – I have been immersed in this environment for almost 3 years, and I think that Russian and US ways of telling stories are on the polar side of the scale in so many aspects, such as length of stories, logic used, level of details, magnitude of emotions, presence of sidelines, etc.

In general – stories told by Russians are perceived to be often long and intertwined from a Western standpoint, but at the same time entertaining in their unique way. Think of "War and Peace" – a famous Russian novel with thousands of characters and details (which only one of my American friends has read as far as I am aware. And very few Russians read every single page as girls usually read the Peace & Love chapters, and boys read War & Battles chapters)

Dissecting Storytelling on Different Dimensions

I once read an article by an American teacher, who had explained the differences between Russian and Western storytelling style very well. She said that the American way of telling the story is in connecting A and B in the most logical and direct way. Russian way of storytelling is very different. A may lead to B, but the way is not necessarily straightforward. There could be side stories and side-characters on the way. And the entire story may lead to C or D in the end.

Also – the "elevator pitch," a brief 30 seconds speech about yourself is something Russians do not know how to do. Telling about yourself is a long story! Telling any story is usually a long story!

Different cultures structure narratives according to their views of the world. We have a sequence of occurred events, and we have to match them with a series of clauses and sentences. It is not the events themselves, it is how we perceive them, based on our culture and experience, that makes the story. Such matching can be done in various ways, and stories always show personal values.

Russian Stories Are Emotional

We do not just give a sequence of events, we also tell how we felt about these events and what we thought of these events. Showing emotions is culturally ok in Russia, people would be surprised if you hide feelings.

Russian Stories Are Almost Never Concise

Yes, we have a saying "Conciseness is a sister of talent," but most of our stories are long, and we expect some listening skills from you. What we tell is important, we put our soul in it and want you to appreciate that.

Russian stories have many sidelines, because if we think of something related, be it another story or a joke – we are going to enhance your experience with it. Storyteller usually improvises a lot, in the course of a narrative.

Russian Stories Are High Context

Many Russian stories are high context. To be fair – many American stories are high-context as well. One needs to have a similar cultural background (as we say – "watch the same cartoons as kids") to get some of the references. I had seen that when I moved to Chicago and for the first year often had no clue which sitcoms my friends refer to.

Maybe Russians Do Not Smile, but We Do Have a Sense of Humor

And this humor does enhance the day-to-day stories. Russian humor is worth a separate post. Some aspects of it were touched upon in the chapter about Russian smiles (or their absence), but it is a very rich topic. We often use "black humor" in situations when other cultures do not joke at all. To the considerable extent, this is our way to cope with stress, and we are really good at that.

Example of the Same Day-To-Day Event Story Told Russian and American Way

Let's say we got in the following situation – we ran out of gas on a highway. Far from the next gas station. How would American and Russian describe that event:

American way: Here is what happened to me today. I ran out of gas on the Highway M40, 10 miles from the gas station. I managed to call a friend, who helped me but was 2 hours late for work. Next time I will make sure I have enough gas in my car.

Russian way: You would not believe, what happened to me today. I am driving along this highway, weather is nice, I am thinking about a similarly great day ages ago when I met my future wife (emotional sideline story about meeting the girl). Suddenly, my car stops. At first, I thought it broke down (emotional sideline story 2 about car mechanics in general and his service guy in particular). But then I noticed that I just have no gas (emotional sideline story 3 about gas level indication system in this specific car and in general). A candid assessment of the situation (PG 18+). Fantastic story of solving the problem in an innovative way (stopped 3 cars – one had a gas tank from which you can suck gas (most modern cars prevent that procedure), one had a pipe, the third one happened to be driven by a long-lost classmate from elementary school (side story 4), In the end – the problem was successfully solved and being a bit late to work under such constraints was not an issue at all, instead it was a miracle I got to work today. I have managed to overcome that great obstacle! If the audience is also Russian – they will also share their stories – describing similar or not so similar, but relevant events, which happened to them.

How to Learn from Differences

To me personally, spending 3 years in the US made me at least try to tell shorter stories. Sometimes I even succeed at that, sometimes I do exploit the fact that my friends are incredibly polite and kind people and do not interrupt long speeches. But at least now I am aware of that issue, and for work, I have mastered the elevator pitch.

If you want to do business in Russia and build working relationships here – develop your listening skills – that is the most critical skill to have here. Meditate, work on your patience. And enjoy the stories – many of them are too long to your taste, but fun. And let me know if you read War and Peace from the first to the last page!

11.4. Time Is Fluid in Russia

A friend called me last week and asked, why is it impossible to set up a meeting with Russians far in advance and be sure that the meeting takes place as agreed. He also questioned why there is always a need to re-confirm a meeting an evening before. I thought that it has something to do with how Russians perceive time and it is a great topic to investigate.

I have found a lot of answers in a fantastic book "What Mean? Where Russians Go Wrong in English" by Lynn Visson, read other articles on the topic and added my personal observations. Here is how Russians perceive time and how our perceptions are reflected in the language:

Time Is Fluid in Russia

Nobody presented fluidity of time better than Dali in his paintings and sculptures. As Lynn Visson writes, the concept of time in Russia is much more elastic and fluid than in the U.S. There are several reasons for that.

The famous American anthropologist Edward Hall described cultures as monochronic or fixed time and polychronic or fluid time. US, UK, and most European cultures are monochronic – in these cultures, time is perceived as a frame for behavior, deadlines are respected, and punctuality is an important trait.

Russian culture (as well as Latin American and some Mediterranean cultures) is polychronic, which means that people like to have flexible plans and value long-term relationships. Change of plans often comes with a request from a relative or a friend to do something for him or her. Requests from friends or relatives are more important than business agreements.

However, Russians do not like to plan far in advance even meetings with friends. The only exception is New Year vacation plans with friends and only because people know that waiting until last-minute may lead to no tickets or high prices. If you call a friend and offer to meet tomorrow or the day after tomorrow – high chances that they will find time to meet with you. But try calling a friend and offering to meet 2 weeks from now – he or she will say "Sure!", but may postpone the meeting last-minute, although they will usually tell you why. That last part is interesting in itself. It is considered not polite to say: "I would not be able to meet with you tomorrow because I already have other plans." A Russian person will give a detailed explanation, why he or she cannot meet – she has to take a child to the doctor, or her boss told her to stay late in the office to finish a project, or he must collect a relative from the airport. There is a cultural need to justify why your plans have changed. However, in general, planning a meeting with a friend or even a business meeting 2-3 weeks in advance is very uncommon. How can I know what I will be doing on that day 3 weeks from now?

The reason why we do not plan far in future is related to our fatalistic view of the world. We have a saying "A person plans, but God has other plans for him." We believe that our future depends on many external factors, which are beyond our control. People do not like to make long-term plans, because "a bad eye" could interfere and cancel those plans. Another popular Russian saying is "Devil sits on your right shoulder and does not sleep." That means – do not reveal your plans and ambitions, be modest, wait until the time comes and then your plans may come true. Russians are superstitious!

Finally – we just do not have a habit of using planners – either in a digital or in a paper form. People, who work in multinational companies do have outlook calendars for business meetings, but even they usually do not add hair dressers appointments or lunches with friends to the schedule. Most Russians just have the timeline of the current week in their heads and "save the date" concept is unknown. And the human brain is not a computer, so confirming a meeting a night before is useful.

We often say: "we will call each other." Usually, that is to re-confirm the meeting. "We will call each other" is a concept that westerners do not understand. For them, it is not clear, who is supposed to call whom and when. However, in Russia, it is very uncommon to set up a specific time for a call (unless a person works in a multinational company and sets up a conference call with a colleague from abroad). Usually, a person will just say – "Sure, call me tomorrow." You are supposed to call and ask if that is the right time to speak. Most often a person will talk to you even if she has guests in the house or the conversation is not convenient for him for some other reason. A lot of Russians will not answer the phone if they really cannot talk (are at a meeting) rather than answer the phone and tell you they are busy. There is also no direct Russian equivalent for the phrase "I'll get back to you."

What are the benefits of being polychronic? Polychronic cultures are more natural with multitasking. For example, you can ask a busy salesperson in a store a question while she is working with another customer. In Russia – a salesperson will always reply and will not be annoyed. In most European countries doing that would be a nuisance for a salesperson.

Punctuality in Russia

For monochronic cultures, time is sacred, being late is considered rude and deadlines are fixed. In polychronic cultures, the man is more important than time and deadlines are flexible. Being late is perceived as abusive in American culture and is not a "sin" in Russian culture. Edward Hall wrote that "if people are late for meetings it may be because they are polychronic, not because they are disrespectful or lazy."

In modern Russia, though, business people try not to be late to the meetings. And if they are running late, the most typical apology is that they are stuck in traffic (which may be true, given the traffic situation in big cities).

It is very uncommon to meet at 6:45 unless it is a meeting at a theater and the play starts at 7 pm. In all other cases, it would be a round number or a half-past. To some extent that is understandable – Moscow is a huge city and traffic is terrible, so it may be not possible to calculate the exact time of your commute.

Some more observations. We do not have am and pm in the Russian language. The day is not divided by noon. Usually, the day is split into either two chunks – before and after lunch (and typically lunch is from 1 pm to 2 pm). Or the day is divided into 4 intervals: morning (any time before noon), daytime – all the time when it is a natural light outside, evening – 6 pm – 11pm, and night – after 11pm-midnight. Since we do not use am and pm, we use military time a lot. So, when texting a friend, we write either "let's meet at 18:00" or "let's meet at 6 in the evening". Any Russian is comfortable with the military time.

When it comes to dates – it is culturally acceptable for a woman to be late. Russian men acknowledge the hard work woman puts in getting ready to go out. If it is a date, a woman is even expected to be late, "that will give the admirer some time to think about her." To say more – a Russian girl would feel very uncomfortable if she is the first one to arrive to a date.

If you are having a dinner party in Moscow – be prepared that most of your guests might be half an hour or even an hour late. In the US if you are invited to dinner at 7 pm, you are expected to be there at 7:15-7:30 the latest. In Russia you are not expected to arrive earlier than 7:30 and 8 pm is a norm, any time after 8pm will be considered late unless you have a good excuse. It is actually regarded as impolite to arrive 10 min earlier than the time or even at the exact time. The hosts may be not ready yet. And very often, when you come to a Russian house, the hosts will still be cooking dinner for an hour or more from the time they specified in their invitation. For them, time is also fluid. They planned to have everything ready by 7 pm but did not calculate time correctly and still have some cooking to do.

I had noticed how different cultures treat time when I studied abroad and had classmates from all over the world. We lived in the same building in Chicago and had a nice lounge on the roof for our parties. If a party was conducted by our American, European or Japanese friends – everything was ready by the time in an invitation, if it were a Russian party – hosts would probably be there on time, but preparations would still be in process. If it was an Argentinian party – you could show up an hour later, and the hosts may still not be there (although when they arrive, they would totally make up for that with the great food and fun atmosphere)

Sense of Urgency

A sense of urgency is another variable, related to time. Lynn Visson writes about a different meaning of a "minute" in the US and in Russia. In Russia in a minute means "soon," in 10-15 minutes, in the US it usually literally means "in a minute." Maria Lebedko writes in her article "Time Perception across Russian and American Cultures" that Russians often answer the question "When am I supposed to do this?" with the word "Yesterday," meaning that the task in question is very urgent.

But in general, nothing is super urgent in our world. And deadlines are treated as "soft deadlines." Most people try to meet deadlines, but if the external forces prevent that, shifting deadlines is considered ok.

I wonder if that starts when people are doing their undergrad. Russian students always spend nights before exams studying. Of course, students all over the world do procrastinate, but in Russia, the entire education system is built so that it encourages procrastination. You do not have many (hardly any) deliverables during the semester, you are supposed to be a responsible adult, absorb the knowledge and do your homework and study on your own. And then – boom!!! Final grade 100% depends on the result of your exam. So, the exam session twice a year turns into long sleepless nights. Similar attitude later applies to the work projects.

Cost of Time in Russia

My American friends would be shocked to know that Russians have no idea how much they make in one hour. We just never think about that. Unless we are paid per hour, which is uncommon, we never divide our salary by the number of work hours. We also do not have a minimum per hour wage in Russia. We have a minimum per month salary. Maybe because of that we rarely think in terms "time is money."

When we consider hiring a cleaning lady, we usually make a decision based on how much we hate cleaning and other household chores and how that weights against an inconvenience of having a stranger in the house, rather than the difference between a cleaning lady's salary and our salary (and that if she does the cleaning, we would be able to work during these hours and make more money).

Status and Time

We have a favorite saying "boss is never late, his/her arrival is delayed" (not an exact translation, but close). In Russia, subordinates are always expected to be on time, but the boss is on his/her own schedule. And bosses often use and abuse that and show up late to work or not show up to work at all. That reflects their status.

I wonder if expensive watches are status symbols because of the same logic. Most Russian businessmen and government officials have exorbitantly expensive watches. If you followed the news recently, you might have read about the $600K watch of Putin's press secretary. You are a boss, you can afford a really expensive watch AND be the master of your time.

Practical Advice

If you are working with Russians – try to break a project in several deliverables with defined deadlines to make sure that the project is done on time. If you have plans with your Russian friends – the most natural thing to do is to plan meetings for the current week. And if you plan far in advance, call us the day before to re-confirm the meeting. Knowing about the cultural differences in the perception of time may not lift the frustration, but at least would explain your counterpart's behavior.

11.5. Role of Branding in Russia over the Last Century

Being a professional marketer, I am fascinated to explore the role of consumer brands in Russia over the last century. That was a real roller coaster ride!

Branding in Tsar Time

Before the October Revolution, during Tsar time, branding in Russia was developing similarly to branding in other developed countries. Department store Mur and Meriliz, in the center of Moscow, just steps from the Red Square, was tempting customers with a wide range of imported goods.

The famous jewelry House of Fabergé was founded in 1842 in St. Petersburg by Gustav Fabergé. Fabergé eggs became world-famous and Russian tsars have developed a tradition to give them to empresses as gifts.

Chocolate factory Einem, opened in 1851 by Ferdinand Theodor von Einem was developing really well and got prizes at the trade events including a Gran-Prix at the 1900 World Fair in Paris. It was also a socially responsible business, which gave part of the profits to charity. By the beginning of the 20th century, Einem had several factories and stores and its confectionary was well-known and loved by consumers.

Revolution of 1917 Changed Everything

Bolsheviks, who came in power as a result of the October Revolution of 1917 loathed bourgeois habits and values. Blue-collar workers and peasants were not used to high society lifestyle and did not have an eye for exquisite things, nor the money to pay for them. The motto of the Revolution was – "Everything around me belongs to people, everything around me belongs to me."

Mur and Meriliz store got nationalized by the Bolsheviks in 1918. The co-owner and director of the store for 50 years, Philip Walter was laid off. Having lost all his money and purpose in life, he died in 1919.

The House of Fabergé was also nationalized in 1918. In early October, Carl Fabergé left Petrograd on the last diplomatic train for Riga and then to German but died soon after. The rest of the family also had pretty grim fortune – some got imprisoned by Bolsheviks, some fled to Finland. Even though Alexander and Eugéne Faberge opened Fabergé et Cie in Paris in 1924, they had a modest success. The good times were over.

Einem was also nationalized after the Revolution and was re-named as Red October in 1922.

First years after the Revolution were turbulent and challenging. The young Soviet Republic lacked management skills, the country was in ruins and for a short while in the 1920s business was sort of allowed again. This was called New Economic Policy, and it was needed to both calm down the people and develop the country. That initiative was productive but it was short-lived. By the end of the 1920s country moved to the planned economy and building socialism.

Branding in Soviet Time

For most of the Soviet time brands were not as important as before. Instead of bakeries, butcheries, etc., named after their owners, we had stores named after the food group, which was sold there: Food, Bread, Milk, Cheese, Vegetables & Fruit, Drugstore, etc. Typical names for the big specialized stores were "House of X": House of Fabrics, House of Porcelain, House of Shoes.

Stores, named "Food" usually had several counters for bread, milk, cheese, sausage, meat and sweets and none of the products were available to self-take. Instead, one had to first stand in line to tell the salesperson, what you want, then stand in another line to pay and then return to collect the purchase in exchange for the receipt.

Distribution was centralized, so most stores had the same assortment. There were, however, some branded stores or service outlets. For example, the chain of food stores, called "Diet," which did not sell any diet food, just normal food. (in Russian Diet has two meanings – one is the weight-loss diet, the other is just a daily ration) Or there was a super popular and prestigious hairstylist outlet in the center of Moscow, called "Charodeika" (Enchantress) although all other stores were called "Hairstyling salons." Or – some department stores in Moscow were named after towns in other socialist countries, such as Leipzig, etc.

Moving to the product level, it gets even more complicated. Most products were unbranded but were divided by category. Let's take bread. A typical assortment in a bread store would include "Nareznoy baton" (white bread, which had "cuts" on top, which gave it the name), "Borodinsky bread" (dark rye bread with cumin, probably named after a place where the recipe was developed initially), "High-calorie pastry" (high-calorie pastry – a name that would've been a complete flop now) and others. All these were not the brand names, but the categories. The same was seen in the sausage group, so dear to Soviet consumers.

Some of the products did have "brand names" though. For example, in the sweets group, there was a toffee named "Golden Key," chocolate candies "Belochka" (squirrel), "Mishka" (bear) and many others and cakes named like "Kiev cake," "Praga," Leningradsky." All these names could also be treated as categories though. "Golden Key" toffee could be made by the famous Red October factory (former Einem), and then it was premium quality or by a no-name regional factory. So, consumers typically asked about the manufacturer, and it was manufacturers' brand that they trusted. The same situation was in all other areas, such as makeup, perfumes, and grooming products. There were "Red Moscow" perfume, "Leningradskaya" mascara, etc.

Sugar, salt, flour, rice, and other staples were sold as commodities, totally unbranded.

However, there were clear standards and recipes for the products, which were developed by and approved by State. Praga cake, a simplified version of a Schwarzwald cake, was always a cake made of chocolate biscuit dough, chocolate buttercream and chocolate glazing on top. It could differ a bit depending on the manufacturer, but it was still recognizable since the recipe stayed the same for years and was approved by relevant authorities.

The most interesting subject in branding in Soviet time was though not the branding of consumer products, but the branding of the country in general, the branding of Lenin and of Soviet values and achievements. It is fascinating that the country, which was so unbelievably good with propaganda and building non-tangible brands completely failed on the level of consumer branding. But on the other hand – who needs brands in the times of deficit, when any product will be bought by a consumer?!

Branding in Modern Russia

In modern Russia branding works very similar to branding elsewhere. Global brands are adapting to be relevant to local consumers, local brands are trying to learn from the international giants. One interesting topic is how the country made a transition to brands and which curiosities existed in that way. But that will be the topic of another story.

12. USSR

12.1. How Lenin Brainwashed Children

What did you think of Lenin when you were a child?

The Soviet Union had created many icons, some of which could be even called brands. However, the most powerful brand before Perestroika was Lenin – famous Russian revolutionary, who led the country in the 1917 Revolution and years after that.

A lot of Russian people, who are in their 20s now do not have a clue about who he was, but for anybody older than 30 his portrait is the most recognizable picture.

The Soviet regime of the 70s and 80s created a cult out of this figure. Each city in the country had a street, named after Lenin, the main square was usually named after Lenin, hundreds of Lenin monuments were mounted both outdoors and indoors, most official organizations and all classrooms had Lenin's portraits.

For a child, Lenin would look at you from the inner cover of your first textbook and from many more books and propaganda materials. However, icons tend to get stale. A person, who is no longer alive, eventually becomes history. Official speeches are not a matter of attention for kids. Lenin's brand needed significant rebranding, the brand needed to connect with the young audience on the emotional level, the brand needed to become relevant again.

One of the widely used methods in marketing is associating a brand with a person. If Coca-Cola were a person, how will she look like, what will she do, how will she behave in everyday situations? Exactly what was done to the Lenin's brand.

First – visualization. It is difficult for kids to associate themselves with an old bearded man. But Lenin was a child once. Soviet PR came up with a drawing of a curly headed boy and placed that image in the center of a 5-pointed red star pin. The first level of membership in a socialist society for a kid was to become an "oktyabrenok" – October child (a reference to the October Revolution of 1917). 7-year-old kids became "kids of October (Revolution)," and now they were responsible for studying hard, behaving well and being good followers of Lenin. In class, we were organized into teams of five people (5 is a reference to the star), teams competed with each other to be the best and also learned how to collaborate.

The next logical step is to learn about Lenin as a child. Who was this boy? What can we learn from him?

Biographers started to dig deep. It looks like stories about Lenin as a kid were based on real stories from his childhood. But these facts were interpreted in a very peculiar way. Any story became an example of a great character, honesty, and bravery. One example, which all Russian people know by heart – Volodya Lenin was playing in the house and accidentally broke a crystal graphene (crystal bottle for water or drinks). He was afraid that he would get punished and lied that he had nothing to do with this accident. But deep inside Volodya was a good boy and felt bad about that. Several days later he told his relatives that it was him who broke the thing. Or, another similar situation – he stole some fruits from the kitchen, ate them, and also confessed only several days later.

How could these examples of behavior be examples of honesty, bravery and a strong character?! But kids are naive and usually believe everything the teacher says. So, nobody questioned the teacher. We were brainwashed entirely and thought that Lenin was a great kid. And it is likely that selecting such stories was deliberate – with each story like that, Lenin became a human being, imperfect at first, but learning how to improve and develop his personality.

How Lenin Brainwashed Children

In the 3rd or 4th-grade school kids moved to the next level of the socialist ladder and became pioneers. The entire concept of the Pioneer organization was copied from the American boy scout organization. Kids learn to be social, be good team players and lead in teams. Scouts had blue ties; pioneers had red ties. The red color of the tie was symbolic – those ties "were particles of our red flag," which in return symbolized the color of blood, which was spilled in the October revolution. Becoming a pioneer was very important; all kids could not wait to become pioneers. Those who did well in school and also were active October kids and showed good behavior were honored to become pioneers first. The ritual for those lucky kids typically happened on the Red Square for Muscovites and near Lenin monument in other cities. Kids had to learn oath by heart. It was a long one, so to facilitate learning, half of the exercise notebooks had it printed on the back cover (the other half had a multiplication table).

Here is a translated text of the oath:

I, First name/Last name, joining the ranks of the USSR Pioneer Organization named after Vladimir Ilyich Lenin, solemnly promise in front of my comrades: to passionately love my homeland; to live, study and fight, as legated by the Great Lenin, as taught by the Communist Party; to always obey laws of Pioneers of the Soviet Union."

After you became a pioneer, you were fed many more propaganda stories about Lenin, mostly about his fight for Revolution. I do not remember most of them, but there is one story, which I think every Russian who lived at that time does remember. Lenin was imprisoned, but he continued fighting with the Tsar regime even from the prison. He invented a smart way to send messages outside – from his ration of food he made ink pots from bread and used milk instead of ink to write letters. Using an iron, his comrades could reveal his thoughts from prison. Kids loved this story, and everybody did experiment with milk and iron.

Only now I understand that the fact that Lenin had a daily supply of milk and bread in his ration was something that never existed later in thousands of Soviet prisons...

12.2. Kolbasa – the Food Symbol of the USSR

If there is one product, Russians are most passionate about – it is "kolbasa" – sausage. This is the food generations of Soviets grew up on. Kolbasa became the food symbol of the USSR and rumors are that it was a change in the recipe that led to the collapse of the Soviet Union. Or at least it was the first sign that the empire is not sustainable.

Russian Kolbasa Has American Roots

After the October Revolution (1917) several decades were extremely tough for the country. The young Soviet Republic struggled to produce enough food to feed the population. Meat was especially in demand since the country's production was not sufficient. In addition to feeding people, the Bolshevik government had political aspirations – to show the entire world that the Soviet Republic is prosperous and to keep the local population happy.

In 1936 Stalin invited Anastas Mikoyan, who was in charge of the food industry and called for innovation and for purchasing technologies abroad. Anastas Mikoyan traveled to the US and visited many food plants. He was a progressive man, eager to learn and adopt new technologies. He liked many innovations, present in the US at that time, and among those was bologna sausage, which he had seen at the meat factory in Chicago. Soon after his return to Moscow, a deal was signed and a first Russian – American sausage plant started to produce sausages of several types. Bologna-kind sausage became the most popular product.

The American recipe was altered though – bologna sausage had a high-fat content, and this sausage was called "Doktorskaya kolbasa" (Doctor's sausage) since it had almost 99% of high-quality meat. The idea was to provide Soviet consumers with high quality, nutritious, healthy and tasty everyday food.

Here is the exact recipe of Doktorskaya kolbasa that was used as an industry standard from 1936 till 1974:

Quantities of ingredients to produce 100 kg of Doktorskaya kolbasa:

25 kilograms of beef meat
70 kilograms of semi-lean pork meat
3 liters of milk
2 liters of eggs
2 kg of salt and 200 gr of sugar
30 gr of cardamom
50 gr of ascorbic acid (color stabilizer)

Manufacturing technology included dicing and mixing all ingredients into a homogenous paste, filling the tubes and later drying and boiling the sausage. The final product was incredibly tasty and quite healthy.

Marketing Communications Campaign for Kolbasa

To ensure faster adoption, the State conducted a full-scale promotional campaign. Sandwiches with kolbasa were sold from street stands and vending machines. There was print advertising, and there was a lot of PR. Recipes which included kolbasa were added to the first edition of the "Book About Tasty and Healthy Food" (first national cookbook). There was even a plan to commission famous writers to write a novel about sausage, but that initiative did fail.

Soviet consumers loved the new product, and Mikoyan's dream that every worker will have a sandwich with sausage for breakfast soon came true. It is interesting that the "ideal kolbasa sandwich" is different in Soviet time and in the present. Now people prefer thin slices of sausage and no butter; before it was always a thick slice of sausage on buttered bread. Btw, unlike sandwiches in the US, our sandwiches are usually open sandwiches, with one piece of bread. In addition to sandwiches, which made perfect breakfast, snack or lunch, people started to use kolbasa in a variety of dishes, from the famous Russian salad to fried eggs.

However, in the 60s and beginning of the 70s, USSR faced tough times again. Bad harvests led to a decrease in livestock numbers. Kolbasa started to disappear from stores. People were unhappy.

You may wonder – why bother? Couldn't people just buy the ham or lunch meat instead of kolbasa? The answer is – there was no ham either. People witnessed empty shelves and had to stay in lines for food. That was a disaster because government propaganda was telling that USSR is ahead of the US in food production, but reality did not match TV reports.

Changing the Recipe of Kolbasa – A Bad Idea

In 1974 the government made the worst decision – to adjust the recipe of kolbasa. Long gone were times when kolbasa consisted of pure meat. The new standard allowed to add bone flour, starch, soya, and other fillers. Needless to say – taste plummeted. However, kolbasa became available again and although consumers noticed the difference in taste – they did not boycott the product.

There were thousands of jokes on the subject though. A very popular one was: "Why do I find strange inclusions in kolbasa, which costs 2 rubles 90 kopecks per kilo? And what do you think – we will take a dog out of a kennel for that money?". The new recipe was never revealed, people said that there are two top secrets in the USSR – composition of the nuclear bomb and kolbasa recipe. And many people still think that either change of kolbasa recipe led to the collapse of the Soviet system or it had predicted it.

Modern State of Kolbasa Affairs

Now store counters are overflowing with a thousand kinds of sausages. However, the taste of even the most expensive ones is mediocre. Manufacturers add stickers that say: "does not contain soy," claim that sausage is produced from the finest ingredients, and heavily invest in marketing. But kolbasa still seems a bit soapy, has a very long shelf life and is avoided by health-conscious people.

Producing kolbasa, according to the standard of 1936, may be an excellent marketing opportunity for one of the brands. I am pretty sure that it will be done sooner or later.

12.3. Packaging in the USSR or Why We Keep Plastic Bags

Some time ago I was in Cuba and bought fresh mangoes and papayas to take to Moscow with me. Finding a wooden or a cardboard box, a scotch tape or even a rope to package all that proved to be a real challenge. That story made me remember USSR time when packaging was scarce and valuable. Now you will learn something that will make you wonder and smile.

Grocery Shopping in the USSR

Living in the world, where all food items are already packaged for you or will be packaged by a store assistant, it is nearly impossible to imagine how you would shop if products were not packaged. How would you carry home eggs, beverages, produce and other stuff?

In a typical Soviet grocery store, only some products (such as milk or kefir) came in bottles or plastic packaging. Meat, cheese, sausage or fish would be wrapped for you in a grey paper. But sour cream or eggs or bread did not have packaging. And nobody gave you a paper or plastic bag with purchase.

So, when going grocery shopping, you first had to bring a reusable shopping bag with you. Or, better, carry a compact grocery bag with you all the time. One of the most favorite grocery bags was called "Avos'ka" – the name comes from the Russian word "Avos'," which is impossible to translate into English. The closest translation is Perhaps (like in "Perhaps there will be something delicious in the grocery store on my way home from work)."

And, if you wanted to buy sour cream, which as we know is a product Russians love – you had to bring with you a glass jar with the lid. Or, let's say you wanted to buy eggs. There was a unique metal bag that you used for that. Or if you wanted to buy Kvas – our traditional non-alcoholic beverage – you had to bring a metal jar "bidon" with you.

People also created different ways to transport some non-food products – for example, one would string 10 toilet paper rolls on a rope to carry them home. Why buy ten at once? Because it was also a "deficit good," so one had to stock on it.

You would ask – why didn't people just use plastic bags? The answer is simple – there were no plastic bags! During Perestroika time plastic bags were among the goods that cooperatives started to produce. These plastic bags usually had catchy pictures (of a Marlboro man or Pamela Anderson) on them and were quite expensive, so people washed them when they got dirty and re-used again and again. I was living abroad with my parents in the end of the 80s, and then returned to Moscow. Of course, I had many plastic bags from shopping in Europe. Guess what – one of my classmates approached me and offered to buy some of my plastic bags. I still remember that she offered 3 Rub per one bag, which was a lot (ice-cream was 20 kopeks, a big cake was 2-3 Rub). I did decline the offer though. I thought that if my parents find out I am selling plastic bags in school, they will not be happy with such a side business of their daughter. (now I think I should've sold the bags)

These times were much more environmentally friendly though. I often wish we had less plastic packaging from food. But the funny thing is that people still do not throw away plastic bags, so each household has a "bag with the plastic bags" somewhere at home. Now you also understand – why!

12.4. Space – Russians' Greatest Pride Revisited

One of the things that make Russians really proud of the country is that we had sent the first man to Space. April 12th, the anniversary of

Gagarin's flight of 1961, is the day that reminds us of that event every year.

Generations of kids in the USSR wanted to be cosmonauts (as we call astronauts, from the word cosmos – space). Space lured and seemed to be one of the most attractive and desired places to work.

Yuri Gagarin – the First Man in Space

A cult figure, a superman with a broad smile. He is famous for saying, "Let's go!" a second before he was launched into space to experience something that no man ever experienced on Earth. His space mission only lasted 108 minutes, but these minutes opened a new era of space exploration.

Not many people know that even his family was not aware that he would be the first man in space. It was a top-secret project, so he could not tell his wife or parents. They learned that Yuri is in space from the radio together with the rest of the nation. He did write a letter to his wife though, but she meant to receive it only if things do not work out, which thankfully was not the case. She had received that letter when Yuri died in a plane crash in 1968. Circumstances of that plane crash are still unclear – he was such a master pilot that people have various conspiracy theories about that tragic accident.

A monument to Gagarin is close to my place in Moscow. I like that monument – it is quite symbolic. You see the tiny capsule in which he traveled in space and an oversized figure of him, raising in the space.

Alexey Leonov – the First Man in Outer Space

Sitting in a tiny capsule 300+ km above the land is scary enough. But going out in the open space, wearing just a space suit – is beyond scary. Alexey Leonov was the first man to go in outer space in 1965.

Read about the life-threatening dangers of his mission! I wonder why there are no movies made on that subject yet – Leonov's space suit expanded outside of spacecraft, and only his inventiveness and calmness saved him from dying and helped him to get back in the spaceship.

I have seen Leonov in person once. He was supporting the release of the Hollywood film "Oblivion". It took place in one of the movie theaters in Moscow. Leonov was wearing some kind of khaki training suit. He was in his 70s, but his appearance caused more applause than the appearance of Tom Cruise at the same stage several minutes before that. And we could see that for Tom meeting with Alexey was a real treat, he talked to him with great respect, after all, Alexey Leonov really did experience all the hardships of space travel which Tom just plays in his scenes at the studio lot.

Alexey Leonov warmly greeted Tom Cruise and said: "Tom is a cool guy, real pilot!" And then he talked about the beauty of our planet and the need to raise awareness for conservation of that beauty and sustainable development. That was a very moving speech.

Valentina Tereshkova – the First Woman in Space

"Sea-gull is speaking," sea-gull was a nickname of the first woman in space that she used in communication with the mission control center. USSR was very modern in gender equality, so sending a female cosmonaut to space was an important thing to do for the government. From that moment on, both boys and girls could dream of a career in space.

Extended Space Missions

After it was proved that a human being can survive a short flight, the next goal was to make long-term space travel possible. That was challenging since human bones, muscles and cardio-vascular system suffer from long periods of weightlessness. But space scientists managed to make extended missions possible.

When I was a child, I met Anatoly Berezovoy, the first Russian cosmonaut, who worked in space for 6 months. He was having dinner at our house, so I had the opportunity to ask as many questions as I wanted. He talked about scientific experiments in space, a need to work out a lot to sustain muscles, communication in the team, views of the Earth in different seasons, missing smells and sounds of Earth and not seeing any aliens (that fact did upset me).

Finally, several years ago I found out that one of my classmates from the School of Biology, Moscow State University, Sergey Ryazanskyi has become a cosmonaut. Such a career is very untypical for a scientist, so it was fascinating to learn how Sergey trained and what he experienced in the space. For example, that cosmonauts have to work out 2 hours every day, but it still takes a lot of time to get back in shape after a long space mission. Or, that most food at the space station is no longer in tubes, rather it is dried. And that Russian cosmonauts do bring alcohol to the space station.

Space Dogs – Belka and Strelka

However, even before humans, there were other mammals in space. The most famous of them – dogs Belka & Strelka (Squirrel and Arrow). Strelka's descendants are still living in the US – Nikita Kruschev gave one of Strelka's puppies to Jackie Kennedy as a present.

Belka & Strelka stuffed bodies are in the museum of Space in Moscow. Seeing the dogs there produced mixed feelings in me. School kids, who visited the museum that day asked many funny questions as well: "So, Gagarin did survive the space trip?! No way!!! And why are the dogs dead? They told us in school that the dogs came back alive!!!"

Other Things That Excited Us

The weightlessness of space. That concept was mind-blowing. We did imagine how cool it would be to float through a living room right now. We were unaware of the terrible toll that this state has on muscles, bones and cardio system over extended periods. It all seemed to be just a fun adventure

Space food. The weightlessness of space implied that you would not be able to eat soup from a soup bowl. All that soup will fly around you in tiny drops. You need special space food, which you consume out of tubes. The cafeteria at the space museum in Moscow used to serve real space food, but now they, unfortunately, serve only real borsch, pies, etc. I was upset about that at first but then realized that being an adult I probably no longer want to consume my borsch from a metal tube.

Hygiene/medicine etc. Even the most ordinary tasks, such as everyday grooming becomes challenging in space. That is why it is always interesting to learn how astronauts manage to shave, wash their hair and what do they do if they have a toothache.

These days most Russian kids no longer dream about becoming cosmonauts, they instead want to go in business. Adults are hesitant as well – in 2012 only 304 people applied for the job (8 people were finally selected for the training). Russia still is a leading space country at Earth orbit, maintaining orbital space station and sending Russian and International astronauts to the station.

12.5. A Typical Apartment of the Soviet Time

USSR with its planned economy was a strange place to live. Everything was standardized, including residential buildings, apartment plans, and furniture. Let's explore what the typical apartment was like during the Soviet Union time.

Irony of Fate – the Movie Which Describes It Best

On the evening of Dec 31st, we always watch the same New Year movie – "Irony of Fate." We have done that for the last 40 years, and this film does not get boring with age. The plot is – a guy plans to celebrate New Year's Eve with his fiancé in Moscow, but he goes to a sauna (Russian version – "banya") with friends before that, and they all celebrate too much… and in the end, send him to St. Petersburg instead of another guy.

He arrives in St. Pete, catches a taxi to his Moscow address, which happens to also exist in St. Pete. He opens the apartment door with his key, and it is the same apartment, just in the other city. That may sound crazy to you, but in fact – that could've been true. Most cities had streets with similar or equal names, all Soviet apartments did look typical, even the lock could've worked. He is still drunk, so he falls asleep on the couch and then the owner of the apartment – a beautiful woman arrives. She is not happy about the stranger, sleeping on her couch in boxers since she is expecting her fiancé to show up. And from there, it is a comedy of situations for the rest of the movie. We usually watch this movie when we cook Olivier ("Russian") salad.

The interior, shown in this movie is a typical interior of the late Soviet Union – the 70s-80s. The main male character probably works in science, the main female character is a teacher in school. So, how come they have identical apartments in different cities?

Typical Buildings in Typical Surroundings

There were just several types of residential buildings and all "sleeping districts" were planned the same. Apartment plans in these buildings were also approved at the state level. Yes, there was a small coincidence – that both families had the 2-room apartment, but the social status of the main characters is very similar, so that makes sense too.

Typical Soviet apartment started with a corridor, which had coat hangers, shoe racks, and a mirror. Bathroom (or bathroom and WC) were accessible from the hallway. There were no master bedrooms with a separate bathroom, a typical apartment had just one bathroom. A kitchen was always small – 5-6 square meters, even though a kitchen usually was the center of the flat and guests were typically entertained in the kitchen and not in the living room. The main living room was the biggest one – about 20 square meters, other rooms (if they existed) were 11-14 square meters. If the number of rooms was less than the number of people, living in the apartment, somebody was always sleeping on a sofa in a living room. There was typically a small balcony, which was mostly used as storage. Apartments without furniture did look the same inside and outside. But how could they select the same furniture? That does not sound believable!

Typical Furniture and How to Get It

I know. In the modern world, where there is rather a paradox of choice than no choice, it is not possible for two different families to choose an identical set of furniture. But we are talking about Soviet time, a time of deficit of everything. A deficit is when you go to a furniture store, and there is no furniture there. Or, you really do not like the furniture that they have and search for better options. Better options were also scarce. Soviet people were not spoiled by either luxury or variety. They had a choice between Soviet-made furniture, which was not good and Czech or GDR (East Germany, German Democratic Republic) furniture, which was more or less decent. The latter was not available in store every day, but if you are lucky or have the patience to stay in long lines or have "connections" in the furniture store – you could score a good set of furniture. That was exactly what most people tried to do. Imported furniture was more expensive, but that was not an obstacle. People had money. The goal was to get access to the desired item. (Now you understand why there was no need for my current profession – marketing at that time)

The most significant object of wish was a furniture piece, called "stenka." Stenka means "the wall." It is a wall of cabinets and dressers that you mount in your living room. A stenka was quite practical – it usually included a dresser where you could hang your clothes and a set of open and closed cabinets, where you could store things. Some of the cabinets had glass doors – you would store crystal glasses and/or books in these cabinets. (both were in a deficit as well). Best "furniture walls" were made in GDR, they had lacquered doors with or without decorations and were uber-chic! Both of the apartments in the movie had "stenkas."

Then you hunt for a good sofa, a good set of arm-chairs and a table. Many apartments, including apartment of my parents, had a glass coffee table for everyday use and a dining table, which surfaced only for special events (such as the New Year's Eve) and spent most of its life disassembled, hidden between stenka and the wall of the room. You also hunt for a good set of kitchen furniture (having a "soft corner" – a corner mini-sofa and a table were best!). You hunt for a Czech set of coat hangers and Yugoslavian bathroom equipment (if it is not white, but blue or beige – even more chic!).

After you are done with that – you do work on decorations. Lamps, carpets (often one rug will be on the floor in the living room, and the other one will be attached to the wall), and accessories. I guess by that point, I do not need to explain that there was not much variety in these either, right?

In the end – if we hunt well – our apartment is super-chic, and it does look super-similar to thousands of other "well-furnished" typical flats.

Did That Make People Depressed?

No, absolutely not. On the contrary – that made life easier! Buying something that was difficult to get was a significant source of happiness. And you had a clear view – what you need to have to "live well." Now it is much more difficult, since the Joneses, living next door may make 10x more than you do and may have seriously better furniture than you do as a result of their income. Nobody likes that. Life was more fair during Soviet time, or at least, it was perceived as such.

12.6. Communal Flats in Russia – Shared Life

When I wrote about the apartments of modern and Soviet time, I forgot to write about communal or shared flats. These were the flats, shared by several families. It is interesting to investigate how families lived in such apartments. That story may surprise you!

What Is/Was a Communal Flat?

An apartment that earlier belonged to one family, but after the Revolution of 1917 was either taken from the owners (if they left the country for example) or more families were moved to that apartment. The idea of the Bolshevik government was that having many rooms for one family is too much luxury. Modern families do not need living rooms, dining rooms, study rooms, libraries, etc. – they just need a roof above their head, a place where they can sleep. 9 square meters per person is more than enough. A lot of families moved to Moscow after the Revolution, and there was not enough of available real estate, so newcomers were transferred to the existing flats.

And now – please imagine. Your family has to share an apartment with one kitchen and one bathroom with several other families. You may have 2 adults in the family, you may also have kids and grandparents, living with you. In any case – your personal private space is one bedroom. The rest is a shared space. How did families work that out?

Day-To-Day Life at Communal Flats

Let's start with visitors. How do they buzz in? There were multiple door rings at the entrance or a note, which specified how many times you need to buzz the ring if you came to see Ivanov or Petrov.

Since you only have one room to entertain visitors and all your family also sleeps in that room – you will have a dining table in the center of the room and beds or sofas near walls. If several generations of the family lived in the same room – using dividers could give at least some sense of privacy. Dresser often works as a divider.

Sacred places in rooms were usually either the icon corner or a TV set. Other emotionally charged items present in the room – photos of family and relatives and decorative items.

Carpets were widely used to add coziness and carpets were both on the floor and at the wall

Lack of space usually meant that the dining table also served as a study table. One could see newspapers, textbooks, medicine, reading glasses and other items there as well as a tea kettle and cups. When guests arrived – the table was cleared, but if the family was having dinner – those items usually stayed there.

Shared space was usually used for coats, umbrellas and street shoes. People also stored bikes or baby strollers there if there was enough space.

Now, let's move to the kitchen. Having several fridges was not typical. Refrigerators were a novelty and were expensive. Some families did not have a fridge at all and stored food outside of a window or below the window sill in winter. "Wealthy people" had their own fridge in their bedroom. If the fridge was in the kitchen and was shared – it would be a dorm-like setup – you have your own shelf or leave notes, attached to your food

Now, the bathroom. In big families, morning time logistics is hard enough. Imagine you have several families, who share the bathroom?! If the relationship is decent, people work out a bathroom schedule and adhere to it, if not – it is an issue. But some people like to take long baths or showers, and in addition to the inconvenience, they may spend more water or electricity. That was also an issue to discuss.

Most often – you just had one landline, and the phone was in the shared space – a lobby or a corridor. Your neighbors would always call you if they answered the call. But they will notice, who called you and will overhear your conversation. And will not be happy if you talk for too long when they are expecting an important call

Implications of Living in a Communal Flat

In general, communal living required a lot of skills:

Cooperation. The best apartments were the ones where inhabitants managed to agree on day-to-day things, such as when to use the bathroom, when to cook and what are the other rules of the house. Following the rules of the house was vital, whatever the rules were. For example, in some apartments washing clothes was to be done in the bathroom, in some apartments – in a separate zone in the kitchen. Having social rules, such as who and when could visit, how loud the visitors could be, etc. also made a lot of sense.

Negotiation skills. Rules are to be discussed. Usually, in communal flats, there was a set of rules, which was developed for years if not decades. But things changed with new neighbors or new circumstances. Being able to re-negotiate the rules was important.

Conflict management. Conflicts happen even in families, among people, who love each other, among relatives. Living in a shared space with strangers, of course, leads to conflicts. And if not managed properly – conflicts do escalate. Most typical stories include spitting in soup in a communal kitchen. To make sure that does not happen – people tried to be kind to each other. For example – if a neighbor asks you, what you are cooking – invite her to try the dish or do a small favor (such as lending some milk or flour or other staple food that she forgot to buy that day). Small favors go a long way.

Privacy management. As you imagine – there is not much privacy in a shared flat. Your neighbors actually have too much information about you – they know when you leave to work, when you return, overhear your phone conversations since the phone is in a lobby, see all your visitors, judge your habits (especially if you have any bad habits), know how you dress and they even know which soap you use and how your underwear looks like (literally, since you hang it out for drying in the bathroom). So, even if you do not talk too much about your life, they see how you live. Usually, the way to manage privacy was to maintain confidentiality in your room and to limit conversations with neighbors to "need to know."

Influence of Communal Living on Russian Mentality

I am sure that there were professional studies on that subject. I will try to find them, and for now – here are some of my guesses:

Personal Space. I always notice that Russian people stand too close to me when we talk. I do not mind that with close friends, but do not feel comfortable when strangers come so close or stand in line right next to me (I spent most of my childhood abroad, that is why I have different borders of personal space). I think that the communal living may be one of the reasons. You get used to sharing your personal space with other people day-to-day, so it shrinks.

Standing in lines. Thankfully the only place where one still has to stand in line in Moscow is the Russian Post Office. But in Soviet times people had to stand in lines daily when they were buying groceries, clothes or anything else. Figuring out a way to manage lines "fairly" was quite like figuring out the schedule of using a bathroom in a communal flat. People, who lived in communal flats, were trained to wait for a lot of things.

Communication/Cooperation. If you can live for decades with strangers in the same home, you become really good at communication. You know how to trade favors, you know how to negotiate, how to keep up relationships. That is definitely a good thing about communal living.

Being judgmental. I already wrote that it is typical for Russia. "I know better what is good for you and I will tell you about that right now" is a very typical Russian behavior. I am not sure whether the roots come from the communal living or it is just our personality trait. But it might be a consequence of communal living. You see the life of several other families as an insider, daily. You see the mistakes they make and privacy boundaries blur with time. You tell your neighbor what you think first (in a direct, "Russian way"). Next time you find yourself telling a stranger on the street, how she should dress her kids! My Personal Experience

I never lived in a communal flat myself, but when my parents were young – they lived in such an apartment in the very center of Moscow. My mom has mixed feelings about that time – on the one hand, they were young and happily married, on the other hand – they had a neighbor, who had dozens of cats in her room and liked to collect garbage on streets. When my parents managed to buy their own flat, which was located further from the center – they were so happy to move out of the communal apartment! It was a 3 room flat, and they had furniture just for one room. So, my mom was moving furniture back and forth until they got enough furniture to fill that apartment. I find these stories super interesting as they are the stories of the life I never experienced myself!

My grand-aunt lived in a communal flat; also steps from Kremlin and I have been to her flat many times. There were 3 bedrooms, a shared kitchen, and a shared bathroom. People, who lived in that apartment knew each other for decades and they had a good relationship, so it was quite peaceful. But the landline phone was in the lobby, so overheard conversations were always commented upon. For example, I remember that her neighbors had a teenage boy and some girl regularly called him and my grand-aunt disapproved of that ("a girl should never call a boy!")

How Did People Get Their Own Apartments in Soviet Time?

There were several ways:

The most straightforward was to wait when the State gives you a new apartment. In the Soviet time, the minimum norm was 9 square meters per person. If a family of several people was living in one room in a communal flat – they were eligible for improving their living conditions. Getting a separate flat involved red tape and a long wait list, but eventually, a lot of people got new apartments free of charge. If you did not want to wait – you could do the following:

- Do something extraordinary – become a well-known singer, writer, artist, etc. The Soviet Union recognized that and could give you an apartment for your talent
- Be very active in Communist party, lead people and get an apartment via your contribution to the Party
- Sign up for a cooperative condo house if you have money (that is what my parents did, they took a loan from the relatives for that)
- Exchange two or three rooms in shared flats for one apartment. That required a lot of business skills but was doable
- After the Perestroika, in the 90s you could just buy an apartment if you had enough money or could negotiate with multiple families and try to improve the living conditions for your family, but also for other families if they agree to move further from the center

There are still people living in communal flats in Moscow, although that is more of an exception now.

12.7. Carpets as Carpets and Carpets as Symbols

One cannot imagine a good Soviet apartment without carpets. The carpet was on the floor in a living room and… often on a wall of a living room. Why?

A Typical Carpet

First of all – what kind of carpets were popular? Traditional, "Persian-style" carpets, mainly produced in Turkmenistan and other former Soviet republics. They were very expensive and were "in a deficit» (hard to find). I guess that the love of the carpets goes from the Asian part of our souls.

Carpets on the Walls

A lot of Soviet people had at least two carpets at home – on the floor and on the wall in the living room. If they could afford that of course, since carpets were expensive. Carpets served a dual purpose – they provided coziness and were a symbol of wealth. I am not exactly sure why people placed carpets on the wall – a logical explanation is that a rug provides extra insulation from cold, but very often carpets were at the internal walls. So, I believe that people just thought that having a beautiful carpet on the wall is a part of a stylish interior design.

Now that habit went out of fashion entirely. But of course, some old apartments still have carpets, hanging on walls. People often repost crazy photos from Russian dating sites, on which candidates are posing with the carpet on the background (which btw is probably the worst background for a photo).

Other symbols of the wealth of the Soviet time included crystal glasses, vases, and crystal lamps, usually made in GDR or Czechoslovakia.

Cleaning Carpets

Cleaning carpets was a special event. Not everybody had a vacuum cleaner and vacuum cleaners, which use water and foam, were non-existent. So, even though Russian people never wear street shoes at home, carpets needed cleaning at least twice a year.

In summer you would take a rug outside, hang it on the metal tube and use a special device to beat the dust out. In winter – you would take the rug outside and clean it with the snow. Cleaning the carpet, using snow was a lot of fun for kids!

Other Types of Carpets

Less affluent people, or people, who lived in rural areas often had different types of carpets on the walls of their homes. Such carpets reminded the medieval gobelins and served mainly the decoration purpose. The most typical ones pictured swans or deer.

There is one thing that really puzzles me about the usage of carpets in Russia. In the US most homes have carpet floors. Of course, carpet floors are also available in Russia, but I have never seen an apartment with carpet floors. And it has nothing to do with our weather – Chicago also has a lot of snow in winter, but most homes there have carpet floors. Also, unlike in the US – Russians never walk in the apartments in the same shoes they wear outdoors. It would've made total sense to have warm carpet floors, but people strongly prefer wooden floors in the rooms and tiles in the kitchen and bathroom. That makes me think, that carpets never served the rational purposes, they instead had aesthetic and status symbol value. Maybe having carpets at home remind us of our Asian roots?

12.8. Life Hacks from Soviet Time or the Story of a Deficit

So, what did Russian people do when there was a shortage ("deficit") of goods and food? I will share with you some life hacks of that time.

What Kind of Goods Were in "Deficit" in the USSR?

Soviet economy was a planned economy. It wasn't based on efficient market principles of demand and supply. So, there was a shortage of a lot of things:

Italian shoes, canned peas, mayonnaise, pantyhose, salami, champagne, sports shoes, underwear, chocolate candies, buckwheat, mascara, construction materials, toilet paper, French perfume, canned salmon, fresh fruit, cars, any nice clothes made in the West, stationery, handbags, theater tickets, etc. This list is endless. The word "deficit" turned into a noun – people used to say, "there is a line in the store – they must sell deficit, let's have a look." Easier to say what was available in stores at the end of the Soviet era.

Typical ("good") grocery store of that time in Moscow would have the following "non-deficit" food: bread, 1-2 types of pastries, milk, kefir, cream, sour cream, butter, 1-2 varieties of cheese, 1-2 varieties of sausage, canned sea cabbage and canned fish, some sort of meat and frozen fish, some non-alcohol beverages and sweets. Anything above was "deficit" (rare and sought-after) goods and created long lines.

Typical fruit & vegetable store (yes, they were separate from grocery stores) would have potatoes, onion, carrots, beets, cabbage and maybe some seasonal fruit. Anything above, for example, bananas or oranges, was a "deficit" and created long lines. For some reason, bananas were always sold green, and one had to wait until they become ripe (if one has the willpower to wait).

Typical "mall" (Univermag) would have shoes and garments which were out of fashion even at that time. Any foreign merchandise was considered to be a "deficit" and created long lines. People often bought stuff they did not need or shoes of the wrong sizes to exchange for something more valuable later.

Typical household stuff store ("Hozyaistvenniy") had cleaning and grooming products and various household equipment, but all of that was "made in the USSR," so quality was low. Polish shampoo would create a huge line as it was in a "deficit" too.

Paradox of the Soviet Time

Nothing in stores, but lots of good things in people's fridges and on the festive dinner tables. How that was possible??

Well, partially that was famous Russian hospitality. You always offer your guests all you have. And, it was a result of making stocks. But in the most part – that was using zillions of life hacks.

Life Hacks of the Soviet Time

It is a vast topic, but here are the main vectors:

1) **Straightforward Approach** – stock on all goods you might need. If you need canned peas and mayonnaise and pickled cucumbers for your Russian Salad – make sure you buy all the ingredients not the day before, but when you see them in store (applicable for food with long shelf life). Yes, you have to stay in line to get them, and there probably will be a limit of how much you can buy (3 cans of peas or 1 kg of chocolate candies). Other people behind you also want that stuff.
2) **Networking Approach** – that approach will be easy to understand for all my B-school friends. Similar as you network to get a job, you network to get special treatment from the grocery store or department store directors or a butcher or even a salesperson in a store. He or she can let you know if they have salami or Italian shoes in store and you can also avoid staying in line to get them (either for money or, exchanging favors. Let's say you can give theater tickets to a famous play in exchange…)
3) **Frugal approach** – best explained in my post about the lifecycle of things or – "balcony, dacha, trash can". You just do not throw away items. An old coat could always be remodeled, nails could be re-used, glass jars from pickles will hold next years' jam, etc. Also, you would've needed an empty glass jar if you want to buy sour cream in the store. You were supposed to bring your own jar, to carry the sour cream home!

Another weird thing – all Russians (even the wealthy ones) still save plastic bags from grocery stores — we never throw them away, since we can re-use them! Literally, every person older than 30 will have a bag full of plastic bags under the kitchen sink! An explanation for that – In Soviet times there were no plastic bags in grocery stores. At all! So, most people had an "Avos'ka bag" with them in case they do grocery shopping during the day. The name "Avos'ka" comes from difficult to explain phenomena, called "avos'." Avos' does not have a direct translation, the closest translation is "perhaps." As in: "Perhaps I come across something valuable in the store, I will need a bag to carry it home." Funny as it may seem – re-using glass jars and having an avoska bag with you for shopping was actually very environmentally friendly.

To give you a further illustration of a frugal approach – let's look at the life cycle of pantyhose (tights). You wear them, but of course, sooner or later you get a hole in them. What do you do if you are living in the USSR? The first thing you do is you reach for the nail polish. And, no, not to do mani-pedi since now you are out of stock of tights. You seal the running of the hole with clear nail polish. And when you come home, you mend the hole. There were even special hooks which were used for mending tights (enormous deficit!).

You use that pair of tights until the holes are obvious. What do you do afterward? Toss them? No, absolutely not. You wear them in winter under trousers! Nobody can see you have tights with holes if you wear pants on top of them, right? And an extra layer keeps you warm.

Ok, even if you are super careful and frugal and spend winter evenings mending the garment – eventually it wears out. Now you toss it, right? Not yet! You wash it and then handicraft other objects out of it!

4) **Handcrafts/Innovation Approach**
Ok, so what exactly could one craft from old tights?! Plenty of things. For starters – one could just use them (after washing) for storing onions. But if you are really crafty you can knit a door mat or even a dishwashing cloth))

Innovation was a primary mode of Soviet people for 70 years. Plastic tubes for IV? You should see the gorgeous fish decorations, made of them! Old ropes? Just give them to me, and I will make a macramé technique owl or a decorative panel picture out of them! Knitting a dress or sewing one – easy! Newspaper hats to protect your hair from paint spills when painting – any kid could do that! Opening a bottle of wine with a pair of pliers and a screw, etc.

Food was an exceptionally creative area. Americans often wonder how people cook from scratch. Guess what?! To make a cheesecake in the USSR, you first needed to make cottage cheese. Out of milk!!! To make a Russian salad sometimes you needed to make your own mayonnaise! Out of oil, egg yolk, pepper, and mustard!

Making home-made jams or baking cakes was considered cooking 101. One of the favorite Soviet films features a story of a single girl, who works in a large state organization and looks for a guy among her coworkers. Hilarious movie! But what is relevant here – workers in the movie did technical drawings at work by hand and need good erasers to correct mistakes. Good erasers at that time were made in Europe, but they were difficult to get and costly. What she did – she soaked Soviet erasers in kerosene, and they became as good and soft as the European ones. And of course, she also cooked home-made biscuits and sweets, since "the shortcut to man's heart is via his stomach."

12.9. What Do Russians Think About the USSR Now?

I often referred to the USSR times in my blog and compared good and bad things from that time with current events in Russia. The question that I often got in emails from my blog readers: *"What do Russians think about USSR now? Are they nostalgic or are they happy USSR times are over?* Really interesting topic, worth writing about.

Couple of years ago I took a fantastic class at Coursera – "Understanding Russians: Contexts of Intercultural Communications", taught by Professor Mira Bergelson and later became Community manager

What Do Russians Think About the USSR Now?

for this course. You may find it quite funny that I took this course being Russian myself and writing this blog. But that is precisely why I did take this course! I could describe many things as an insider, but I could not explain a lot of them.

One of the many things that surprised me – two distinct groups feel nostalgic. One group – people who were young in the times of USSR. They feel nostalgic since youth is the time when everything was bright and rosy. The other group – really young folks, who were born after USSR collapsed. They haven't lived in this time themselves but heard a lot of good things from parents and other relatives, and also re-construct Soviet reality based on movies of that time. Middle-aged people are not so fond of USSR times since we do remember the end of the empire and the uncertain Perestroika times of the 90s.

How good or bad was USSR in reality? Challenging to be fair, but I will try to outline the main positives and negatives:

Pros of Living in the USSR:

- Free education
- Free medical services
- Free use of resorts once a year (Sochi, Crimea, etc. – a month of "all-inclusive fun at the sea")
- A lot of stability – your job was secure, nobody was going to kick you out of your apartment, etc.
- A lot of pride (and patriotism) for the country – space, ballet, army, etc.
- No "keeping up with the Joneses" (none of your neighbors were buying Lamborghini)
- Lots of intellectual discussions with your friends and real quality time – since that was the era of 3 TV channels, no gadgets, and no cell phones
- Feeling you had savings and had security for retirement
- A path to success was clear, you could have planned for decades
- No traffic jams since the number of cars were limited (chances are you do not have one too though)

Cons of Living in the USSR:

- Free medical services were a good concept, but to get proper medical services, one needed to use networking and sometimes also pay
- You had plenty of money but couldn't buy whatever you wanted freely. You either needed an approval from the State or needed to do networking to find product/services you wanted to buy. And, you spent a lot of time standing in lines
- You could travel freely in the country, but going abroad was problematic – you needed to show a lot of compliance to travel even to Eastern European countries and opportunities to work abroad were limited to a very few people
- Freedom of speech was officially banned. You turned off the landline and talked with friends in a whisper in your kitchen. Communist party ideology replaced religion and any other values in the official mainstream
- You did not own any real estate (your apartment and dacha were in your use, but belonged to the state)
- Since your personal achievements did not bring more money, you tended to slack. Money was not a goal though at that time. More important – your ideas and your work were evaluated not by your peers, but by the Communist party members. You felt isolated from the world community in your field.

This is not the full list on both fronts. But hopefully, it gives you an idea about living in the USSR.

12.10. Propaganda in Russia and Abroad

Propaganda definition: ideas or statements that are often false or exaggerated and that are spread to help a cause, a political leader, a government, etc. (Merriam-Webster Dictionary)

In recent years opening the Facebook, the timeline makes me sad. I see that many of my friends from Russia, Ukraine, and other countries have opposing views on the current political events.

I am stunned to see that – most of my 900+ friends on FB are well educated, smart and thinking people. How can their opinion on the same events differ so much? And why does that remind me so much of the time of Cold War? What is going on?

What is going on is called Propaganda. Propaganda machines are working at full speed both in Russia and in the West. One of my Russian friends wrote that he hates when people say – "the truth is somewhere in between." His point was that there is only one truth; all the rest is just a manipulation of facts.

One of my American friends said: "if we live in a system where propaganda is EVERYWHERE and permeates so many facets of our lives, how will we know much better? Our discussion really made me think not only about Russia but also about other countries and societies – communist (at the time) or not – and how their systems work to get people on board with specific ideologies."

Most People Believe to Be Immune to Propaganda

All my consumer research studies show that the majority of people think that advertising does not influence their buying choices. The same thing happens with propaganda – if you ask, people usually acknowledge that propaganda is a powerful force and it does impact others' opinions. But it does not influence views of that particular person.

That is what is most scary. Well-planned propaganda is communication, intended to shape perceptions, manipulate cognitions, and orchestrate behavior. But it does so in a subtle way, leaving the impression that you think on your own and form independent opinions.

How is that done? The key to successful propaganda manipulations is that a news piece is never 100% false, on the contrary – it usually contains 50 or more percent of truth or real facts. But any facts could be manipulated, especially in the modern world.

Are Russians More or Less Prone to Be the Victims of Propaganda?

I do not know the answer to that question. From one point of view the main media – Russian TV is state-controlled. From the other point of view – in the USSR while all media was state-controlled and foreign media were banned – a lot of people were able to read "between the lines" and form their own opinion.

Now everybody who wants to read opposing opinions can find those either online or in foreign media, but do people actually look for other opinions?

Is Propaganda Always a Malignant Thing?

If we use the above definition of Propaganda – yes. Manipulating facts is never a good thing. However, every country and especially democratic countries need to create some kind of positive PR to form and transmit the central philosophy that can unite the nation. "American Dream" is an example of such PR, but that is a positive idea, which teaches the "can do" attitude to people.

Sochi Olympics and FIFA World Cup PR efforts were a good thing since they have shown the other, better face of Russia and have portrayed Russians as friendly people, who can joke, play sports and welcome visitors.

State Propaganda rarely reflects the sincere wishes of the population
One of my friends wrote the following on FB:

"I have no idea what to expect or how the political situation will evolve. And in the midst of this uncertainty, I would like to say this.

The recent actions of the Russian government have nothing to do with the majority of the Russian people. Like any other nation in the world, we value peace above all, and none needs or wants this craziness. Certainly not me, or my friends and family.

I can't do anything about what's going on or going to happen. But I can lcast say it here."

I believe that the statement above is correct.

A Personal Story on a Propaganda Case

At the end of the 90s, I was on a trip to Bryansk – Russian city, in 6-hour train ride from Moscow. Bryansk used to be a prosperous little city in the Soviet times; most citizens were employed at one of the three large defense plants. After the disarmament, everybody lost their jobs and had to find other ways to feed their families.

I went to Bryansk with a Canadian radio journalist, Karen, whose mission was to make a program about people's lives in that city. It was a crazy 14-hour day. We had 11 meetings with people, living in Bryansk – from a former director of a weapon plant to a retired couple to young businessmen, who have air-conditioning, computer and other businesses to students.

When we were sitting at the train station late at night, completely exhausted and waiting for our train, Karen said: "They gave me a title for the program beforehand – "Russia – the Winter of Tears." When I come home, I will speak about changing that title. What I have seen here is more about people being optimistic about their future and trying to adapt to the new realities." I was shocked to know that Karen had the title of the story even before she went to Russia. That was an example of Propaganda. In the same time, I liked that she had formed her own opinion of what she had seen and dared to talk to her editors about that.

What to do?

First of all, we all should understand that Propaganda does influence any of us, whether we live in Russia, in Ukraine, in the US or in any other country.

It is not possible to be physically present at all the world events. But it is possible to assemble the vision of the world, by learning facts, listening to opposing opinions and thinking. The final view will never be 100% free of Propaganda ideas but will be much closer to the truth.

12.11. Guest Post: American Perspective on the Soviet Union

Understand Russia is thrilled about having a guest post from friend and colleague from the business school Andrew, who writes the blog about wise investing, www.thestockyfox.com. Andrew shared with us his impressions of the Soviet Union from the time, when he was a kid, growing up in California. Let's dive in this exciting time-travel adventure!

Soviets as the enemy

I was born in 1977 and grew up in Southern California. My first impressions of the Soviet Union, formed when I was about 6 or 7 years old, was that it was the enemy. I never had any distinct concerns regarding the USSR—I never seriously feared the idea of them launching nuclear missiles at us or a Soviet invasion—but it was just a general feeling. As a little boy I obviously "knew" the US was the best country in the world, and the USSR represented the opposite of that.

As so often is the case, many of these perceptions were formed by television and movies. Top Gun (1986) had faceless Soviet fighter pilots (you never saw their faces because of their helmets) attacking Maverick and the Americans "unprovoked." War Games (1983) and Project X (1987) were based on the premise that the Soviets would attack, probably with nukes, and we had to be ready. Red Dawn (1984) and Rambo: First Blood, Part II (1985) showed that it was always the Soviets who were ultimately behind the evil plots.

When we played "army" it was always the Soviets that we were fighting. On the playground, if you wanted to insult a classmate, you'd call him a "communist" or a "Soviet." A lot of the video games had us playing the character of an American freedom fighter taking on the Soviet Union.

I went to a pretty diverse elementary school, and as kids are always competitive, we would argue about which of our ancestral countries were best. The Hispanic kids bragged about Mexico, the Asian kids about China and Japan, the black kids about Africa, and the white kids about European countries (my heritage is Dutch, so I fought hard for the Netherlands). But there were no kids who confessed to their Russian heritage or bragged about the Soviet Union. Of course, there were plenty of kids with Russian heritage living in Los Angeles, but that was just something you would never acknowledge on the playgrounds in the early 1980s. No sense needlessly exposing yourself to the unrelenting ridicule that would surely accompany admitting your family was from the Soviet Union.

But if you asked me why I felt the way I did, I wouldn't have known what to say. Our teachers and parents never said anything that specifically bad about the USSR, but they never said anything positive either, and you got the sense that by their silence the Soviet Union was "bad news."

Soviets as the opponent

When I was eight or nine years old, in 1985 or 1986, my impression started to change. The Soviet Union had evolved from being our enemy to be being our competition. I was getting older and had started competing in sports, so the opponent analogy certainly made sense to me. Also, by that time there seemed to be a thawing of relations as President Reagan, and General Secretary Gorbachev began the dialogue which would ultimately relieve the world's fear of nuclear Armageddon.

The US and the USSR were still competing for world powers, and it was our job as Americans to beat the Soviets, be it on the battlefield (which seemed less and less likely) or in the sports arena. As sports became more important to me, I quickly learned the story of the 1980 US Olympic hockey team that defeated the Soviets, probably the single most hallowed victory ever in US sports. My dad and I were big basketball fans, so it was with great delight that he told me the US Olympic men's basketball team had never lost before . . . Except in the gold medal game in the 1972 Olympics when the Soviets "cheated" to win.

(The Americans protested the final play and refused to accept their silver medal. To my knowledge, this is the only time this has happened in Olympics history, and it's a travesty. I hope the 1972 team stops being sore losers and accepts their medals along with the Soviet victory.)

When you played arcade hockey, you always wanted to be the US team in white and not the Soviets in red. When you imagined sinking the game-winning shot, you were always playing in the Olympics against the Soviets.

I remember watching WrestleMania III in 1987 when Hulk Hogan overcame the odds to defeat Andre, the Giant. Hogan epitomized American guts and winning spirit, while Andre represented the Soviet strength and size that just couldn't prevail. As it turns out, Andre was French, but at the time all I knew is that he talked funny and looked foreign, so he must be a Soviet—shows you how perceptive a nine-year-old is.

The Soviets were still bad, but it wasn't because they were evil or that they were trying to hurt us. It was more that it was them and us, and we wanted to win.

Soviets as a friend

By the time I was 11 or 12, in 1988 or 1989, there seemed to be a major change, and now the Soviets were becoming our friends. It was pretty obvious by then that the US and USSR were never going to go to war. Also, every day it became clearer that in the geopolitical game that the US ideals and way of life were going to "win."

These events allowed us to start to think of the Soviets as friends, slowly but surely. In 1989 MTV, pretty much my sole source for pop culture was giving a ton of coverage to the Moscow Music Peace Festival. Some of my favorite bands were playing—Motley Crue, Bon Jovi, Skid Row—so I followed it pretty closely. The Soviets were totally digging the same bands I was into. And they even had a couple of heavy metal bands of their own like Gorky Park. Those guys had the same hairsprayed long hair and earrings as the American bands, and I'm sure they freaked out the Russian parents just like my bands freaked out my dad. Maybe these guys weren't all that different from us. Bon Jovi and Gorky Park showed heavy metal knew no national borders!

Also, during that time the geopolitical narrative changed. It was less the Soviet Union and its people who were our adversaries but its leadership; we started to think that the Soviet people were okay but it was just their form of government that had to go. When President Reagan made his famous speech in West Berlin, he didn't ask the people to tear down that wall, he asked: "Mr. Gorbachev, tear down this wall" (at 1:34).

It was a sentiment that was even in the movies. In Rocky IV (1985) it turned out that Ivan Drago wasn't a bad guy after all. He was just wanted to be a boxer like Rocky. It was his managers that were the problem. That seemed like a perfect analogy for all of the Soviet Union. This was confirmed in The Hunt for Red October (1990) which depicted the captain and officers of a Soviet nuclear submarine attempting to defect from the totalitarian regime to live a simple life in America.

The Soviet Union splits up

After the Berlin Wall came down in 1989, it seemed like just a matter of time for the Soviet Union. Even though I was only 12 at the time, I definitely felt that major changes were going on in the world. I remember my history teacher talking about the reunification of Germany and saying "this is something that we've been waiting for 50 years. And I bet there are even bigger changes coming."

In the summer of 1991, I was 14 then and about to enter my freshman year of high school, I remember seeing the coverage of the coup on the news. My dad and I chatted about it, hoping that "everything would turn out okay," but beyond that, I didn't really know what to think and was quickly distracted by the things that distract 14-year-old boys (14-year-old girls).

When Boris Yeltsin emerged, it seemed everyone wanted to portray him as a new brand of Russian leader (now we were told the country was Russia, not the Soviet Union) who embraced democracy and would "be our friend." He seemed like a nice enough guy, and everyone seemed to be thinking that the Russians were okay, so that was that.

Plus, Saddam Hussein had invaded Kuwait the year before so our American psyche could make Iraq our national antagonist instead of the Soviet Union.

As an adult I did visit Russia, flying into Moscow, climbing Mt Elbrus, and then flying out of St Petersburg. It was an amazing two weeks.

Printed in Great Britain
by Amazon